PARIS AS REVOLUTION

PARIS AS REVOLUTION

WRITING THE NINETEENTH-CENTURY CITY

PRISCILLA PARKHURST FERGUSON

University of California Press

Berkeley · Los Angeles · London

843.09
F35p

University of California Press
Berkeley and Los Angeles, California

University of California Press, Ltd.
London, England

© 1994 by
The Regents of the University of California

Library of Congress Cataloging-in-Publication Data

Ferguson, Priscilla Parkhurst.
    Paris as revolution : writing the nineteenth-century city /
Priscilla Parkhurst Ferguson.
        p.   cm.
    Includes bibliographical references and index.
    ISBN 0-520-08642-2 (alk. paper)
        1. French literature—19th century—History and criticism.
    2. Politics and literature—France—Paris—History—19th century.
    3. Literature and history—France—Paris—History—19th century.
    4. Revolutionary literature, French—History and criticism.
    5. French literature—France—Paris—History and criticism.
    6. Paris (France)—Intellectual life—19th century.   7. City and
    town life in literature.   8. Cities and towns in literature.
    9. Paris (France)—In literature.   10. Revolutions in literature.
    I. Title
    PQ283.F46   1994
    843'.709324436—dc20
                                                            93-44374
                                                                CIP

Printed in the United States of America
9 8 7 6 5 4 3 2 1

For RAF

Contents

Illustrations

Credits

The Bibliothèque Nationale, Paris, for the photograph of the Porte and Place de France.

Rare Book and Manuscript Library, Columbia University, for the photographs of two flâneurs from *Les Français peints par eux-mêmes* and the title page of the *Physiologie du flaneur*.

The Henry Lillie Pierce Fund, the Museum of Fine Arts, Boston, for the photograph of Gustave Courbet's painting *La Curée*.

The Houghton Library, Harvard University, for the photograph of the frontispiece of *Le Nouveau Paris*.

The Library of Congress for the photograph of the frontispiece of Victor Hugo, *L'Année terrible*.

The Photothèque des Musées de la Ville de Paris and ARS, New York/SPADEM, Paris, for the photograph of Victor Hugo.

Special Collections, the Van Pelt-Dietrich Library, the University of Pennsylvania, for the photograph of the destruction of the statue of Louis XIV in the Place Vendôme.

Giraudon / Art Resource, N.Y., for the photographs of Gustave Courbet's portrait of Jules Vallès from the Musée Carnavalet, Paris, and of the Eiffel Tower from the World's Fair of 1889.

Roger-Viollet for the photographs of the Colonne Vendôme and Émile Zola.

Acknowledgments

Undoubtedly, all books should be considered a form of collective action. Certainly, every author depends on a vast network of people and institutions, and I am happy to acknowledge the institutions that supplied the time to work on *Paris as Revolution* and the individuals who kept me at it.

A fellowship from the National Endowment for the Humanities combined with a sabbatical leave from the University of Illinois in 1988 afforded time to start the project. Work in Paris was greatly enhanced by time spent at the École des Hautes Études en Sciences Sociales at Pierre Bourdieu's Centre de Sociologie Européenne. A month at the incomparable Bellagio Study Center of the Rockefeller Foundation in the summer of 1992 enabled me to write chapter 5 far more expeditiously than would have otherwise been possible and in surroundings that approximated Rabelais' Abbaye de Thélème. A leave from Columbia University gave me the needed time to finish the manuscript.

In this work so strongly driven by place, I should like to record my appreciation of two special places. The glorious painted beams of the Bibliothèque Historique de la Ville de Paris in the Hôtel Lamoignon encouraged a sense of history that the very helpful staff assisted with unfailing courtesy. Finally, as the Bibliothèque Nationale turns into the Bibliothèque Nationale de France, it is fitting to acknowledge the privilege of working rue de Richelieu. I will find the unparalleled collections in the new library across the Seine, but I will not find the reading room with its wonderful vaulted ceiling that tempted me to speculate about the many generations who worked there before me, including many of the writers whom I write about.

An earlier version of chapter 2 appeared in *Literature and Social Practice*, edited by Philippe Desan, myself, and Wendy Griswold (Chicago: University of Chicago Press, 1989). Aspects of chapter 3 have also been published in *Home and Its Dislocations in Nineteenth-Century*

France, edited by Suzanne Nash (Albany: SUNY Press, 1993); and in *Cultural Participation: Trends since the Middle Ages,* edited by Ann Rigney and Douwe Fokkema (Amsterdam: John Benjamins, 1993). I am grateful for permission to use this material.

Of the many colleagues, students, and friends who have helped me test my ideas, refine my discussion, and polish the prose, I owe a particular debt to Suzanne Nash and Henri Mitterand and especially to the two exceptional readers for the University of California Press, Jonathan Beecher and Catherine Nesci. Susan Suleiman saw what the title should be. For the second time, Doris Kretschmer shepherded a manuscript of mine through the University of California Press. Every author should be so well served.

My greatest debt, once again, is to Robert A. Ferguson. If, like the ship on the seal of Paris, this book rides the waves, it is surely because of his navigational skills, his enthusiasm for the project, and above all his certitude that the boat was really sailing.

Prologue: Writing Revolutions

Das XIX Jahrhundert ein Zeitraum (ein Zeit-traum)
Walter Benjamin, *Das Passagen-Werk*

The nineteenth century—a time-space, a dream-time.

The year 1789 made Paris the city of revolution, and it remained so for the century that followed. The city had been the theater of the Revolution in the 1790s, and for almost the whole of the nineteenth century it set the stage for revolution yet to come. The nineteenth century could neither contain the Revolution as a current event, though it would try, nor relegate it to the immobility of the past. The Revolution was, instead, a vital social phenomenon that had to be reengaged, redefined, and reimagined by each succeeding generation. And if Paris was, in Walter Benjamin's brilliant characterization, the "capital of the nineteenth century," it was because revolution haunted the present and the future of the city even more than its past. The history of the French Revolution was always written in the present tense. Nineteenth-century observers could scarcely escape the confrontation of city and revolution. The profoundly urban character of the Revolution, contemporaries agreed, had a great deal to do with the decidedly revolutionary nature of the rapidly transforming urban scene. Given the connection, it was imperative that Paris be explored and known again and again. Knowing, in this sense, would always be a complicated business.

Inevitably caught up in the turmoil, writers focused so obsessively on the city because it seemed to hold the key to an explosive past no less than to a bewildering future. *Paris as Revolution* locates the originality of nineteenth-century fiction in this convergence, in the intense commitment of these writers to knowing the city and to dramatizing that knowledge. Seen as revolutionary performances themselves, the great works of Flaubert, Hugo, Vallès, and Zola that I discuss in the chapters below stand as the extraordinary, vital elements

1

of a vast urban text. Paris produces far more than the background for the tales these novels tell; it furnishes the terms of the narrative itself. These writings do not just talk about revolution in the city; they stage the city as itself revolutionary, and on many levels at once.

Paris served quite literally as a revolutionary stage. The site for the most dramatic as well as the most emblematic events of the Revolution—from the storming of the Bastille to the executions of the Terror—the city offered an ideal space for the daily practice of revolutionary ideals. The concentration of energies and institutions, like the density and volatility of population, exacerbated the inherently public character of the Revolution. From the Festivals of Reason and Federation on the Champ de Mars to the carts of prisoners trundled about Paris, the Revolution put the political on display. So much of what has come to be thought of as modern about the events of 1789 derived from the translation of politics into everyday life, where every move, every speech, every article of clothing, made a public statement. Every engaged citizen appeared on stage at every moment.

These politics of publicity connect Paris in revolution to modernity. The delicately balanced, even at times slightly perverse relation of the observer to the observed, which Baudelaire made so important a feature of the modern metropolis, actually begins in revolution and then proclaims itself in the revolutions that disrupted Paris after 1789. In the public arena, it became as essential to be seen, and be judged, as it was to see, and judge. Sorting out the signs of revolution meant ordering the city in a complex interaction of political identity, social setting, and cultural practice.

A convenient label after 1789, "postrevolutionary" begs more questions than it answers. Where should we stand to determine what revolutionary meant, and might mean still? After which revolution? 1789? 1830? 1848? 1871? Do we mean revolution in the city or revolution of the city? Must postrevolutionary imply that revolution has somehow ended? From the vantage point of the late twentieth century, "prerevolutionary" is surely as appropriate at any given moment prior to 1871 for a society that overthrew or established three monarchies, three republics, and two empires in just over eighty years. Radical political dislocation consumed the century, and its concomitant, revolution, became the antithesis of a discrete event. Revolution became a state of mind, a heightened consciousness of the fragility of social institutions, and an acute sense of the possibility of continuing and constant transformation. In the course of time, that possibility became a probability that demanded action and reaction, again and again, from both the individual and the collectivity.

If revolution disquieted, it also exhilarated. For sheer intensity of creative energies, nineteenth-century Paris had no rival. The emerging urban discourse compelled critical strategies of accommodation to an ever-shifting milieu. Although cities had long been associated with both political unrest and intellectual innovation, nineteenth-century Paris was unique, and not least because its narratives presumed to tell the story of the modern world. The great novelists of the nineteenth century did not simply write about the Paris that they knew (or hoped to know); they confronted the human condition in that time and place, fully confident that they could fix the meaning of the largest transformations through the multifaceted phenomena of revolution and urbanization. Their narratives of the modern city also transcribe an emerging modernism. The fragmentation of vision, the disintegration of experience, the primacy of individual expression over collective belief—these are the signs that mark these novels as chronicles of the modern. These works are, in consequence, essential to an appreciation of both the urban setting and the changing form of the novel.

Yet, for all the modernity that twentieth-century readers recognize in them, these works are very much of their century. The fragmentation of vision is countered by an assumption of narrative authority, an authority that rests, I shall argue, in the assumed role that revolution plays in narrative. Revolution was a virtuoso metaphor that gave the nineteenth-century city and also the nineteenth-century novel an originary source, a dramatic contemporary context, and an interpretive model. It could explain the city and make sense of its apparent contradictions. It could comprehend the city as a whole. Since revolution related at once to the past, the present, and the future, it touched every aspect of politics, society, and culture. Specific political assessments aside, revolution was imagined very differently depending on whether revolution was grasped as the historical events that followed more or less directly upon 1789; perceived as the contemporary and continuous political agitation that brought into being the regimes of 1799, 1830, 1848, 1851, and 1871; or, yet again, filtered through the fears and hopes of dramatic change still to come.[1]

At issue in every explication were the connections between the several dimensions of revolution. How were the changes of regime tied to the escalating impact of industrial capitalism? How did both impel the literary and artistic turmoil that so altered modes of artistic production and the products themselves? That there were connections was obvious to the most indifferent observer, but the exact nature and meaning of the linkages were a subject of great debate. The choices within the vast semantic and sociological field of revolution charted the range of both literary options and political positions from the beginning to the end of the century. Assuredly, the world of literature was not what it had been, and even if there was little agreement on what literature had been under the ancien régime, every change at hand was intimately linked to revolution. The indissoluble connection between literature and politics was already a commonplace when, in 1802, the vicomte de Bonald made his celebrated proclamation that "literature is the expression of society as language is the expression of man."[2] But the continuing fact and presence of revolution gave the idea irrefutable and constant confirmation. The connection became almost an article of faith for the century that followed, regardless of political or aesthetic position. Revolution on the street, revolution on the page—the two were inevitably found together, even if the relations were far from transparent and the correlation was often indirect.

Attitudes toward revolution are always problematic, but in nineteenth-century Paris they were as consuming as they were at least in part because they were also confused. Passionate involvement with revolution in its many guises turned Paris into an engrossing object of cultural speculation. As a result, the city comprised much more than the subject and backdrop that it had provided for writers and painters for close to six centuries.[3] From the background of cultural performance, Paris moved to center stage, and it did so through urban narratives that focused importantly, if not exclusively, on revolution as the deciding factor in the changes marking Paris on virtually every street. The great social and political reconfiguration that followed upon 1789 bestowed upon the city a status that it held for a century: the permanent but ever-changing site of the Revolution gave birth to the city of revolution.

The capaciousness of the concept made both its literary and its sociological fortune. Revolution proposed such a seductive model for literary interpretation because it constructed social change simultaneously as a function of time and of space, the very elements that form the foundation of any narrative. Revolution is the perfect *chron-*

otope, the rhetorical figure proposed by Mikhail Bakhtin that fixes the interaction of historical time and space in a work of literature. Understanding how chronotopes work in particular texts is fundamental, Bakhtin argues, to figuring out how genres work.[4] If we accept Bakhtin's claim that particular genres are distinguished by their chronotopes, we realize that revolution may well give us the distinctive chronotope of nineteenth-century urban narratives. For in rendering the triangulation of time, space, and text, revolution suggests the decisive context for thinking about the city in nineteenth-century France. A three-way definition of self, society, and political identity is always at work in the nineteenth-century authors who write about Paris, and the controlling frame of reference is invariably the place that each constructs in a revolutionary tradition.

Whether present or repressed, implicit or explicit, revolution determines what Benjamin calls the "time-space" and the "dream-time" that define nineteenth-century Paris.[5] But these definitions are necessarily multifaceted in both theory and appeal. Any appreciation of revolution as paradigmatic chronotope must be an interdisciplinary process. Literary criticism, historical interpretation, and sociological placement join in any realization of the symbol system that is constructed in and around nineteenth-century Paris, and it helps to keep these disciplines in play in our own awareness of nineteenth-century conflations.

The genres that work out these historical and spatial interconnections most fully are the journalistic essay and the novel, which together constitute something of a "collective autobiography" of Paris and Parisians as they confronted a rapidly changing world for which they were often ill prepared.[6] To read these prototypical genres of the modernizing city is to do more than discover the great number of revolutionary and revolutionized urban texts that recount the city and tell stories about the Revolution. These profoundly urban genres make the city itself into a revolutionary text. To speak of an "urban genre" or a "revolutionary text" is to do more than indulge in metaphor. Or rather, this particular metaphor takes on a theoretical life of its own. If reading the city has become a commonplace, we do well to remember that we are able to undertake such readings, as Michel de Certeau reminds us, only because of the properties the urban text shares with written or more specifically literary texts.[7] Urban and literary texts alike display the never-ending dialogue between author and work, between work and reader that also inheres in the practice of the city. Each exhibits the contest between fabrication and interpretation; each exemplifies the shifting affinities between text and intertexts. Moreover, reading urban space in terms of a literary narrative comes easily to nineteenth-century Parisians who struggle with the vitality of revolution in order to represent, to explain, and, finally, to make sense of their city.

The power of what is in sum a political aesthetic lies precisely in the expression these works give to a collective memory or tradition. At the same time, these texts anchor and thereby perpetuate that memory. They provide a "social frame," to take Maurice Halbwachs' term, on which society hangs its beliefs and its practices. But, as Halbwachs also argues, the social memory—in this case, revolution—remains alive only to the extent that it is reactivated by and through current social structures.[8] The names of the city scrutinized in chapter 1, the guidebooks of chapter 2, and the novels of Flaubert, Hugo, Vallès, and Zola analyzed in subsequent chapters—all of these manifestations of the written word, from the ephemeral journal article to the most complex literary work, are means by which the present activates the past and keeps it alive. Revolution was contemporary in nineteenth-century France not only because of the recurrent political conflict and the repeated changes of regime but also because so many texts supplied a continuous social frame and literary narrative for the revolutionary tradition.

These works were not the only means of communication, and it is certainly true that they rely on other kinds of social frames that also kept revolution alive. Even so, I shall argue, the power of these texts lies in their capacity to mobilize revolution in the present—even, at far remove, today. In the construction of revolution and in the elaboration of the symbol system attached to Paris, the texts examined in *Paris as Revolution* played a critical role for contemporaries, and to the extent that these texts are read still, they perpetuate revolutionary Paris a century and more later. To the degree that the Revolution remains a touchstone in French culture (a matter of much current debate), these texts will resonate within that culture. They, in turn, will have something to do with keeping revolution alive.

Much of the power of these works derives from the sense of authority that they radiate. These writers are confident that they can know Paris. However different Vallès, Hugo, Flaubert, and Zola are, they all write from knowledge of some sort and, more important still, they write from a presumption of knowability. For them, the city is readable, and they write within this conviction of legibility.[9] The assurance of legibility governs the work of some—Balzac, Hugo, and Zola—more obviously than others—Flaubert and, perhaps, Vallès. But this faith—and it is indeed a faith—makes all of these writers figures of the nineteenth century.

There is, of course, much criticism, both of individual writers and of nineteenth-century fiction more generally, that rightly stresses the complexity of representation and the awareness of these writers of that complexity.[10] Reading backward from Proust or Joyce, Sarraute or Beckett, the twentieth-century reader finds the authority of the omniscient narrator not so unimpeachable after all. The urban narrative that I identify in effect mediates between the necessarily simplifying perspective of the controlling author (the "bird's-eye view" of the omniscient narrator) and the muddled, fragmentary perspective from within the labyrinth of the city (the incomplete, obscure point of view of the protagonists in these works). That these writers at times acknowledge the fragmentary and therefore faulty nature of the knowledge that their works convey does not lead them to renounce the larger project of understanding. For the writers of revolutionary Paris, the possibility of knowledge of the city, its fundamental knowability, is a requisite article of faith. When Paris ceases to appear knowable, as it does by the end of the century, when revolution no longer offers an explanatory principle but becomes one of many available images in the cultural archive, this revolutionary tradition comes to an end. At that point, revolutionary energies turn in other directions, twentieth-century journalists and novelists look to other models and other aesthetics, and they imagine other cities.

Paris as Revolution follows these urban narratives from the First to the Third Republics, from the expansion of the city beginning in the First Empire to the demolition and reconstruction during the Second Empire, from the political triumphs of 1789 and 1830 to the revolutionary defeats of 1848–51 and 1870–71, and to the Dreyfus affair at the end of the century. The political parallels are not fortuitous. Each of these major events redefined Paris, its topography, its sociology, its iconography, its systems of representation. Each of the chapters below analyzes this nexus of the political, the cultural, and the iconographical at a particular historical moment. I shall not have much to say about the actual alterations of the topography or the political or social landscape of Paris over the nineteenth century because I am concerned above all with the means by which that landscape was understood and with the rhetorical frame that conveyed this understanding. I want to know how Paris was represented and how Paris was known.

The most obvious change in Paris appears in urban iconography, and particularly in the names by which the city represented itself. As the monarchy had claimed symbolic authority over the city by imposing its favored names, so the revolutionaries of the 1790s contested that authority by proposing their own politically correct names and images to control the stage upon which revolution was to play itself out. The strident battles over nomination and representation, which recurred at every stage of revolutionary change in Paris, underline the issue of ideological control that will emerge in a more muted form in literary and journalistic writing.

The literary guidebooks that proliferated from the beginning of the century worked to secure the transformed and ever-transforming social landscape. A crucially important genre in the writing about the city in the nineteenth century, these proto-novels of the city responded to the new Paris that demanded to be named, defined, and explored, enterprises that became increasingly problematic as the city itself was reconfigured. The guidebooks of nineteenth-century Paris reached for images that would render a larger meaning in narratives that were consciously partial and soon outdated.

Whereas the guidebooks wander about Paris and ramble over the text, the novel aimed for rhetorical control. To clarify how the novel commanded the revolutionary city, I have focused on a number of classic writers and texts, each of which confronted Paris at a moment of political crisis, at a time when revolutionary hopes fell. For Flaubert in *L'Éducation sentimentale,* it was the failure of 1848 and the coup d'état of 1851 that turned the jaunty *flâneur,* prototype of the artist in control of the urban environment, into the failed artist, the hapless soul lost in the city. For Zola in *La Curée,* it was the Second Empire, which unleashed unprecedented speculation and set Paris on the course to defeat; in *La Débâcle,* it was the war and the Commune in

1870–71. For Hugo in *Quatrevingt-treize* and Vallès in *L'Insurgé*, it was, once again, the Commune, the civil war that pitted France against Paris. Finally, Zola, in the novel named simply, but superbly, *Paris*, confronted the city as it faced the twentieth century.

These times of political crisis accentuate the inevitable disparity between the vision of a city and urban realities, between the dream of political change and the actuality of politics. Representations of the city, too, are caught in discrepancy, between the emblems that work to fix the image of the city and the narratives that endeavor to capture its movement. For nineteenth-century Paris, revolution afforded a dynamic principle, at once a principle of explanation and of representation, simultaneously vision and reality. Static representations of the city—the names, the seals, the icons—remain locked in the past, attached to a particular moment in time and to a particular definition of revolution. The great works of urban narrative, however, conceive revolution as an active narrative force. One might even say that the great novelists Flaubert, Zola, Hugo, and Vallès, whose works I shall discuss, conceived revolution as a precept of representation. For these writers revolution did not pose a problem so much as challenge their powers of representation. They needed, and they created, the kind of narratives in which Benjamin's time-space and dream-time could become one. In the process, they gave artistic force to the legendary verdict handed down by Emperor Charles V in 1540 that Paris is not a city but a world.[11]

1

Paris: Place and Space of Revolution

1789. Depuis un siècle bientôt, ce nombre est la préoccu-
pation du genre humain. Tout le phénomène moderne y est
contenu.

                                          Victor Hugo, *Paris-Guide*

1789. For close to a century, this number has preoccupied the
human race. It contains the whole phenomenon of modernity.

The Revolution made Paris unique among the great cities of the
world. Other cities may be more impressive, more important, more
beautiful, but none can claim revolution as its very principle. For the
whole of the nineteenth century, Paris could make that claim, and it
did. The storming of the Bastille in the northeast corner of the city
on the 14th of July 1789 announced the first modern revolution, and
the perception of the modernity of the phenomenon has a great deal
to do with the decidedly urban character of the most central events
of the 1790s. The Revolution played out in an urban spectacle of
unparalleled and willful drama. Revolutionary governance took place
in public, in the street, in the square, in the assembly hall. Its urban
setting—from the trial and execution of the king to officially staged
ceremonies like the Festival of Reason—set the tone of the Revolution at the time and for the century to come.

Urbanity was not ancillary to the Revolution. Quite to the contrary,
the role that devolved upon Paris turned out to be absolutely crucial
to the profound reconceptualization of French society that followed.
Neither the English Revolution of the seventeenth century nor the
American Revolution of the 1770s sought to redefine the individual
and the whole understanding of society with anything like the fervent
conviction that animated the entire political spectrum of the first
French republic. Still more significant in the long term, the concentration of people and the intensification of energies in the city
merged revolutionary ideals into the practice of everyday life. The
language of the urban center set the standard for the rest of the

country, as it had during the ancien régime, but thenceforth it was sustained and incomparably magnified by the educational institutions established in the crucial first decade of the republic. Taking over cultural as well as political supremacy from Versailles, Paris determined the course of the Revolution by always being the place of revolution.

Paris could represent the Revolution because the Revolution, in its turn, remade Paris in its image. The dramatic temper of revolutionary events fixed powerful new images and associations in the city, associations that shaped public perception for the better part of a century. Whatever other associations it might acquire, and whether it was feared or revered, Paris persisted as the city of the guillotine, the city of popular riots and coups d'état, the city that staged revolution as a matter of course, and of principle.

Paris bore the conspicuous marks of its monarchical origins. The monuments, buildings, palaces, churches, the very streets of this revolutionary city, kept in full view a social order that the new age worked so sedulously to consign to the past. It was inevitable that revolutionaries should seek to remake the city in the image of their revolution, a Paris that reached beyond its most obvious role as the site of revolutionary incidents. The new Paris would constitute the space in which the Revolution was inscribed. In a word, Paris was meant to signify the Revolution.

Altering topography offered the most evident answer to the dilemma of imposing the new city on the old, and a number of buildings besides the Bastille were in fact destroyed. Yet, despite the visions of barbarians sacking Rome raised by the neologism *vandalism,* Paris saw far less destruction than some had feared and others had desired. In any case, short of building a new capital altogether (the route followed by the American Republic) or razing the city and starting from the ground up (such a suggestion was, indeed, ventured), reconstructing Paris as the pure signifier of revolution was quite out of the question, even if one could achieve agreement on what that signifier should look like.

By shifting topography to toponymy, from the relatively fixed to the inherently mobile, revolutionary fervor converged on phenomena particularly susceptible to modification. Energies were not directed at things themselves so much as at the ways those things were conceived, perceived, and used. Rather than destroy aristocratic palaces, the new government was more likely to convert the property to properly revolutionary function as a public building. With their inscription of the revolution on the cityscape itself, words, names, and eventually texts, offered an immediate and economical means of turning urban space to revolutionary account. The many texts of a revolutionary urban discourse produced in effect a new, revolutionary landscape.

Every regime thereafter followed this paradigm of redefinition. Each of the major political revolutions of the nineteenth century— 1830, 1848, 1871—reconfigured the landscape to fit the altered structures of power. Writers joined architects, urban planners, and government officials in molding the distinctive cultural practices of the new city. For the city was at once text and pre-text as it engaged writers in a concentrated effort of reinterpretation and re-presentation. In the very act of bearing witness to the transformations of the city, writers and their texts pushed those transformations further.

The insistent rewriting of the city was at once the result of the experience of modernity and an agent of that modernity. For the city was far more than the place where central revolutionary events occurred. Paris became the archetypical city of revolution not because the Bastille fell in one corner of the city and the guillotine rose in another but because so many different kinds of texts infused this space with an aura of revolution. The urban discourse that evolved over the nineteenth century in the novels, the articles, and the literary guidebooks that poured into the literary marketplace sought to contain revolution and to fix change. The names bestowed on the city over the century continually revised and in revising retold the never-ending tale of Parisian revolution.

I

Je remplis d'un beau nom ce grand espace vide.
J. Du Bellay, *Les Regrets*

I fill this great empty space with a beautiful name.

To create is to name. The reverse also holds. To name is to create, since nomination presupposes as it signifies the right no less than the privilege of creation. Whatever form it takes, nomination makes a primal gesture of appropriation. The Book of Genesis accordingly makes nomination at once inseparable from, and a requisite of, creation. Adam's naming of God's creatures (including Woman) is the act that places them under his dominion. Genesis similarly insists upon the intrinsic connection between language and space. Although Adam names the creatures of the earth, God alone names the earth and does so before every other creation. Bestowed before the Fall in both instances, the first names given by God and Adam bespeak a perfect world, and every nomination since harks to this harmony between the creator and the work. Every naming holds out the hope of starting anew, for every creator wants to say, in essence, "and, behold, it was very good" (Genesis 1:31).[1]

The biblical vision of nomination, with its power justified and sustained by unimpeachable authority, haunts every act of nomination. It is especially relevant to the naming of space. For spatial nominations express as they formulate a certain sense of the collectivity. More or less obviously, they fit within a larger system of representations through which the collectivity defines itself, to itself and to the world beyond. Names crystallize identity. But the space that they create can open into conflict as well as community. Whose space for whose community? These names play out the tensions between the individual and the collectivity, between the ideal and the real. While these tensions play out in every spatial nomination, they are, perhaps, most pronounced in cities. Small enough to make the whole visible and large enough to accommodate a multiplicity of parts, the modern city articulates its history in the network of names that signal possession of space.

Cities require names for many purposes. They need to name the whole, and they need to name the parts. But a single name cannot comprehend the polyphonic, polymorphous, polysemic city. If it identifies, the single name offers no entry into the intricate urban text. The ordinarily fixed name of the city contrasts sharply with the mobility, and the volatility, of the names for the parts within a city. In one sense, the single name comprehends all the others. But these others do not project an image. They tell tales, the tales of the city. Names within the city recount its history, its heroes, its battles, its culture. They spin the threads of the evolving urban narrative, woven over many years, decades, centuries.

There is perhaps no better single gauge to the larger significance of these nominatory connections than city street names. Like the other signs of urban civilization—from obvious icons like statues, monuments, and buildings to the grid of streets and districts—street names confer meaning on urban space. Obvious signs *to* the city, street names are at the same time signs *of* the city. Certainly, the naming of streets affords a crucial opportunity to affirm, or to contest, control of the city. It arrogates the authority to fashion the city. Beyond identifying location, names on streets socialize space and celebrate cultural identity. They historicize the present and preserve the past. They mediate between local and ambient cultures, between individuals and institutions; they play politics and articulate ideologies; they perpetuate tradition; and they register change. In sum, street names offer a privileged field to examine the continual process of recording and interpreting the city. In the extensive notes he made for his unfinished magnum opus on nineteenth-century Paris, Walter Benjamin stressed precisely this kind of linguistic definition of space. The city, for Benjamin, accumulated a privileged class of words, a nobility of names. Through language, the ordinary—the street—becomes extraordinary. The city thus becomes a universe of language or, in Benjamin's dramatic conception, a linguistic cosmos.[2]

A linguistic cosmos? Or, more modestly, a text to be read metaphorically as well as literally? Names narrativize the environment and in so doing concur in the construction of a properly urban text. To speak of the "urban text" is to do more than indulge in metaphor. Or, rather, the metaphor makes good theoretical sense. We can read the city because of the properties the urban text shares with other texts. The one and the others display the never-ending dialogue between author and text, between text and reader. Each exhibits the contest of fabrication and interpretation; each exemplifies the shifting relations between text and intertexts.

Should we object that the city has no author, we would see that the commonsensical dichotomy is open to question. Although cities themselves are the work of many hands, planned cities have authors of sorts, and urban planners certainly have ambitions that can only be seen as authorial. Meanwhile, for the written text, contemporary criticism directs us away from the author to the many different intertexts. Written texts, like cities, unfold through long, and often painful, processes of creation. In both cases the text changes. With cities, the basic text *has* to change to accommodate the requirements of new users—a dynamic not always present for the new reader of an old written text.

Names make important connections between these two kinds of texts. For names appropriate the urban text much as an author marks a written text. As the biblical model makes clear, nomination presumes authority, and it supposes as well an agent to exercise that authority. Its many names make the city a striking illustration of the multivocality, or heteroglossia, that Bakhtin assigns to prose and, particularly, to the novel. The basic contours of the urban text as of the written text are determined by the tensions between the authority of the nominator and the interpretations continually fabricated by the users of those texts. The heteroglossia of the text contests the authority of the author. Every reading of any text must balance the competing claims of authorial constraint and interpretive freedom. Reading the city is no exception to that rule.

II

> Habiter Athènes, Corinthe, Sienne ou Amsterdam, c'est habiter un discours. . . . La ville est un langage.
>
> Jean Duvignaud, *Lieux et non lieux*

> To inhabit Athens, Corinth, Siena or Amsterdam is to inhabit a discourse. . . . The city is a language.

That streets should have names is not self-evident. For centuries, most villages and towns felt no need to name their streets, and even today a major urban center like Tokyo manages to do without them. The rethinking of urban space entailed by the naming of streets suggests a relatively extensive geographical area, a population of a certain density, and a varyingly complex array of social and commercial activities. Street names were one outcome of this (re)conceptualization of the urban whole. The debates over street names during the Revolution became so strident because the monarchy had so strongly marked the Parisian text. Rewriting that text to make the city consonant with revolutionary ideals was an enterprise all the more fraught with conflict because the monarchical text proved impossible to efface. Contrary to the way the American revolutionaries were able to proceed at about the same time when they built a capital city from the ground up, French revolutionaries had to contend with the past on every corner.

In their beginnings many towns made do with one or a very few names—la Grande Rue, la Petite Rue, la Rue Basse, la Rue Haute, or, in early American settlements, the inevitable Main Street. Street names became general in Paris beginning in the twelfth century, but elsewhere in France the written record indicates few names before the thirteenth century. No other city at the time came close to the population of Paris. By the end of the thirteenth century, the city could boast over two hundred thousand inhabitants and over three hundred streets—three hundred ten "real streets" according to the testimony of Guillot's poem *Le Dit des rues de Paris*.[3]

How were these early streets designated? As in older cities generally, streets in medieval Paris bore "local" or descriptive names, that is, names that made some sort of connection to the site. Consider the following names in Paris and their often tangled origins:

Location—Contrescarpe (on an escarpment), Saint-Denis (the road leading north to Saint-Denis), Grève (near the bank, i.e., *la grève,* of the Seine)

Topography—Rosiers (rose bushes), Serpente (serpentine street), Pavée (paved, therefore remarkable)

A building or domain—Louvre, Monnaie (the mint), Notre-Dame; or owners thereof—Capucines (Capucin monks), Croulebarbe

Merchandise sold or trade exercised—Mégisserie (tanneries), Ferronerie (ironmongers), Verrerie (glassmakers)

A store sign—Epée-de-bois (wooden sword), Croissant (crescent moon)

Inhabitants—Anglais (English scholars in the Latin Quarter), Mauvais Garçons ("bad boys" or ruffians), Grande Truanderie (big-time ruffians and criminals).

These often colorful names satisfy on several levels. The evident link between name and space renders the name essential, a manifestation, as it were, of the space. The name justified the space, which in turn authorized the name. In the perfectly harmonious world these connections implied, signifier corresponded to signified, sign coincided with referent.

The evident connection between name and place enabled another, between place and history. In their original form, such names were so many features of a genuine popular culture. The users, that is, the inhabitants, took care of the names. But when another generation of users took over, street names shifted to reflect their use of the space.

Orality makes popular culture singularly unstable, so that until street names entered the written record, they were subject to the vicissitudes of population movement and topographical alteration and to the vagaries of human memory. Semantic corruption set in almost as soon as the original basis for the name vanished.

The name that we see on the street today may have no connotative connection to the original, despite the tales that may be (and usually are) advanced to sustain a connection. In the Paris of the thirteenth century, the street Gilles-Queux told of an important inhabitant, Gui-le-Queux, that is, Guy the Cook. Without the cook and his cooking to anchor the name, Gui-le-Queux turned into Gille-le-Cueur, which metamorposed into Gilles-Coeur (Gille Heart), then to its present name, Gît-le-Coeur (Here-lies-the-heart), the last generating innumerable stories about a putative mistress of Henri IV who supposedly lived there when the name entered the written record. Egyptienne, taken from the chapel of Sainte-Marie l'Egyptienne, became Gibecienne and later Jussienne; and among the most savory, Pute-y-muse (Whores' Walk) became the Petit-Musc (Little Musk) that we come upon in the fourth arrondissement today.

The list could go on and on. Moreover, so strong was the sense of placement, so powerful the belief that word and object ought to correspond, that early chroniclers of Paris made a point of tracing back through topographical and semantic changes to reestablish the authentic connection. By the early fifteenth century there was already a need to set the record straight. The historian Guillebert de Metz, for example, had frequent recourse to the phrase "properly speaking" to disentangle the subsequent narratives and establish what he determined were the true origins of certain Paris street names.[4]

The expansion of Paris occurred along with the consolidation of the French monarchy. Indeed, royal appropriation of the city marked the entry of Paris into the modern age. Street names were its insignia, yet another sign of royal power, a means of impressing dominion on topography itself. The force of the revolutionary reaction on the streets a century and a half later was very much a function of this initial exercise of what can be taken as symbolic eminent domain, the creation of a "sacred geography" designated by and dedicated to the monarchy. This sacred geography was at the same time a "landscape of power" that inscribed the power relations of the larger society.[5]

The ascendancy of Paris took a decisive turn with the decision of François I to settle in Paris. In 1528 the impecunious king notified his "Very Dear and Well Loved Friends" in the rich municipality that his intention from then on was to reside in "our good city of Paris" more than in any other part of the kingdom. To this effect, the Louvre was to be repaired and made fit for royal habitation.[6] Once the definitive conquest of Paris seventy years later ended the wars of religion, the first Bourbon king, Henri IV (1594–1610), went about making his Paris the symbolic center of a reunited France. He and his energetic minister Sully launched the first Parisian urban renewal, building some sixty-eight new streets and developing whole new areas, most spectacularly the Place Royale (now the Place des Vosges) and the Place Dauphine on the Ile de la Cité.

Fittingly, it was Henri IV who introduced the honorific model of topographical nomination, which removed nominatory powers from the users to the government, where they have resided ever since. As it reached further and further into the quotidian, the state assumed the expression and almost the constitution of a collective consciousness. The new streets of the new Paris confined their honors to the royal family: the rue Christine, named for the daughter of Henri IV and Marie de Médicis; the rue and the Place Dauphine, for the then Dauphin, Louis XIII; and at one remove, the rue Sainte-Anne, named for the patron of the queen, Anne of Austria. Aristocrats close to the Crown might fall under the royal mantle of honorific recognition (the rues Richelieu, Mazarine, Vendôme, Colbert), as did certain especially important entrepreneurs who opened new sections of the city (the rues Charlot and Villedo, the Pont Marie). Glorious happenings completed the roster of nominatory possibilities (Place des Victoires, and Place des Conquêtes for the Place Vendôme). In the eighteenth century, the municipality added city officials (the rues Vivienne and Feydeau, the quai d'Orsay). But though those honored came to include "lesser" individuals, dispensing that honor remained a royal prerogative.

So strong was the sense that the city belonged to its masters and its makers that the dramatist, essayist, and seemingly ubiquitous journalist Louis-Sébastien Mercier predicted outrage on the part of the city fathers when the first honorific street names fell outside of these official categories. It is logical, Mercier agreed, that the streets sur-

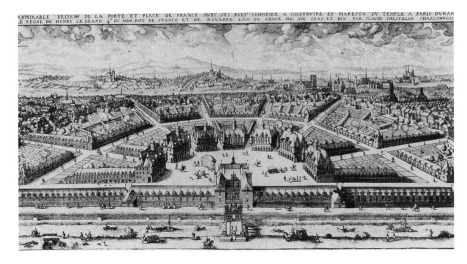

Plate 1.   The Porte and Place Porte de France. An engraving of 1640 taken from a 1615 design for the Place de France, a synecdoche for France. Henri IV planned the Place for the area near the northern city wall, but it was never built. Each of the twenty-four approaching and connecting streets was to bear the name of a province, the significance of the province determining the size and centrality of the street. The eight main streets leading into the place represented the largest provinces; the seven concentric connecting streets took the names of the lesser provinces; and the smallest interconnecting streets were allotted to the smallest provinces. No wonder a later commentator called it "the most national, the most French idea that any French sovereign had ever conceived . . . a sort of national Pantheon." (Photograph courtesy of the Bibliothèque Nationale, Paris.)

rounding the new Théâtre de l'Odéon in 1779 should bear the names of illustrious French dramatists. But as he foretold the brouhaha, Mercier confidently insisted that the scandal would not last. City officials, he conjectured, would soon get used to seeing Corneille and Molière as the "companions of their glory."[7]

The royal practice of urban nomination found its clearest expression not in any site or name that we can recall today but in Henri IV's extraordinarily ambitious project for the Porte and Place de France. In this vast semicircular place to be located immediately inside the northern city wall, each of twenty-four approaching and connecting streets was to bear the name of a province. The size of the street correlated with the geopolitical importance of the province: the eight main streets leading into the center of the place bore the names of the greater provinces (Picardie, Dauphiné, Provence, Languedoc,

Guienne, Poitou, Bretagne, Bourgogne); the seven concentric connecting streets stood for the lesser provinces (Brie, Bourbonnais,
Lyonnais, Beauce, Auvergne, Limousin, Périgord); and finally, the
smallest interconnecting streets signified the smallest provinces (Sain-
tonge, La Marche, Touraine, Le Perche, Angoulême, Berri, Orléans,
Beaujolais, Anjou).

Perhaps the Place de France represented royal hegemony too perfectly; or perhaps its conception of toponymical relations was too abstract for the early seventeenth century. In the event, Henri IV was
assassinated before he could proceed, and his successors let the venture drop. The plan was not even printed for another thirty years. But
it is a remarkable document, striking for the modernity of its conception; for the Place de France, in effect, reduced to a single text the
political program that concerned all of the regimes over the nineteenth century. It was, to take the exalted terms of a nineteenth-
century commentator all but overcome with patriotic fervor, "the
most national, the most French idea that any French sovereign had
ever conceived." Had it been realized, this observer enthused, France
would have had "a sort of national Panthéon" before the fact, a monument to "strike the imagination" and propagate edifying "moral
and political ideas" among the populace.[8]

Whether these pedagogical considerations were those of the first
Bourbon monarch or, more likely, those of a nineteenth century fairly
obsessed with creating national unity, the moral and political idea
that drove this experiment was indubitably the integration of France
and its capital. The Place de France made synecdoche visible, since
it, like the honorific model of nomination more generally, tied the
street to ideology. As a consequence, the Place broke the link of street
to site and severed the connection between toponymy and local urban
practices and personages. The Revolution changed the ideology, but
the first rebaptism of a Paris street in 1791 followed the principle of
symbolic control established by the monarchy over a century and a
half before.

In turning into an act of state, the naming of streets reverted to
the adamic model. Nomination presupposed creation. Presumably,
usage followed. But how do city dwellers know their streets other than
through usage? Registration of street names entered them into the
public record, but those early records were unlikely to affect many
users directly. Moreover, the scarcity of reliable maps and their lack

of portability complicated inordinately any venture out of one's immediate vicinity. The Swiss visitor to Paris in 1663 who took three hours to reach his destination was neither the first nor the last to find himself in such a predicament. The colorful, striking store signs helped only after one reached the right street.

Hence, the single most important measure for the integration of the street and the neighborhood into the city, and the first step toward rationalizing use of the urban text, was the decree that the name be fixed on the street itself. The first real street sign dates from 1643, when the Dominicans requested permission to mark the street on which their convent was located "Rue Saint Dominique formerly Cow Street." Surprisingly perhaps, not until 1728 did the lieutenant général de la police order names placed on the first and last house of every street in Paris. The often vehement resistance to the decree revealed the still very weak sense of the city as a whole to which individuals subordinated their personal affairs. To foil the recalcitrant owners who tore off the metal plaques nailed onto their houses, an ordinance in 1729 directed that the name of the street and the number of the *quartier* be chiseled in a stone set into the wall itself. Many of these inscriptions can be seen still today, some with the same name as on the contemporary sign, others with names that invoke the older city. In 1823 metal plaques with white letters on a black background replaced the names in stone, and beginning in 1844, enamel plaques with white letters on a blue background replaced the first plaques. The current signs in Paris are flimsy metal imitations of these blue and white enamel plaques.

The formal street sign dealt the final blow to popular nomenclature. Although registration tended to sanction usage, in the long term it was inscription that decided usage. The written language fixed the urban text, quite literally writing that text. The evident disdain for and fear of popular culture come to the fore in the "sanitizing" of some of the earthier appellations. The Dominicans did away with the cows that had once pastured in the area, and some two hundred years later Voltaire campaigned (to no avail) to replace *cul-de-sac* with *impasse*. Tire-vit (Pull-Prick) had already been euphemized to Tire-boudin (Pull-Sausage) by the fourteenth century, but some found even that unseemly. Obscene names were, first of all, unworthy of a civilized society. From his position as a spokesman of the Age of Enlightenment, Mercier peremptorily declared that the obscene names of the older streets "attest to the turpitude of our ancestors." On the other hand, with his characteristically titillating rhetorical flourish, Mercier held out little hope to change the ways of people who gave "obscene forms" to the pastries they baked![9]

The Revolution made the divide between past and present even more absolute, for the old regime was not simply the past, it was a past that had been repudiated. The sense that a new society required a new toponymy is especially acute in a guide to Paris published in 1801 by one J. B. Pujoulx, man-about-town and all-purpose man of letters. More anxious than Mercier to break with the inappropriate past and more aware of the larger mission of Paris in the world beyond France, Pujoulx worried that from the "obscene names that dirty the corners of certain streets" visitors would infer the immorality of the present inhabitants.[10] Naturally, Pujoulx roundly condemned Tire-Boudin, although he had to admit that it was a decided improvement over the previous name, which he declined to specify. (Tire-Boudin soon became the rue Marie Stuart.) Thus modernizing Paris went about the task of civilization, of making itself into the image of the new world fit for the new century. As Norbert Elias argues in *The History of Manners,* such measures demonstrate that the march of "civilization" compelled dissociation from the (inferior) past and eradication of practices that did not measure up to the standards of the present. The present day was clearly superior in the eyes of contemporaries, and every precaution had to be taken to make that superiority evident to all.[11]

Pujoulx, good son of the Enlightenment that he was, deplored the "incoherence" and "bizarreness" of Paris street names as a whole even more than he did the indecency of one or another street. They were a "ridiculous assortment," a "salmagundi," and the present name was almost always at odds with the present situation or destination of the street. To straighten out the streets by providing "reasonable" names, Pujoulx endorsed turning all of Paris into a geography lesson. All the streets would bear the names of major towns and cities in France. The size of the street would correspond to the size of the city, with the longer streets running through several *quartiers* reserved for the major rivers. Through its street names, Paris would be France, and topography would once again signify as it had in the medieval, descriptive names.

The difference was crucial. Henceforth, the city would signify not as nature but as ideology. Two centuries after the fact, Pujoulx extended to the entire city the rationale of Henri IV's Place de France (to which Pujoulx seems to refer, if rather elliptically), transforming the streets of Paris into the map of France. The eighteenth century transformed this preoccupation with coherence into a system for the entire city. Pujoulx's proposal of 1801 stands as a clear demonstration of the strength of these convictions and the force of this vision of the city as an integrated, intelligible whole, as a distinctive testimony to the forward march of civilization.

Pujoulx, apparently unwittingly, reiterated a project a half century old. The *Géographie parisienne* elaborated by the abbé Teisserenc in 1754 had elevated the principle of Henri IV's Place de France into a system to comprehend all of Paris and all of France. (The enthusiastic abbé went so far as to suggest that the system could be carried to every state in the whole world!) The typically prolix eighteenth-century sub-title told it all (or almost): *En forme de dictionnaire, contenant l'explication de Paris ou de son plan mis en carte géographique du royaume de France, pour servir d'introduction à la géographie générale; méthode facile et nouvelle pour apprendre d'une manière pratique et locale toutes les principales parties du royaume ensemble et les unes par les autres.* (Dictionary, Containing the Explanation of Paris or Its Map Turned into a Geographical Map of the Kingdom of France, to Serve as Introduction to General Geography; An Easy and New Method to Learn in a Practical Manner and on the Spot All the Principal Parts of the Kingdom as a Whole and Each Through the Others). Because he recognized that names are "arbitrary signs" and easily altered, the abbé Teisserenc held strongly for a system that best suited the public good. Pujoulx admitted that an acquaintance had made the connection between his plan and another "about like it," but disavowed any knowledge of such a project. Still, he readily conceded that the basic idea was so elementary that it might have occurred to a good many others. He was, in any case, less interested in being first than in being the one to bring a rational system of nomination to public notice. Perhaps his plan would work.

The key word is system. Rationalization showed up on the obverse of the coin of royal appropriation of the city. Not just a few streets or a square, however splendid, but the entire city was intended to signify within a larger urban strategy. All Paris was to serve a larger, nobler purpose. The jumble of street names made all too obvious the inevitable discrepancy between the actual city and the city as project, between the real and the ideal. The utopian nature of these nominatory projects became clearer in the plans drawn up for new cities. The grid on which so many new cities were laid out in Europe as well as in America from the seventeenth through the nineteenth centuries was the very emblem of a rationalized topography modeled against the norm. But with their roots in the densely populated and overbuilt central sections and intricate network of medieval streets, the older cities thwarted every attempt at rational planning. Even in the early seventeenth century, the Place Royale and the Place Dauphine had to be constructed on vacant land distant from central Paris. The work of centuries and of many hands, these old cities were irrational in the extreme. The poorly designed layout, the odd proportions, and the crooked, uneven streets prompted Descartes' observation that these old central cities looked more like the work of chance than reason.[12]

A comprehensive name scheme provided a signal means by which to negate, or at the very least camouflage, topographical irregularity. It suggested the unification of the city around a grand design, which would turn it into a product of reason rather than chance. This newly coherent city would achieve human mastery of nature and society. The ideal city would be rational, and it would be ideologically coherent. The Revolution offered an unprecedented opportunity to do just this, to redesignate, and thereby, to redesign the city.

III

Nous aurons toujours un Voltaire, et nous n'aurons plus jamais de Théatins.
                    Marquis de Villette, 1791

We shall always have a Voltaire, and we shall never again have Théatin monks.

The most immediately striking aspect of revolutionary nominatory revision, which was also the Revolution's nominatory legacy to succeeding generations, was the intense politicization of everyday life. Children were given first names taken from the revolutionary calendar (Floréal), revolutionary virtues (Liberté), heroes (Franklin, Voltaire, Ami du Peuple, Brutus), or a combination (Brutus-sans-culotte-marche-en-avant). Among the over forty models of revolutionary playing cards, one set had Voltaire as the king of diamonds and Rousseau as king of clubs; Justice, Temperance, Prudence, and Force took the place of the queens of hearts, diamonds, spades, and clubs. One "revolutionized" chess game replaced the king with a tyrant, the queen with an adjutant, and castles with cannons; checkmate resulted from a "blockade." Over three thousand communes (out of forty thousand) brought their names into line with revolutionary order—Villedieu became La Carmagnole, after the popular revolutionary song, and Saint-Denis became Franciade. Revolutionary conviction transferred to language and invested discourse with a veritable mystical power. In this process of politicizing, the everyday street names played their part. From instruments of symbolic social control, street names became one more weapon in the intense battle for ideological allegiance waged over the nineteenth century. Well before 1789, Mercier complained that street names did not instruct inhabitants as they ought to.[13]

The Revolution provided that opportunity. The original reforms were born of enthusiasm and a passionate will to inculcate the Revolution by example. In 1791, the marquis de Villette, in whose house Voltaire had died in 1778, solicited formal approval for his own alteration of the street name on his house from Théatins (after the religious order located nearby) to Voltaire. "We shall always have a Voltaire, and we shall never again have Théatin monks," went his impeccably revolutionary reasoning. Moreover, the marquis urged the "good patriots" of the rue des Plâtrières (Plasterers' Street) to honor *their* titular republican deity: "It is important for sensitive hearts and ardent souls crossing this street to know that Rousseau used to live there on the fourth floor, and it scarcely matters that plaster used to be made there." Villette's enthusiasm fired others. Royalty and saints were swept away by authentic republican saints (Montmartre to Montmarat, Hôtel Dieu to Mirabeau-le-Patriote, Sainte-Anne to Helvétius) and republican virtues (Princesse to Justice, Richelieu to La Loi). If there was an association between site and name, as with the streets honoring Voltaire and Rousseau, the attachment invariably translated ideological considerations. It was perhaps inevitable that republican habitués of the Café Procope reportedly submitted names of royalist writers for all the sewers![14]

However well intentioned, piecemeal alterations violated every notion of system. They could never satisfy a regime that sought, as the abbé Grégoire put it in his later report to the Assemblée Nationale, to deal with "every abuse" and to "republicanize everything." Moreover, driven by the passions, enthusiasms, and manias of the moment, these changes ran the risk of being made incorrectly in a climate of such volatility. Mirabeau-le-Patriote was an appropriate substitution for Hôtel-Dieu in 1791; a mere two years later, the disclosure of Mirabeau's counterrevolutionary activities made it a dreadful embarrassment. Mirabeau quickly lost his street (along with his place in the Panthéon). La Fayette posed similar problems. Neither he nor Mirabeau, Grégoire noted, had withstood "the purifying vote of posterity."[15]

The chaos and uncertainty introduced by myriad namings and renamings brought dissatisfaction all around, prompting several motions for total nominatory reform. There exists no more striking emblem of revolutionary utopian impulses than these amazing proposals for extensive reform of street nomenclature. As nomenclature could reform topography, it could rewrite history. The entire city would be renamed and, hence, recreated. One Citoyen Avril despaired of the "barbaric or ridiculous or patronymic" names of Paris streets. Worse still, these names were "insignificant" and left the whole with no "motive." So anarchic had the renaming become that Avril urged the suspension of all naming until a comprehensive plan had been adopted. His own scheme combined great men whose memory would "perpetuate the revolution" with a variant of the abbé Teisserenc's geographical toponymy. The next year Citoyen Chamouleau went even further in his proposal to rename every street in the whole country. Each street was to bear the name of a virtue: Notre-Dame would become the Place de l'Humanité républicaine, surrounded by the rues de la Générosité et de la Sensibilité; la Halle would become the Place de la Frugalité républicaine, and so forth. "Thus the people will ever have virtue on their lips," the idealistic orator intoned before the Assemblée Nationale, "and soon morality in their hearts."[16]

The Comité de l'Instruction Publique responded to these instances with a charge to the abbé Grégoire to consider the problem, and it adopted his report in January 1794. After a review of the history of street naming from Peking to Philadelphia, Grégoire made several recommendations. He agreed that patriotism required new names. However, he insisted that "calm reason" establish not a name here and a name there but a "combined system of republican nomenclature." First, Grégoire emphasized, names should be short, comprehensible, euphonic, and appropriate; and second, they should be morally correct: "Each name ought to be the vehicle of a thought, or, rather, of a sentiment that reminds citizens of their virtues and their duties." System got citizens to the proper place and got them there properly, that is, with a lesson in mind. "Is it not natural to go from the Place de la Révolution to the rue de la Constitution and on to the rue du Bonheur?"

Lessons compelled system. Reasonable street names would instruct more effectively than a salmagundi of names with no necessary connection to one another and less connection to the whole. System alone enabled the mind to connect the parts and the whole. The whole would then present an ensemble such that the first name led directly to the other. Grégoire was by no means dogmatic. He advocated system, not a particular system, and exhorted each commune to choose the system best adapted to its particular situation. Every commune in France was "invited" to put these recommendations into practice, and a fair number did. If relatively few streets were involved in these changes—no more than 6 percent according to one estimate—these alterations included a large number of the major thoroughfares. The sense of disruption was considerable if not extensive.

All of these plans for nominatory reform testify to the pedagogical thrust so conspicuous in revolutionary enterprises. The elaborate revolutionary fêtes staged in Paris and in the provinces similarly sought to mold consciousness. The indefatigable Grégoire also wrote an immensely influential report on the French language, which insisted on an idiom common to all citizens as a vehicle of patriotic sentiment and state power. Every one of Grégoire's reforms responded to the twin demands of a modernizing state, ideological control and administrative efficiency. Street-name reform would dot the urban landscape with "emblems capable of exercising the mind, acting on the heart, and bolstering patriotism," and it would do much more, Grégoire hastened to add, by facilitating business and travel, postal service, police surveillance, and tax collection. To this end, he advocated placing signposts at entry points into cities and numbering each house on a street (street numbering did not occur until 1805). These various acts only seem to be unrelated. In fact, they all aim at tightening republican unity. That rationality was in a sense the prime republican virtue made opposition to the rationalization of the city tantamount to protesting the republic. Irrationality was counterrevolutionary. There could be no objections to the numbering of houses as there had been in the ancien régime by aristocrats who, as

Mercier tells it in his article on street signs ("Les Écriteaux des rues"), disdained the "vulgar numbers" that would lend "an air of equality" to their streets.

The highly self-conscious manipulation of symbols made manifest the ambitions to move beyond reform to creation. Symbols entered practical politics, and they did so marshalled under the banner of reason. The Revolutionary calendar gave new names to months divided into equal units of thirty days, themselves divided not into *semaines* of seven days but into *décades* of ten days, with names derived logically from the numbers (*primidi, duodi,* etc.) rather than the gods of another era. The day was divided into ten units, some new clocks showing both the twelve and the ten hour divisions. Money was put on the decimal system and "nationalized" (the franc taking the place of the pound); weights and measures were standardized. The passion for system went hand in hand with the obsession with symbols. To be effective, the Revolution required both.

Thus, to the royal concern for creating a city in the image of the monarchy, the eighteenth century joined its own brand of didacticism. The abbé Teisserenc's model brought the user into the picture not as the source of significance, in this case, street names, but as the recipient of a superior wisdom. Grégoire modified the expression of this sentiment to suit revolutionary times, but the key attitude did not change. "The people is everything, everything is to be done for the people." Details exhibit the "paternal solicitude of the government toward citizens and philanthropy toward foreigners." Iconography was one of these details of representation. The users—the people actually in the streets—were to have no interpretive latitude in reading the authoritative text, which was to direct their lives as well as their footsteps. More than ever in these toponymical utopics, the Revolution imagined the city as a sacred geography. More visibly than ever, the city reproduced by the Revolution projected a landscape of power.

Street names and other symbols, Grégoire reminded the Assemblée Nationale, provided the revolution with the means to do what no regime had ever done—institute reason and popular sovereignty, each as a term of the other. Grégoire urged legislators to seize the unprecedented opportunity, to establish a system of republican nomenclature. "No model for such an enterprise exists in the history of any people."[17] If the layout of the streets could not be rationalized—that would await Haussmann more than a half century later, and then rationalization would be partial—nomenclature might yet proclaim the revolution. If it could not be the heavenly Jerusalem, Paris might nevertheless approximate the heavenly city of the Enlightenment. A comprehensive system of names might then just possibly realize what Descartes thought impossible a century and a half before; it could build the city anew.[18]

These attempts to suppress the multivocality of the city were bound to fail, and they did. Descartes was enshrined in the Panthéon, but his ideal city, as far as Paris was concerned, belonged to the realm of the ideal. The inherent heteroglossia of the urban text won out, as Pujoulx's postrevolutionary lamentations confirm. Urban renewal at midcentury notwithstanding, nineteenth-century politics dissipated dreams of a rational city. From revolutionary nominatory practices subsequent regimes took the lesson of overt politicization, not that of system. Streets became weather vanes in the political winds. As successive governments strove to repudiate the past and legitimate the present, the honorific system of nomenclature became as unstable as the medieval one that it had replaced. Mirabeau's displacement from the Panthéon was only the first of many dislocations. (Surely, it was meet and fitting that the abbé Grégoire be accorded the ultimate honor of interment in the Panthéon during a ceremony in December 1989 marking the end of the bicentennial of the French Revolution.)

The new city envisioned by the revolution was not to be. It was not, properly speaking, a dream so much as a utopia, or the discourse that Louis Marin has labeled "utopic." This discourse, or narrative, designates a place that exists in, through, and as a text. The more coherent the text, the more integrated the system and the weaker the correlation between toponymy and topography, that is, between the "inside" and the "outside" of the text. Beyond the obliteration of particular names, revolutionary schemes rejected the very idea of connection between site and sign. Despite the stress laid by Grégoire and others on the practicality of these nominatory systems, these schemes impress the modern reader by their abstraction. The text obscures rather than illuminates topography, the name hides the place. The requirements of the system, and of the text, override the desires of the users, the readers, whose room for maneuver is more and more narrowly circumscribed. Blueprints for an ideal society, these comprehensive plans for rationalization gave no heed to urban practices and disregarded entirely the strife to which these practices invariably lead.

IV

L'espace possède ses valeurs propres. . . . Cette quête des cor-
respondances . . . propose au savant le terrain le plus neuf.
                                    Claude Lévi-Strauss, *Tristes Tropiques*

Space possesses its own values. . . . This search for connections
. . . offers the scholar the newest of territories.

The vision of a unified, rational city projects the new beginnings that are, in one sense, what revolution is supposed to produce. But if the past can be condemned, it cannot be so easily eradicated from everyday life. Like most of the institutions that touched daily life in the city, Paris streets negotiated past and present as they continued to act out the Revolution. However many projects aimed at transforming the urban text into an ideological whole, the city resisted. Paris, like French society as a whole, was almost equally consumed by the past and the future. A very different revolution was needed to create a capital city truly emblematic of the new country, a revolution that could face resolutely forward. Washington D.C. was what Paris could never be, a city that figured the republic. It is precisely the differences between these two capitals that tell us why, if Washington is the city of the republic, Paris is the city of revolution.

The rational city came closest to realization in the new, planned cities. Only previously unsettled terrain could offer the unencumbered space necessary for Descartes' engineer to sketch out an urban ideal. While the French talked endlessly about rationalizing cities, it was the Americans who effectively built most of those planned cities. America offered up for settlement an entire continent, which had, comparatively speaking, few vestiges of the past to encumber the present. These cities of the New World obeyed a different aesthetic from that of the archetypical European city, with its layers of settlement; its dirty, crowded central section; its crooked, winding streets; and its multiple-dwelling, and often multistory, housing stock. The aesthetic of containment that enclosed the European city between a center and fortifications around the periphery was quite foreign to the aesthetic of expansion that presided over the American town.

To put this aesthetic into operation, American cities relied on the grid of right-angled streets, recommended by the ease with which lots could be surveyed, built up, and sold. Like the heavenly city described in such luxuriant detail in Revelation 21:16, which many city fathers certainly had in mind, the archetypical American city "lieth four-square." So strong was the presumption of suitability that the grid was imposed even where the irregular terrain did not especially lend itself to such geometric severity (most strikingly in San Francisco). Expansion was written in this text from the beginning. Barring natural obstacles, American cities had only to follow the logic of the grid and push forth in every direction. The vocation of the city, the grid announced, was commerce and communication, not magnification of the great. To be sure, the American town was a landscape of power, but the power relations inscribed by the grid were more diffuse, less striking than those in cities designed around dramatic vistas and imposing central squares.

Street names played their part in this aesthetic, and they too heeded the logic of the grid. American cities owed their characteristic combination of numbers and greenery to William Penn's plan for Philadelphia in 1682, which rejected names of prominent personages for streets as unworthy of a Quaker creation. In the city itself, High Street (now Market Street) and Broad Street, which figured on the original plan, were augmented by numbered streets going in one direction and by cross streets named for, in Penn's words, "things that Spontaneously grow in the Country." The names from the country tied the city to the surrounding area. The numbers too served double duty, First Street, for example, recalling First Day, the Quaker Sunday.

The abbé Grégoire, concerned with devising logical systems of nomenclature, was greatly impressed with the way that Philadelphia Quakers had "imprinted their dignified character even on their streets." Quaker disapproval of glorification and distrust of patronymics resonated broadly in the new world. To be sure, American streets carry the names of individuals. But if American streets honor, they seldom glorify. As de Tocqueville recognized, the democratic impulse levels rather than raises, and Americans manifestly have felt uncomfortable with the hierarchy so salient in Paris street names replete with full names and titles.[19]

Moreover, the American Revolution entertained a very different relationship with the past than did its French counterpart. There was no urgency to eradicate vestiges of the past. The nominatory conservatism characteristic of the American Revolution is worlds apart from the symbolic radicalism of the French Revolution. No one paid much attention to the radical revisions suggested from time to time, and the royal titles mostly remained in place. Responding in 1794 to a correspondent who urged eradication of prerevolutionary street names, the editor of a New York newspaper sensibly, and prudently, maintained that all streets and their names belonged in the historical record. Popular sentiment evidently concurred with Thomas Jefferson, who revealed a keen sense of a sacred geography that one tampers with at one's peril: "I am not sure that we ought to change all our names. And during the regal government, sometimes, indeed, they were given through adulation; but often also as the reward of the merit of the times, sometimes for service rendered the colony. Perhaps, too, a name when given, should be deemed a sacred property."[20]

The striking exception to the usual course of American urban planning was, and is, of course, Washington, D.C. With its name taken from the "father of the country," the capital city recalled the paradigmatic patronymic origins of the city, precisely the connections that William Penn had so emphatically rejected for the City of Brotherly Love. Washington himself was very much involved in the planning of the city that would bear his name (which he always referred to as the "Federal City"). He chose the site, and he chose the planner for the capital that was to exemplify the new nation and the very structure of the new government. The plan that Major Pierre Charles L'Enfant submitted to President Washington in June 1791 started with the Philadelphia grid but superimposed broad avenues like the Champs-Elysées in Paris, as well as diagonals and multiple focal points reminiscent of those in Christopher Wren's plan for rebuilding London.

The originality of the plan struck everyone, one commentator going so far as to praise the "genius" that had made an "inconceivable improvement upon all other cities in the world." The same observer accorded particular praise for the avoidance of the "insipid sameness" that made Philadelphia so dull.[21] The vistas, the broad avenues, and the monumental public buildings inscribed the plan of Washington within the tradition of Saint Peter's Square or Versailles. But, instead of pope or prince, this city of the New World glorified a republic.

Contemporaries readily grasped the symbolic significance of the planned city. "Un citoyen des États-Unis," writing in French in 1795, elaborated a striking semiotic interpretation of the new federal city. L'Enfant, noted this author, had made visible the relations between city and country and those between the three branches of the government. Placing the Capitol on a hill with several broad avenues radiating outward made it unquestionably the center of the city, much as this city was to be the center of the new country. As former President (and then Chief Justice) William Howard Taft noted in 1915, L'Enfant's capital city was the very image of the federal Constitution adopted in 1788, infinitely adaptable to "the greatest emergencies and the most radical crises that could possibly confront a nation."[22]

In this projection of nation, nomenclature played its part. The plan impressed the regularity of the grid upon topography even more forcefully than in Philadelphia by dividing the city into quarters and placing letters on north-south streets in addition to the numbers for east-west streets. To counter the monotony of the numbered grid, the diagonal avenues that cut through plazas or converged on a central point like the Capitol and the president's house bore the names of the then fifteen states. The location of these avenues followed their geographical location in the country, north to south (which was also the order in which delegates from the several states signed the Constitution in 1787). The three longest avenues, which traversed the entire city from east to west, represented three of the largest states, Massachusetts, Pennsylvania, and Jefferson's own Virginia.

The layout of the streets may or may not have been Thomas Jefferson's idea, but like the plan of the city as a whole, it gave emblematic expression to the republican ideal that he and the Founding Fathers sought to establish in the new United States. Whatever the origins, the streets of Washington constituted a dazzling symbolic ploy to reconcile the states of the Union to the federal city that figured as it sustained their union. The nomenclature wove the states into the very fabric of the city just as the Constitution merged the states into the federation. It was this city in the New World, not Paris, that executed Henri IV's conception of the Place de France almost two centuries after the fact. The city and its grid, like the Constitution, resolved what remained unresolved in Paris and in France. They settled the nature of the relationship of the part, the province or state, to the whole, the nation. Toponymy and topography joined in a grand national scheme of unity. Surely, the abbé Teisserenc and the abbé Grégoire would have been pleased.

The uncontested brilliance of Washington lay in the exceptional coherence of a design that, like the Constitution itself, was exceptionally suited to future needs, symbolic as well as urban. L'Enfant conceived the space in terms not of enclosure but of organic expansion. To the rationality that the eighteenth century so ardently desired and the ideological coherence that French republicans struggled to effect, L'Enfant joined a distinctively American preoccupation with growth. The Federal City, he reported to President Washington, would "soon grow of itself, and spread as the branches of a tree." Like all city plans and like the original Utopia, L'Enfant's plan for Washington was itself a *utopic,* that is, a place that came into existence not simply *through* a text but *as* a text in the strictest construction of the term. As such, it is emblematic of all texts, an edenic vision of a world to which words and works give form and substance.

In no way could the new, planned city of Washington serve as a model for the many-layered urban palimpsest of Paris, with its legacies from so many regimes, its vestiges of so many events and so many populations. L'Enfant's plan proclaimed Washington's vocation as capital of the Republic. In contrast, every map of Paris pronounced it as much more than the capital of France. The singularity of Paris as a city of revolution resides in its torturous relationship to the past, to the many pasts of the city and of the nation. The existing society and the existing city had to be made over in the image of the revolution, and yet could not be. The past was too conspicuous to be elided and too conflictual to be assimilated.

The modernity commonly ascribed to nineteenth-century Paris is rooted in this sense of movement, the perpetually unfinished, always provisional nature of the present and the imminence of change. Paris, not Washington, figured the age of revolutions. The battles on and over Paris streets strike a vivid contrast with L'Enfant's peaceful vision of organic growth for the American capital. By inscribing conflict onto the urban text itself, the Revolution of 1789 set the stage for the revolutionary Paris of the nineteenth century. The sense that change was at once inevitable and unpredictable translated into a veritable obsession with revolution, with fixing change, with arresting movement into order to make sense of the city and of the revolution by which it had come to be defined.

2

Mapping the City

Guide-books, Wellingborough, are the least reliable books in
all literature; and nearly all literature, in one sense, is made
up of guidebooks.

Herman Melville, *Redburn*

On 2 Pluviôse, Year II of the republic (21 January 1793 on the prerevolutionary Gregorian calendar), Louis Capet was driven from the
Prison du Temple to what had been inaugurated as the Place Louis
XV but was then the Place de la Révolution (and would subsequently
become the Place de la Concorde). The journey lasted nearly two
hours. The closed carriage and its full military escort passed through
streets lined with citizens armed with spikes and guns. The beating
of drums attached to the horses muffled any possible expression of
sympathy for the man who had been Louis XVI, the sixth member of
the House of Bourbon to reign as King of France and Navarre, great-
great-great grandson of Louis XIV, the monarch known as the Sun
King. At the scaffold, the condemned man asserted his innocence
and absolved his executioners, but his attempts to say more were
stifled by more drums. The deed accomplished, the severed head was
paraded before the impatient bystanders whose shouts of "Vive la
liberté" and "Vive la république" brought to a close this performance
of what Michel Foucault so aptly called the "Spectacle of the Scaffold."[1]

The personal and dynastic drama and its compelling political consequences consumed observers at the time and focused commentary
on the properly national significance of the execution. For in be-
heading the king, the Revolution simultaneously abolished a central
symbol of country and obliterated a vital emblem of the city. It is those
urban consequences, the crisis of authority that necessitated redefinition of the city, that concern this chapter. Once the king's city—
the city earlier kings ritually appropriated as "our good city of
Paris"—Paris became the city of the Revolution. But what did, what

might that mean? Whose "good city" would Paris be henceforth? At least since the sixteenth century, monarch and inhabitants alike had boasted of Paris as the "capital of the kingdom." Was it also the capital of the Republic? Decapitation deprived the city of a *chef*, of its symbolic head. Paris became an organism without a head, truncated, incomplete, in sum, a monstrosity. So strong was the association of the city and the monarchy, so visible the imprint of royalty on the topography and the toponymy of the city itself that the execution made much of Paris a symbolic nonsense. Clearly, the crown and the fleurs-de-lys that figured on the seal of the city had to be discarded. But what would replace them? Whose city was it? Who now would, or indeed could, comprehend it? The city, in a very real sense, had to be rewritten before it could once again be read.

Most obviously, one regime took over from another and went about the business of creating institutions and ideologies in its own image. Accordingly, revolutionaries destroyed a number of the more egregious emblems of the past (the term *vandalism* was coined at the time). But transition entailed more than demolition. Given the imprint of the monarchy upon Paris, iconographic regeneration posed problems of major proportions. The Revolution had somehow to accommodate the past. The execution of Louis XVI functions as a larger symbol of urban crisis, one that bespeaks an immediate need for symbolic re-representation, a drastic rewriting or resymbolization, of the urban text.

Writers of many different persuasions and commitments took up this challenge in the nineteenth century. Claiming a new authority over the city as text, they sought to guide their readers through the newly unfamiliar passages of the city and to explain, if possible, its disconcerting capacity for continual change. The role of guide through a fearful place was not, of course, a new one. Virgil's guidance of Dante through hell supplied the model regularly invoked through the centuries, and never more insistently than in the first part of the nineteenth century, when Paris itself reverberated from the repeated, and intensified, disruptions of revolution. The writer simply assumed, or arrogated, the intellectual authority to map the postrevolutionary city.

That authority was necessarily also political, so nineteenth-century writers cast themselves in a position of leadership, guiding readers through the perilous territory that only they knew as they insisted it be known. The special relationship of the writer and the city does not originate in this postrevolutionary period, but it is then that writers learned to press their claims with especial urgency. There was a void to fill, and it was filled by the self-conscious authority of the author and by texts that presented themselves as authoritative. The nature and the consequences of this immense self-confidence are prime elements in an understanding of the urban discourse that began to emerge in early nineteenth-century Paris. The stories that the city came to tell, in new genres like the guidebook and eventually the novel, became part of its history, just as the history of the city was integral to the very notion of the genre. The urban discourse elaborated in nineteenth-century Paris builds on just this crosscutting of genre and history. The Revolution made the interaction of the two more obvious, and more imperative, but the relation was already well established by 1789.

I

Naître à Paris, c'est être deux fois Français.
Louis-Sébastien Mercier, *Tableau de Paris*

To be born in Paris is to be doubly French.

No city exists apart from the multitude of discourses that it prompts. Topography is textuality. One reads the structured space of the city as one reads the structured language of a book. But more than analogy is at work in this dual textuality. In the modern city the two models of urban texts—the "text" of the physical city and the writings about that city—coincide, overlap, comment upon, and at times contradict each other. This intertextuality becomes increasingly intricate as the city expands, builds, and demolishes and as writing about the city draws upon ever more diverse, ever more sophisticated, and ever more established traditions of texts. As these urban texts become more various, meaning proliferates and turns the city into a palimpsest, that is, a textual expression of the labyrinth. Indeed, readings of the palimpsest weave the magic thread that enables the individual to find a way through the labyrinth.

Such reading requires guidance of a sort different than the directives proffered in more conventional narratives. As early as the mid–sixteenth century, it became evident that the city of Paris needed another kind of narrative to make sense of its increasing diversity. There was no lack of histories and legends and myths to trace the origins of the city and of its name. In fact, chronicles of ritualized praise had been part of a Parisian discourse for centuries. But these celebrations of Paris make no connection to the explicitly topographical expositions like Guillot's *Dit des rues de Paris* at the very beginning of the fourteenth century. The guidebook as it took shape in the early nineteenth century emerges from the conjunction of these two very different urban texts, the chronicle and the topographical exposition. But the genre that arises from this alliance does not merely join one text to another. More than juxtaposition is at work. For the guidebook to take its place among city texts first requires that the city as a whole be rethought.

Like most practitioners of the genre since, the authors of these early guidebooks assume that unmediated contact with the city is inadequate at best, and probably dangerous as well. The frequency of reference to Paris as hell in the nineteenth century—it was a cliché by the time Balzac got to it in the 1830s in his celebrated opening of *La Fille aux yeux d'or*—bespoke a pervasive fear in a city beset by evils with unknown consequences. The writer of a guidebook supplied the essential link between text and reader and between city and inhabitant. Gradually, the nineteenth century raised this affinity between the writer-guide and the city to a principle of literary-urban conduct. The literary guidebook became a characteristic genre of postrevolutionary Paris.

Under the ancien régime, guidebooks were less complex undertakings. To the extent that the control of proliferating meanings was less problematic in the ancien régime, it derived from the increasing emphasis on the imposition of royal authority. Guidebooks undertook to define the city in terms of the evolving landscape of power and to direct attention to the sacred geography of monarchical Paris. The importance of the postrevolutionary literary guidebooks can be gauged only against the background of three centuries of guidebooks that magnified the monarchy. Like the postrevolutionary battles over street names, the reconceptualization of the guidebook, its promotion to something of a literary status, went hand-in-hand with the far larger work of reconceiving city and country after the Revolution.

Appropriately enough, the first guidebook of Paris appeared only four years after François I officially settled in his "good city" of Paris and two years after publication of the first map of the city. In 1532 the bookseller Gilles Corrozet printed what seems to have been the first guidebook of Paris. *La Fleur des antiquitez de Paris* (*The Flower of Parisian Antiquities*) set a model that served for two centuries and more.[2] Corrozet elaborates in specifically topographical terms the extension of monarch's authority over the city of Paris that is illustrated so strikingly in the evolution of the seal of the city. The original seal, that of the water sellers, dating from the early thirteenth century, shows the simplest boat, emblem of the water merchants' trade. A century later, the seal of the Prévôté des Marchands, the overall municipal governing body, displays the same boat, but with the significant addition of two fleurs-de-lys above the now full (though still single mast) sail. In this way, the monarchy literally impresses its signature on the seal of the city.

Corrozet follows this lead, insisting upon the connection between all the inhabitants of the city, but particularly that between the bourgeois and the king, who now honors the city with his presence. In what we might now call a semiotic analysis of the Paris seal, at the end of *La Fleur des antiquitez de Paris* Corrozet lists the inhabitants who count: "men of learning, . . . merchants, . . . priests, bourgeois, nobles, clerics, and men of arms." Yet Corrozet begins by placing his work under the aegis of the king. He will, he notifies the reader at the outset, first present the history of the city and then "all the most laudable things accomplished in Paris by princes and kings, and all the edifices made by them from the time that it was first inhabited until the time of the very Christian king of France, Francis the First of this name." He ends with a truly marvelous genealogy that traces the reigning king, François I, back to Paris, son of Priam, thereby substantiating the legendary origin of the city in the royal line of Troy and, incidentally, making good on his dedication of the work to the "Nobles, bourgeois, of Greek or Trojan origin." The forced conjunction of bourgeoisie and monarchy stands as a reminder that the decision of François I in 1528 to settle in Paris is determined by his need for the funds that only the city fathers could supply. It is, then, entirely appropriate that Corrozet's analysis of the city seal should see the boat on the seas as a sign of "inestimable wealth."

The first edition of *La Fleur des antiquitez de Paris* follows the tradition of the chronicles. It is all legend and history and testimonial

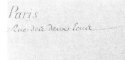

REGISTRE. 3.

Nᵒ 550.

PAR ORDONNANCE RENDUE

le 27 du mois d'octobre de l'an 1699 par Mᴹˢ les Commiſſaires Généraux du Conſeil députez ſur le fait des Armoiries.

Celles de la Ville de Paris

Telles qu'elles ſont ici peintes & figurées, aprés avoir été reçuës, ont été enrégitrées à l'Armorial Général, dans le Régitre cotté Paris, *en conſequence du payement des droits reglés par les Tarif & Arreſt du Conſeil, du 20ᵉ de Novembre de l'an 1696. en foi dequoi, le préſent Brévet a été délivré A Paris par Nous* CHARLES D'HOZIER, *Conſeiller du ROI, & Garde de l'Armorial Général de France, &c.*

d'hozier

Plate 2. Seal of Paris, 1699. The seal as officially registered under Louis XIV, with gold fleurs-de-lys against a blue field over the merchant ship representing Paris, on a silver sea against a red background. The superimposed fleurs-de-lys signaled the dominion of the king over the city. The ship first appeared in the thirteenth century as the sign of the Water Merchants Guild and, hence, of the commercial vocation of the city. The fleurs-de-lys first appeared on the seal in the fourteenth century. (Photograph by the University of Chicago Medical Center, A.V. Department.)

about the city and contains no topographical information whatsoever. Corrozet was an astute bookseller who identified a market and at the same time created a genre. Accordingly, the second edition, which he brought out only a year after the first, turned *La Fleur* into a true guide to urban space. To the legends, history, chronicles, poems, anecdotes, heraldry, and epitaphs of the great, Corrozet added important topographical information, notably lists of all the streets, churches, and colleges in the city. The next twenty years saw a total of five reprints of the 1533 edition, the last two with an updated list of streets and other relevant topographical details.

In 1550 Corrozet printed the far more substantial *Les Antiquitez, histoires, croniques et singularitez de la grande & excellente cité de Paris, ville capitalle & chef du Royaume de France* (*The Antiquities, Histories, Chronicles, and Singularities of the Great and Excellent City of Paris, Capital City and Head of the Kingdom of France*), which he dedicated not to the bourgeois of *La Fleur* but to "the noble and illustrious Families of Paris." So great is Corrozet's pride of place—Paris is "the most magnificent, largest, most populous and sovereign city of France, indeed of all Christendom"—that he admonishes Parisians for their ignorance of their city. It is not enough, Corrozet impresses upon readers who might be tempted to shirk their duties as Parisians, to declare peremptorily that one is from such a place. One must be able to discuss its "prerogatives and beauties," and these, in Corrozet's Paris, are once again the work of the monarchy. He claims the honor of writing for "the very Christian Crown of France & the exaltation of your families," and *Les Antiquitez* stresses more than the earlier *La Fleur* the debt of city to the monarchy. From the buildings the first kings built to the tombstones and epitaphs that their successors dedicated to them, Corrozet explains, "you will find how much our Kings have enriched and decorated this capital city with privileges, with buildings, and with their own persons, even after their death," the last in reference to all the "sepulchres and epitaphs" promised in the subtitle. *Les Antiquitez* too enjoyed considerable success. Corrozet printed a second edition in 1561, and another bookseller brought out a third edition in 1577, after Corrozet's death.

Later guidebooks celebrate the monarchy in a more sophisticated mode, but celebration it remains. François Colletet organized the *Abrégé des annales de la Ville de Paris* (1664), as the subtitle of the work tells us, by the successive reigns of French kings. It was entirely logical as well as absolutely appropriate for Germain Brice, author of the most popular guidebook of the century—nine editions and five reprints between 1684 and 1752—to begin his tour of Paris with the official residence of the king in Paris, the Louvre, "the most remarkable place, which is the principal ornament of the city by its vast extent and by the quantity of edifices of which it is composed."[3]

As the growth of the city modified urban space, urban genres began to specialize. Serious historians too confronted the varied strata of urban topography and toponymy. Thus Henri Sauval's *Histoire et recherches des antiquités de la ville de Paris* (1724) quickly became the standard to which later generations (including Victor Hugo for the documentation of *Notre-Dame de Paris*) would return again and again. Other works addressed other uses of the city. Compendia of various sorts emphasized the practical, supplied street names and useful addresses, and included summary statistics for the individual who needed to negotiate the city while contemplating its past glories.

The guidebook proper occupies a space between these two poles of past and present. It usually presents a historical sketch of some sort—the term *antiquités*, so important for Corrozet, continues to figure in numerous subtitles—along with a modicum of more or less useful information. Whatever the specific orientation, from history to almanac to guidebook in the broadest sense, these urban genres sought to systematize as well as to glorify and to make it possible for readers to make their way around the city.

In 1759 and 1760 two works appeared, by the same author and with almost the same title, that point to the prevailing sense of the guidebook as an urban genre. M. Jèze's 1759 *Tableau de Paris* offers above all information. It is resolutely tied to the present, since the material consists of, as Jèze announces in the preface, "the details most subject to variation." The author offers his *Tableau* as a "work that is useful for some, necessary for others." Jèze invites readers to help him keep subsequent editions up to date. The 1760 *État ou Tableau de Paris* is by design not a history (Jèze cites Sauval) and not a description (he cites Corrozet and Brice) but rather a state (état) of knowledge about the city. This is a book to be used, to be studied, and to depend upon (it is at once a "book for use, for research and for commodity"). Jèze insists again and again, here in his "Preliminary Discourse," on the systematization of the information that he provides. That information, much of it familiar from the 1759 *Ta-*

Plate 3.   Seal of Paris, 1811. In the First Empire, the fleur-de-lys and the blue
of the monarchy disappear in favor of the eagle and bees associated with
Napoléon. The Egyptian goddess Isis on the prow of the ancient, silver ship
against a red background brings the Egyptian military successes of Napoléon
in full view as well as the classical associations with imperial Rome, which also
conquered Egypt. The other parts—the crown that recalls a fortified castle,
the eagle, and the two garlands (oak leaves on the left, olive leaves on the
right) tied by red ribbons—were shared by all French cities of the First Order
(*bonnes villes*). (Photograph by the University of Chicago Medical Center, A.V.
Department.)

Plate 4.   Seal of Paris, 1817. The monarchy that returned to France after Waterloo replaced the Napoleonic eagle and bees with the emblems of the ancien régime. The seal reproduced the basic 1699 escutcheon but replaced the ship with an elaborately rigged military vessel and retained for the outer section the now familiar château-crown, while adding lilies to recall the flowers with which Parisians greeted the return of Louis XVIII. (Photograph by the University of Chicago Medical Center, A.V. Department.)

bleau, is presented systematically. The goal is not simply to supply more information but to present a rational system of knowledge about the city. As the subtitle tells us and a large fold-out map graphically illustrates, the city is "considered relative to the Necessary, the Useful, the Agreeable, and the Administration." If the last category seems somewhat anomalous in the series, Jèze, in his 1759 *Tableau,* makes a point of signaling, among the many claims of Paris to preeminence, "the wisdom of its Government and its Police."[4]

These urban works and others that followed served the larger purposes of government insofar as they fit within the larger goal of rationalizing the city and bringing it, and its sometimes rebellious inhabitants, under control. Whether or not they articulated these urban concerns, the guidebooks participated in the work of the monarchy, even as the king moved the court from Paris to Versailles. They fixed its imprint in a written text that would survive topographical and social change. By virtue of being systematically organized in a text, street names, monuments, statues, and other urban icons acquired a permanence that guaranteed their survival as text even as the city itself altered, built anew, and modified urban space. The guides fixed the city and in so doing arrested potentially idiosyncratic definitions of place. So usual do these administrative prerogatives appear to the latter-day reader that we forget just how recent the notion of a fixed urban text is. Guidebooks, histories, and practical compendia comprised but one element in the fixing of that text, but they were an important element, indeed, all the more so for the indirect nature of the connection they compelled.

II

Variété, mon sujet t'appartient.
Louis-Sébastien Mercier,
Tableau de Paris

Variety, my subject belongs to you.

The struggles over the designation of city space gave a distinctly urban resonance to the larger political conflicts that played out in postrevolutionary France. The successful contestation of authority opened the city to redefinitions from every quarter. The execution of one king and the defeat and subsequent flight of his successors in

1814, 1815, 1830, 1848, and 1870 dramatized the fragility of political authority. Having lost its central authority, the urban symbol system fell into disarray. Into this void, writers stepped with surprising assurance to assert the authority of the written word to interpret the modern city and the society that it both represented and expressed. In this continually manipulated urban space, guidebooks found a ready market, among the provincials arriving in Paris to undertake the work of the new representative government and among a good many others hopeful of profiting from the new state of affairs. Parisians themselves, many of whom seldom ventured outside their neighborhood, stood in need of instruction. They were often lost, as Mercier noted before the Revolution, in the swelling multitude of provincials and foreigners. Native and visitor alike desperately needed direction in the changed and rapidly changing milieu. If this need was apparent to Mercier in the very last days of the ancien régime, it was palpable after the Revolution and in the new century.

Not the least problematic aspect of the new Paris was its inhabitants. The Parisians of the revolutionary and postrevolutionary eras were not those of prerevolutionary yesterday. Indeed, description of place presented less of a challenge for the urban accountant than did analysis of people. If writings in and about postrevolutionary Paris went on at length about the "ruins" of the old Paris, the psychic emphasis nevertheless fell on the new city, and particularly on the changed and changing customs (*moeurs*) that characterized that city. One P.-J.-B. Nougaret presented his *Paris, ou le rideau levé* in 1798 "to serve the history of our former and present customs." In *Paris à la fin du XVIIIe siècle* (1801), J. B. Pujoulx opened the century with promises of a "historical and moral sketch" of monuments and ruins, disquisitions on the state of science, art, and industry, "as well as the Customs of its inhabitants." In 1814 Louis Prudhomme's *Voyage descriptif et philosophique de l'ancien et du nouveau Paris* announced not only "historical facts and odd anecdotes about the monuments" but also much concerning the "variation of the customs of its inhabitants over the past twenty-five years," that is, since 1789.[5] And so on.

To be sure, earlier guidebooks did not altogether neglect the Parisians. Corrozet, we have seen, addressed his Parisian public directly, and a century later, Brice undertook to defend their character. Over the eighteenth century, newspapers and novels found Parisians an inexhaustible source of inspiration. Lesage's novel *Le Diable boiteux*

(*The Lame Devil*) (1707) was immensely popular at the time of its publication (Lesage kept adding to it until 1726) and became an important model for a whole line of nineteenth-century literary guidebooks. What better figure for the guide to the inner city than his device, a not very threatening junior-grade devil whose ability to remove rooftops revealed the inside story? Montesquieu was another literary ancestor, not of course through the sober, magisterial *Esprit des lois* (1748) but through his satirical epistolary novel of 1721, *Les Lettres persanes* (*The Persian Letters*). Marivaux, best known as a dramatist (witness the street named in his honor near the Théâtre de l'Odéon that created such a commotion in the 1770s), also joined this group of explorers of Parisian mores in his novels, *La Vie de Marianne* (1731–42) and *Le Paysan parvenu* (*The Parvenu Peasant*) (1734–35), and in a direct steal from the journalism of Joseph Addison and Richard Steele, *Le Spectateur français* (1721–24) and *Lettres sur les habitants de Paris* (1717–18). Yet, however much these works tell us about Paris, none makes an explicit claim as a guide to the city, and none resembles what we might now call an ethnography of the city.

It fell to Louis-Sébastien Mercier (1740–1814), poet, playwright, novelist, chronicler, and all-purpose man of letters, to make, and make good on, both claims. The first, one-volume edition of the *Tableau de Paris*, which appeared in 1781, contains 105 short, definitely quirky sketches that explore Paris and examine the mores of Parisians. Here was the literary ancestor to whom every subsequent urban ethnographer turned; this work was the model against which subsequent works were measured.[6] Mercier does not address foreigners who seek their way around Paris so much as he tells Parisians about themselves and their neighbors, about people and places, which they may not know at all and which, in Mercier's view, they ought to know. "Many of its inhabitants are like foreigners in their own city; this book will perhaps teach them something" ("Préface"). The public obviously agreed with the author's assessment, for the popularity of the first volume was such that the indefatigable Mercier brought out a revised edition in four volumes the very next year, four more volumes in 1783, and four more in 1788.

The epigraph to the fifth volume boldly states his credo: "Variety, my subject belongs to you." There is something quite extraordinary in the assertion. Instead of claiming a hierarchical focus as an ordering control—king, country, or other symbols of authority—Mercier takes on the whole range of the city around him and makes *himself* the control. Everything is relevant within an authorial self-possession that becomes its own reason for being. The quasi-ubiquitous and extraordinarily prolific urban explorer alone is in a position to cover and to render the whole city, and through the city, the larger society. Moreover, ubiquity is suddenly a virtue instead of a problem. The controlling perspective in the *Tableau de Paris* is, to use a neologism of the 1780s, that of *ethnology*. Mercier justifies a striking comparison between life in Paris and the life of natives in Africa and America by the fact that two-hundred-league hunts and arias at the Opéra Comique are practices that are "equally simple and natural" ("Préface").

Ethnologist *avant la lettre,* Mercier looks down at the street dwellers as well as up at the great and shows no hesitation about venturing into the most insalubrious and potentially dangerous corners of the city. He will not, he warns the reader, disdain the lowly, the miserable, the disquieting, or the distasteful, for his research covers "all classes of citizens" ("Préface"). Introducing the article "One-eyed cabarets" (7), Mercier knows full well that his "delicate readers" will not come to such an ill-famed place. Now there is no need to do so: "I went there for you. You will see the place only in my picture, which will spare you some disagreeable sensations." And indeed Mercier writes often of places and people that few of his readers will or will have wanted to know: "Beggars" (3), "Rats" (5), "Prisons" (3, 8), "The Executioner" (3), "Cemeteries" (9), "Public latrines" (7, 11) (notably, the absence thereof), "Sewers" (7), and so on and on.

Instead of a place, Paris has been transformed into a multiform experience, one that Mercier describes in such a way that no Parisian need feel left out of that experience. By the same token, every Parisian can also feel more richly involved in a complexity that is less intimidating because it is now experienced—if only vicariously through the printed word. Behind or within each aspect of the narrative lies a larger claim of still greater importance. "This is what we now are," Mercier seems to say, inviting everyone to take both comfort and pride in the cohesion and identity that reading *his* experiences can bring.

In short, Mercier renders the city in terms of both the vagaries and the concrete possibilities of everyday life and through the occupations of ordinary people. He favors public space over private enclave. The places that attract him are not the palaces of royalty or the *hôtels particuliers* of the elite but rather the gardens and boulevards and promenades open to all, the shops of the bourgeoisie, the cafés, and the cabarets, places of natural urban promiscuity, where the urban spectacle is at its most lively. The individuals he crosses as he traverses the city from one end to the other are not, with a very few exceptions, the well known or highborn. The personages of the *Tableau* are the many who fill the multitude of tasks on which the city depends: the water carriers, pawn brokers, charlatans, booklenders, cooks, governesses, authors, maids, prostitutes, working girls, dentists, midwives, lackeys, authors. The *Tableau* emerges in the act of reading as a vast compendium of the everyday practice of the city, where the ordinary may be the extraordinary, and where, under Mercier's pen, the extraordinary becomes ordinary, the stuff of everyday life, from the "Mobility of the Government," "Visits," and "Civility" to "Moving" and "Miracles."[7]

The broad net cast by the *Tableau de Paris* gives the work a decidedly modern flavor. Over a half century before the "Avant-Propos" to the *Comédie humaine* and the extended parallels Balzac will later draw between the animal and the human kingdoms, Mercier asserts that the human being "is an animal subject to the most varied and most astonishing modifications . . . whence the infinite number of forms that transform the individual according to the place, circumstances, and time" ("Préface"). Like Balzac, Mercier takes those transformations as his subject, and, like Balzac, he also receives considerable criticism for the reach of people and behavior of which he takes serious account. The most celebrated jibe comes from Antoine de Rivarol, man of letters and author of the most famous celebration of the French language, *De l'universalité de la langue française* (*On the Universality of the French Language*) (1784). To a writer who flatly decrees that "what is not clear is not French," the *Tableau de Paris* must have appeared obscure and confused. Certainly he objects strenuously to what he viewed as its irremediable vulgarity. This is, Rivarol scolds, a work "thought up in the street and written on the street sign," whose author "has depicted the cellar and the attic and bypassed the salon."[8]

Rivarol is not totally off target. The street is never far from Mercier's eye. The street sign, as we have seen, is an apt analogy, and the streets themselves of eighteenth-century Paris are, and not just by Mercier's account, dirty. There is a good deal of dirt in the *Tableau*, both real and metaphorical, from the chapter entitled "Manure" (2) to the startling assertion that the proud city of the Enlightenment used to be called "Lutetia, city of mud!" ("Décrotteurs," 6). Mercier's city needs its garbage men, and Mercier sees that his *Tableau* gets them ("Boueurs," 5). Readers accustomed to the decorous guidebooks that implicitly glorify the monarchy and explicitly praise the city must have been disconcerted, and quite possibly appalled, by the *Tableau*. Mercier concedes that his is a revisionist view and acknowledges that he has painted a more somber picture than readers are used to, one filled with "chagrin and anxiety" rather than the "joy and gaiety" traditionally attributed to Parisians. But he swears that his paintbrush renders faithfully what he has seen with his own eyes. Not for this ethnologist the "indeterminate and vague speculation" of experience that comes from books. He has, as he tells us, written the *Tableau* with his legs ("Mes Jambes," 11).

In walking the *whole* city, Mercier also bespeaks the implicit democracy of the coming revolution. Everything is of interest, and every layer of the city, every social group, receives its due. Privilege and poverty exist side by side. The importance accorded the lowly in this insistence upon a parallelism is almost unthinkable within the ideological (and therefore aesthetic) confines of the ancien régime. With the actual revolution, this same stress becomes part and parcel of a broader and inevitably more dynamic urban experience. One may go farther. Paris is almost incalculably more vital when everything is worthy of description. Mercier predicts, in every sense of the word, a revolutionary city of infinite possibility.

It is not simply *what* or *whom* Mercier talks about that explains the success of the *Tableau de Paris* among contemporaries or made it a model for literary guidebooks a half century later. The literary program that Mercier sets for himself in the 1780s echoes throughout the 1830s and 1840s. Mercier's is a new kind of *Tableau de Paris*, not the *tableaux* of Jèze, nor the many inventories or catalogues that seek to rationalize the city, but the tableau of the painter, with its varied palette and different brush strokes. No more *annales*, no more *descriptions raisonnées* or *dictionnaires*, no more *antiquitez*. Mercier marks his dissent from the tradition of guidebooks by his determined refusal to take account of topography or history: he has produced "neither *inventory* nor *catalogue*." He will not talk, he informs his readers at the outset, about the already fixed, about the monuments and buildings that mark urban space. (Ever-obliging, however, he supplies the name and address of a bookseller where a four-volume dictionary can be purchased.) He will himself fix the transient, the ever-changing public and private behavior, the "fleeting nuances" of comportment and "public and private customs," and everything else that strikes him in "this bizarre heap of customs that may be crazy or reasonable but always changing" ("Préface"). Mercier disavows satire; he is not, he tells us, a latter-day Lesage, however easy it would be to indulge in satirical sallies.

In a credo that looks ahead to and perhaps paves the way for the nineteenth-century realist novel, Mercier certifies that he will restrict himself to what he sees. There will be none of the intellectualizing that mars the work of so many of his contemporaries. His tableau is the product of "the brush of the *painter*," not "the meditation of the *philosophe*." Unlike so many others, he does not dismiss the world around him. His own century, his own country, his own city, interest him far more than the "uncertain history" of the Phoenicians or the Egyptians. And since it is, after all, with his contemporaries that he must communicate, the *Tableau* by rights concentrates on them. In a proclamation that points both ahead to the journalistic principles and the realist practice of the next century and back to the pedagogical thrust of the Enlightenment, Mercier asserts and justifies his unremitting focus on the present, on the "current generation and the physiognomy of my century" ("Préface").

It is here, in his concentration on the present and the exclusion of the past, that Mercier at once continues and revises the guidebook. New editions allow guidebooks to keep pace with the shifting urban scene. But these standard guides tend to place the changing landscape of the city within a fixed history. Fixed by a monarchical past, the changing present is defined and anchored by an established, conventional past and a rationalization of the present (remember that Jèze boasts that he considers Paris systematically, "relative to the Necessary, the Useful, the Agreeable, and [in the wonderful apparent non sequitur] the Administration").

Mercier's *Tableau* parts company from contemporary urban discourse in its elimination of the anchor that had stabilized the city text at least since Henri IV in the beginning of the seventeenth century, namely the monarchy. Thus, even before the destruction of the Bastille actually altered the cityscape, Mercier undertook to remap Paris. His reinterpretation of the city, and of the larger society, reaches well beyond the specific criticisms of the government made with considerable verve (Mercier writes from a prudent self-imposed exile in Switzerland). Like the good philosophe that he is (despite his disclaimers), Mercier stakes his claim to glory on the "few useful verities" contained in his observations, which, he fervently hopes, will lead "the zealous administrator" to correct some of the more egregious abuses he points out ("Préface").

The reconfiguration of ethnologist turns out to be far more significant than the didacticism of the philosophe. Mercier's Paris is more various and more diverse than the Paris produced by the usual guidebook exactly because it has no focal point. In the *Tableau,* all classes, all occupations, meet and mix. The focal point is the author himself, whose subject, as he himself tells us, is the variety that he finds. The consequent jumble of the text faithfully reproduces the disarray of the city. Both, in Mercier's aggressively egalitarian view, repudiate the hierarchy and chronology that implicitly or explicitly order the conventional guidebook.

Mercier conceives his writing of a piece with his perception of the city. His language adheres to classical norms no more than his rendition of the city follows classical conceptions of urban design. Tellingly, if the word that he needs does not exist, Mercier makes one up. Language changes like the city, and Mercier connects the two fields of action in his *Néologie ou vocabulaire des mots nouveaux, à renouveler ou pris dans des acceptions nouvelles* (*Neologia or Vocabulary of New Words, to Be Renewed or Taken in New Senses*), published in 1801. The clutter of the *Tableau* reproduces the confusion of the quotidian in a large city. If the *Tableau* can be seen as a harbinger of the Revolution, it is because this work exposes the neat distinctions between the first, second, and third estates for the fictions that they were. High and low born mixed in the public spaces of the city frequented by Mercier, and by his readers. As Mercier's city encompasses all walks of life, so too his *Tableau* mixes genres, tones, and modes. At once and in turn reporter, ethnographer, philosophe, man of letters, gossip columnist, journalist, redoubtable pedestrian, watchdog of government, and more, Mercier sets a paradigm for urban observers for a century to come.

It is scarcely surprising that a work by someone who ten years before had written a utopian treatise (*L'An deux mille quatre cent quarante*, 1771) should adopt a prospective rather than a retrospective view of society. Mercier is by no means unaware of history. But his is a history in the making, a history of the present for the future, and he writes about the present as a past in the making. Thus, far beyond the ken of most of his contemporaries, Mercier addresses posterity, confident that a hundred years in the future readers will return to his work to find out about his century and his city.

This confidence, perhaps Mercier's greatest asset, was not misplaced. The *Tableau de Paris* inaugurated a new genre and served at once as model, standard, and norm for innumerable later works about Paris. Louis-Sébastien Mercier was one of the first to write the diversity of the city. Almost alone, he created the essay-reportage, the urban genre that fascinated and inspired generations of urban explorers with its insistence upon the vitality and the meaning of turmoil and confusion. Not surprisingly, then, the "literary guidebooks" that proliferate in the early nineteenth century take the *Tableau de Paris* as a touchstone, as the work that they have to confront, as the model they must rewrite if they are to come anywhere near Mercier's achievement.

Mercier also sounds one more theme to which later Parisian guide-commentators will turn again and again, that of the special relationship between the writer and the city: "Paris is the country of a man of letters, his only country" ("Paris, ou la Thébaïde," 12). More than this, however, Mercier's practice sets the example for nineteenth-century literary urban explorers: affirmation of the diversity of human, and particularly urban, experience and affirmation too of the equality of interest of all those experiences. Where writers in the 1830s and 1840s differ from Mercier, why Mercier himself cannot repeat the achievement of the *Tableau de Paris* after 1789, what makes his later writing at once more timid and more aggressive, is the colossal fact of actual revolution — 1789, 1799, 1804, 1814, 1815, 1830. Mercier anticipates the event but not the many changes of regime that will soon impress upon writer and reader alike the ever-present possibility of violent social change.

III

Avec ce titre magique de Paris, un drame, une revue, un livre
est toujours sûr du succès.
            Théophile Gautier, *Paris et les Parisiens au XIXe siècle*

With this magic title of Paris, a play, a journal, a book is always
sure of success.

The Revolution generated an immense amount of writing about
France, and the production about Paris increased astronomically.
Many contemporaries must have agreed with J. B. Pujoulx, who noted
in the first chapter of *Paris à la fin du XVIIIe siècle* that no period
favored the observer more than the present: "Everything is new."
Paris became the indisputable center of French political, economic,
and intellectual life. Its population augmented at a faster pace than
ever before, doubling between 1801, when the first official census was
taken, and 1850 (and this despite a serious cholera epidemic). Political volatility exacerbated the sense of urban instability. In a space of
less than seventy years, France moved through an impressive number
of political regimes. Two monarchies, two empires, and three republics were ushered in variously by two revolutions (1830 and 1848),
two military defeats (1815 and 1870–1), one coup d'état (1851), and
one civil war (1871). But, as for the Revolution of 1789, the city of
Paris was the theater of all but one of these events (the Prussian army
laid siege to but did not actually occupy the city in 1870–1).

The great number of guidebooks to Paris that appeared in the new
century testifies to the need for guidance, not simply because of the
altered topography but also, and more urgently, because of the radically altered character or, to use the term favored by contemporaries,
the "physiognomy" of a city that had been shaken to its foundations
by revolution. The extraordinary popularity of the Hermit series inaugurated by Étienne de Jouy, beginning in 1811, reveals a dramatic
combination of anxiety and curiosity about the city that was changing
before the very eyes of the writer and the reader.[9] Jouy's hermits gave
the guidebook, or what I shall call the "literary guidebook," a formula
that seems to bring Mercier up to date (the later Hermite de la
Guiane acknowledges his connection to Mercier). But the filiation is
trickier than this explicit reference allows. The *Tableau de Paris* remains unique because Mercier's city has a decided and marked unity,
a coherent physiognomy.

Such cohesion is exactly what the quarter century between Mercier and Jouy has shattered. The volatility of politics has rendered the task of the would-be observer of customs uncommonly difficult. "The French nation no longer has a physiognomy," complains another one of Jouy's personages, Guillaume le Franc-Parleur (William the Frank Speaker), writing a month after the final defeat of Napoléon at Waterloo and the reestablishment of the Bourbon monarchy. "The convulsions of suffering have altered its traits so profoundly and so completely denatured its character, that it has become entirely un-recognizable." Returning to Paris after an absence of twenty-five years and despite having lived in the city for thirty years before that, a friend reports to Guillaume with considerable distress that "Men and things, everything is changed, displaced, confused: I look and recognize nothing; I speak, and people barely hear me."

The chronicler-protagonists of the Hermit series exhibit none of Mercier's enthusiasms, few of his quirks, and little of his ambition. The politically circumspect Jouy moves with the times and the re-gimes. Royalist fervor wins out when "the august family of the Bour-bons is given back to us." Jouy kills off his Bonapartist original Hermit de la Chaussée d'Antin just as Louis XVIII enters Paris as king. Guil-laume le Franc-Parleur, the new Hermit, is younger, a politically cor-rect monarchist who, "like all France," had been the "dupe" of Bo-naparte's promises. The trenchant criticism and the overreaching ambition to comprehend the course of the city in history had to wait for the great novelists of the July Monarchy, for Balzac and Stendhal and Hugo. Jouy's Hermits have a far less intense relationship to the city than either Mercier before him or Balzac and Hugo after. Like Mercier, the Hermit "paints" customs. But he seeks to depict society as such and not a given society, and his concern is with "classes, spe-cies and never individuals."

In all his various incarnations, the Hermit is a genial character whose regular sorties into the city take him into unaccustomed places and bring him into contact with a broad range of people but, as the name implies, without ever involving him deeply. The affable tone of the essays and the title warn the reader that this observer sets himself apart from the city. Very much unlike Mercier, who is passionately involved in every event, every individual, every city space, the Hermit remains aloof from the scenes that he himself observes. It is this dis-tance from his material that enables the Hermit to travel through the provinces as easily as Paris. For, whether at home or abroad, the Hermit is essentially a traveler (he proudly tells of his trip around the world with Bougainville). He most definitely is not, as Mercier so proudly is, a man of letters. And he is certainly not, again as Mercier so assertively is, much interested in reform.

Jouy's extraordinary success pointed to a pervasive bewilderment over the state of urban society, a state of affairs that other writers by the score also sought to address. If, as Victor Hugo insisted in the 1820s, a postrevolutionary society compelled a postrevolutionary aesthetic, a postrevolutionary urbanizing Paris dictated an urban aesthetic. Just how that aesthetic might be revolutionary was a subject of great debate as writers sorted out genres and styles, publics, publishers, and politics. But that it must be revolutionary in some fashion admitted of no doubt. Histories, guidebooks, essays, novels, and poetry about Paris glutted the market, which then asked for more. Every person able to pick up a pen seemed to rush to take up Pujoulx's implicit invitation when he declared at the beginning of the century that however much had been written about Paris, no time was as interesting as the present. The result, predictable enough, was a surfeit of publications on and about Paris. In 1856, by way of justifying yet another anthology of Paris explorations, Théophile Gautier took stock of a situation that was surely not new: "With the magic title of Paris, a play, a journal, a book is always sure of success. Paris has an inexhaustible curiosity about itself that nothing has been able to satisfy, not the fat serious books, nor the thin publications, not history, . . . not memoirs, not the novel."[10]

Guidebooks proper, with maps and details on the location of streets and sights, generally confined themselves to tracking topography and institutions. As Paris expanded and built (Napoléon I started significant building projects virtually as the century began), guidebooks proliferated. Typical of what we now immediately recognize as an example of this most conventional of genres was *Le Nouveau Conducteur parisien ou plan de Paris* (1817) with maps, listings of hotels, means of transportation, sometimes statistics of one kind or another, and useful information ranging from hours and locations of restaurants, museums, and libraries; numbers of houses, streets, and inhabitants; locations of translators; the street numbering system; and so on. *Le Nouveau Conducteur*, like most of its predecessors in the ancien régime and indeed most of its successors, addressed largely foreigners, referring those in need of more information to the sixth edition of *Le Conducteur de l'étranger à Paris.*

Little cultural information is included beyond reassurances to the apprehensive visitor that drinking the water from the Seine "does not indispose Parisians with its slight laxative quality" and, moreover, has no ill effects on foreigners so long as they drink it mixed with wine or a drop of vinegar. (Mercier had already pointed to the "purgative" powers of the Seine [1, 4].) The title points to the difference. For this guidebook is, as announced, a conductor, not a guide. A conductor gives precise directions to a specific, known, charted terrain (note that the subtitle of *Le Nouveau Conducteur* can be translated "map" or "outline"). A guide imparts as well a larger sense of direction. The conductor may be far in the lead; the guide, closer by, imparts wisdom as well as direction through unknown and uncharted terrain. The archetypical image is, of course, Virgil's guidance of Dante through the Inferno (Dante addresses Virgil in canto 2, line 10, "Poeta che mi guidi . . "). *Le Nouveau Conducteur* has no author. There is no guide. The modern guidebook makes no moral claims, confines the advice it offers to practical, readily verifiable information, and assumes no responsibility for conduct beyond its confines. We are at the antipode of Mercier's idiosyncratic, opinionated reports about the city and equally as far from his ambition to render the "physiognomy of [his] century." Perhaps these new writers of guidebooks agreed with Jouy that France in the early nineteenth century no longer had a physiognomy.

Without an author, these guidebooks essentially renounce any claim truly to guide the individual in Paris. Modern equivalents of Jèze's tableaux, these works content themselves with the obvious, with surface detail, which, although abundant, says nothing about the nature of the urban experience and nothing about revolutionary Paris. We are miles from the excitement and the wonder that pervade Mercier's *Tableau,* and still further from the intense explorations of the city by Balzac and Hugo. All of these authors, in however different a mode, stamped the city with their strong personalities.

The link between Mercier and Balzac or Hugo, then, comes not through conventional guidebooks, but by way of what are more aptly called "literary guidebooks." These works are not really guidebooks, since, unlike either *Le Nouveau Conducteur* or Jouy's Hermit series, they offer significant directions to the new society emerging in Paris after the Revolution, and especially after the July Revolution of 1830. Topography is the least of the matters taken up in these works, from the fifteen-volume *Paris, ou le livre des cent-et-un* (1831–34) to the work that caps and exhausts the genre, *Paris-Guide*, published for the World's Fair of 1867. For Parisians as interested as they were anxious about the world changing before their very eyes, these works offered both information and assurance. Where Mercier gave an *état présent*, nineteenth-century commentators reveled in change, in the new characters, personalities, customs, and behavior that characterized contemporary urban life.

At the same time, no single authorial voice grounds the interpretation of the city text. These were aggressively collective endeavors, multivolume collections of vignettes on people, places, events, and institutions. The anthologies capitalized on the expansion of the reading public, which also made the serial novel so successful a formula at about the same time, beginning in the 1830s. Publishers raced to get out the next compilation, and writers from all corners of the literary world joined in, from Chateaubriand and Charles Nodier among the older generation to Lamartine, Balzac, Gérard de Nerval, Alexandre Dumas, Victor Hugo, and a host of others. Foreigners too, Goethe and Fenimore Cooper most prominent among them, were pressed into service. *Paris, ou le livre des cent-et-un* saved the publisher from bankruptcy, and each volume of *Les Français peints par eux-mêmes* carried a front page to all the contributors from the "Grateful Publisher." By the 1840s these literary guidebooks carried lavish illustrations by Gavarni, Henry Monnier, and Daumier, to mention only the best known.

The pieces themselves run the gamut from the sketches of urban character types known as *physiologies* (Balzac's "Histoire et physiologie des boulevards de Paris" in *Le Diable à Paris* or the "Physiologie du flâneur," to which I return in chapter 3), to serious, and generally unimaginative, delineations of sometimes picturesque institutions (the morgue, the insane asylum at Charenton, public libraries) to incidents (the cholera epidemic, the funeral of the scientist Cuvier).[11] Like the city that they strove to represent, these collections offer something from and for almost everyone.

The nominal model of the new urban journalism is Lesage's satirical novel, *Le Diable boiteux* (1707 and 1726), which recounts the adventures of Asmodée, a minor devil of lust and lechery, as he removes the rooftops of houses in Madrid (read Paris) to flaunt his control over human lives. Immensely popular from its publication, *Le Diable boiteux* offered a convenient tag for the literary guidebooks and, perhaps, in the figure of the devil, an emblem of authorial perspective. Asmodée is uninvolved; he comes from another world. When Jules Janin signs "Asmodée" to his introductory article to *Paris, ou le livre des cent-et-un* (1831), he signals his connection to a genre that looks at the city from afar, and when Gavarni places a devil standing over the map of Paris on the title page of *Le Diable à Paris*, he too suggests distance as the operative mode of urban interpretation in the texts that follow (though it must be admitted that the devil in question bears no resemblance to the description that Lesage gives of his Asmodée).

Yet, if Lesage supplied the emblematic figure for these collections, it was Mercier who furnished the literary model. Fifty years after the publication of the *Tableau de Paris*, the publisher, Ladvocat, placed *Paris, ou le livre des cent-et-un* under Mercier's aegis: "We must do for the Paris of today what Mercier did for the Paris of his time." But politics has intervened in that half century, and Mercier's brush will no longer do. "Another pen besides Mercier's is needed." It is not simply a question of finding a contemporary Mercier. No single pen can comprehend the postrevolutionary city. Indeed, how could any individual render the multiplicity of "tricolor Paris?" Is not this urban multiplicity inscribed on the flag itself? Does not the very flag of France join the white of the monarchy to the red and the blue of the city of Paris? Who can possibly render the "drama of a hundred different acts" of this revolutionized city? What guide could possibly lead us through the "long gallery of modern customs, brought into being by two revolutions?" The publisher's solution—the solution of this particular genre on the edge of literary respectability—counters diversity of subject with diversity of execution, which is why the literary guidebook stands as the paradigmatic genre of urban exploration.[12]

Jules Janin begins his introductory article, "Asmodée," by insisting on the association between new times and new modes of presenting them. Since everyone has taken to observing contemporary society, nineteenth-century Paris wants not one but many observers to reveal it all: "It is through this revolution in the study of customs that the new lame Devil will get something out of us. . . . It is through the collaboration of everyone that he will write once again the story of our failings.''[13]

Yet collaboration placed definite limits on urban discourse. Although Mercier clearly gloried in the exuberant diversity he found on all sides, he remained confident of his ability to contain the proliferation of the city. His nineteenth-century epigones—overwhelmed by diversity, by sheer numbers, by strange sectors of society and their stranger inhabitants—could not sustain his sense of certainty. Insofar as the fragmentation of the city precludes encompassing the whole, these works could only enumerate their findings. No single point of view prevails. The classical unities, and the more modern ones as well, no longer obtain. The social and political revolution calls for the collaborative interpretation: "Unable to get a comedy out of one man, we have set out more than a hundred strong to make a single comedy; a hundred of us or two: what's the difference? As far as unity is concerned, it comes down to the same thing." Less unified perhaps, the resulting production is more interesting.

To judge by the number of works that appeared in this format, including reprints of previously published articles, multiple authorship made good commercial sense, and it made good sociological and aesthetic sense. Jules Janin obviously thought so, for ten years after *Paris, ou le livre des cent-et-un,* he undertook the introduction to undoubtedly the most ambitious of these works, *Les Français peints par eux-mêmes* (five of the nine volumes concern Paris), which appeared between 1840 and 1842 and was billed as an *encyclopédie morale du dix-neuvième siècle.* Not only the rapidity of change but also and especially the fragmentation of Parisian society, Janin asserted, force a new approach to the city. In one hundred years (the same period Mercier allotted for his own work), "people will recount that this city, so proud of its unity, was divided into five or six sections ('faubourgs'), which were like so many separate universes, separated from one another far more effectively than if each were surrounded by the Great Wall of China."[14] Things do not seem to have changed much on this score since Jouy affirmed that in no city except Peking and Lahore do the classes and neighborhoods live so separately (*L'Hermite de la Chaussée d'Antin,* 12 June 1813).

Janin also echoes Jouy (and other conservative writers, such as Balzac) in pointing to contemporary politics, and specifically the Revolution, as the source of division. "This great kingdom has been cut

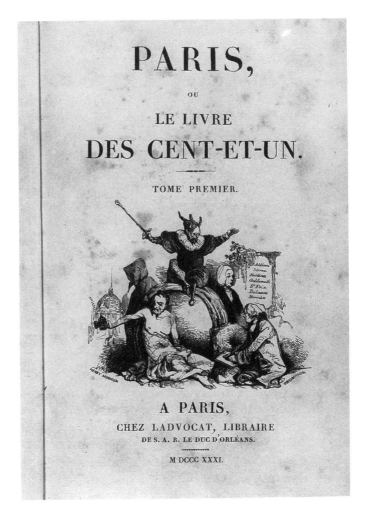

PARIS,

OU

LE LIVRE

DES CENT-ET-UN.

TOME PREMIER.

A PARIS,

CHEZ LADVOCAT, LIBRAIRE

DE S. A. R. LE DUC D'ORLÉANS.

M DCCC XXXI.

Plate 5. Title page by Henry Monnier, *Paris, ou le livre des cent-et-un* (1831). Among the ancestors invoked for this miscellany of sketches on the city that opened with the July Monarchy, English writers predominate on the tablet in the background (Addison, Sterne, Fielding, Goldsmith); St Foix and Dulaure are historians of Paris; and the incomparable Mercier is the author of the *Tableau de Paris*. The peg-leg devil, who overlooks the scene in the foreground, is taken from Lesage's novel of 1709, *Le Diable boiteux*. He will acquire more contemporary demeanor and dress in later collections. (Photograph by the University of Chicago Medical Center, A.V. Department.)

Plate 6. Title page, *Le Diable à Paris* (1855). The devil, in somewhat more modern dress and no longer lame, straddles a map of Paris, lamp in hand to light his way. His basket literally overflows with the articles of the writers contributing to the collection listed under the title. (Photograph by University of Chicago Medical Center, A.V. Department.)

into as many little republics." A single writer could grasp the unitary nature of the king's domain; many chroniclers are needed to comprehend the warring, squabbling republics of a postrevolutionary age. Just open any chapter of *Les Caractères,* Janin urges, and you will be convinced that representation of France in the July Monarchy must be divided among many authors. Contemporary society boasts, or despairs, of innumerable phenomena that La Bruyère never imagined. Today, in postrevolutionary society, there are multiple cities within the city, and they are all changing all the time. A portrait has to be drawn every hour because yesterday's is already out of date.

Yet the most fundamental questions remain. What and where is Paris? How is the city to be imagined, defined? How in fact are we to read these texts, and the city beyond? I would suggest that tables of contents (*tables des matières*) provide just the unity that the city text requires, a unity that encounters diversity in much the same way that a map imposes an artificial, constructed unitary view on three-dimensional space. The order of the text is *logical* in the primary, etymological senses of theory (*logia*) and discourse (*logos*). More accurately, this order is *physiological* because each table of contents is itself taken as an overgrown *physiologie.* That is, each table of contents offers a particular entry into urban life, a singular, necessarily reductive angle of vision on the vast complex of the city. Like the *physiologies* that reduced individuals to types, these multiauthored collections reduced urban society to a string of character types.

The very vogue of these works testifies to the failure of the definitions they propose, the failure, in sum, of what may be termed an "aesthetic of iteration." In these texts the divers parts of the city fail to cohere.[15] Jouy made this aesthetic his guide: "The best, or rather the only means of knowing [Paris] well is to examine each part in isolation" (*L'Hermite de la Chaussée d'Antin,* 12 June 1813). But at least Jouy could claim that his pages would make the connections. The chorus of voices of multiple authors fails to provide that minimal focus. The aesthetic of iteration founders on the descriptive because there is no authority to turn the list of description into the order of narrative. There is no guide, no authority, to interpret the city.

Absent that guiding authority, the order of these works becomes *sociological,* the order / disorder of society complacently, uncritically duplicated in an urban text designed to reassure. The multiple authorship vaunted by Janin and so strongly supported by publishers and readers alike reproduces, as indeed it is meant to, the diversity and the disorientation of urban life. The city is laid out before the reader like the merchandise displayed in the arcades that Walter Benjamin takes as another emblem of modernity and of Paris. By design the display of the guidebook diffuses attention onto as many points as possible, to entice the potential consumer or spectator to sample at random and at will. The power is in the hands of the consumer, not the author.

I suggest that synecdoche is the basic trope of these jumbled urban texts. The table of contents, with the chapter titles listed one after another, is to these works as the view from Notre-Dame is to the city itself, a simplification, perhaps a distortion, but one that is necessary in order to conceive the city as a whole. The table contains the entire book and itself offers an interpretation of that book, and of the city. (This interpretation may be confirmed by the actual articles or modified or, for that matter, contradicted altogether.) The table of contents constitutes an urban planning of a sort, a utopia, though of real enough places and institutions, in any case a fiction. The table of contents negotiates the text and, by extension, the city. The strange becomes familiar, the familiar becomes amusing. These texts depend upon one reading of the city—that contained in the table of contents—and produce another as the individual devises an interpretation within textual constraints.

IV

> Il n'y a plus au monde que le Czar qui réalise l'idée de roi, dont un regard donne ou la vie ou la mort, dont la parole ait le don de la création.
>
> Balzac, "Ce qui disparaît de Paris"

> There is no longer anyone except the Czar who embodies the idea of king, whose gaze gives life or death, whose word has the gift of creation.

Whether expressly instrumental like *Le Nouveau Conducteur* or more narrative like *Le Diable à Paris,* the guidebook could not cope with the city of revolution. Understanding that city required more than lists or descriptions. In place of enumeration nineteenth-century Paris craved interpretation. Collections of miscellaneous texts failed to satisfy that need. Because they diverted attention from the essential, they could never provide the focus necessary to a coherent urban discourse. Individual writers, however, might and did assume that authority. The great novels of Paris that drew their strength from this arrogation of authority became the privileged vehicle of urban interpretation. Novelists defined the role of guide in the strongest, virgilian sense of the term, as they took their readers into the inferno of the city and led them out again, sociological tour and moral lesson completed.

Clearly, the model for the narrator in these works was no lesser devil, but the highest authority. Rewriting revolution demands a special kind of imagination, one that sees beyond the parts to the whole. The great novels of the nineteenth century do just this, and their richness depends, in good part, on their assumption—quite the contrary of Janin's—that the city exists intact and that, however much attention must be paid to the parts, Paris is more than their sum. For the aesthetic of iteration characteristic of the literary guidebooks the novel substitutes an "aesthetic of integration." The novelist claims to produce in narrative the whole fragmented by the Revolution, reaching to a larger authorial vision.

Balzac, in his piece "Ce qui disparaît de Paris" ("What's Disappearing from Paris") for *Le Diable à Paris* in 1844, explicitly connects the transformations in the city, in particular its losses, to the dereliction of royal authority. The definition of city space once imposed by the monarch no longer obtains. Latter-day kings no longer possess the powers of invention. In the Europe that appeared after 1789, only the czar fully realizes the *idea* of kingship, which Balzac locates in a *gaze* capable of giving life or taking it away or in a *word* endowed with the gift of creation. Obviously, Balzac has a replacement in mind, himself, the writer, the one individual endowed with the power to resurrect old Paris.

The conjunction of literature and the city is already a commonplace by the nineteenth century. Indeed, urban discourse of every sort threatens to overwhelm the city itself. In one hundred years, Jules Janin fears, "people will say that in this capital all time was spent talking, writing, listening, reading" ("Introduction," *Les Français peints par eux-mêmes*). Into an urban space flooded with discourse of every sort the novel brings a reimagined city. In place of the fragments of a city the novel affirms its intention to make the city whole. This paradigmatic urban genre simultaneously expands the narrative to

contain the city and constricts the city to fit the narrative. The simplification involved in these rhetorical strategies of containment is a
necessary feature of the governance and use of symbols. Without such
stylization, the city muddles the reader looking to decipher the urban
text in much the same way as it disorients the individual inhabitant
or traveler endeavoring to negotiate the city.

The metaphorization of Paris does not begin in the nineteenth
century, but metaphors and images of the period take on a decided
intensity.[16] The characteristic and appropriate trope for the city is
metonymy. For metonymic figures, in particular synecdoche, construe the familiar sights of the cityscape that topographically and sym-
bolically tie its many parts: the Seine, the sewers, the catacombs, the
cemetery, and in the long term, the métro are, like the printed page,
networks that bring the scattered fragments into a whole. All of these
figures reduce the city to a part, but a part that in turn contains the
city. The reciprocity of synecdoche is vital to the way these metonymic
figures define the city in its entirety.

One of the most frequent strategies of writers and tourists alike is
to view the city from afar, most strikingly from a height. Early maps
tend to place the observer somewhere on the horizon, at a point of
view that no one at that time could possibly have. Mercier was not the
first to climb the towers of Notre-Dame to observe the city from above,
nor was he the last.[17] In the nineteenth century an adventurous soul
might take a balloon ride. Or read novels. The view of the city from
afar becomes a staple among topoi in the nineteenth century, an urban
variant of the more general romantic taste for panoramas. The most
famous of these is assuredly the "chronicle inscribed in stone" that
Victor Hugo details for medieval Paris in "A Bird's-Eye View of Paris"
("Paris à vol d'oiseau") in *Notre-Dame de Paris* (1831) (bk. 3, chap. 2),
which he counters thirty years later in *Les Misérables* (1862) by "the
deadly harmonies" of the 1832 Paris insurrection in "An Owl's-Eye
View of Paris" ("Paris à vol de hibou") (pt. 4, bk. 13, chap. 2). The
mirror image of the aerial panorama is the labyrinth in Hugo's celebrated presentation of the sewers in *Les Misérables,* the one and the
other *not* the "real" city but a projection of that city.

Of Balzac's Parisian panoramas, the most striking views, the most
pregnant with meaning, are those from the cemetery of Père-
Lachaise, which is both in and above the city.[18] These scenes—Jules
Desmarets' meditations at the burial of his wife in *Ferragus* and Eu-

gène de Rastignac's defiant challenge at the very end of *Le Père Goriot*—elaborate the topographical contrast between the subterranean and the aerial city into an analogy between the city of the living and the city of the dead (complicated by the location of the cemetery *above* the city). The cemetery is a *site de passage* and a *rite du récit*, a rite and a place of passage, a modern example of the medieval dance of death designed to impress the living with the vanity of life. At Père-Lachaise the grieving Jules Desmarets for the first time comprehends the Paris that he sees at a great distance. The cemetery becomes a city unto itself, a microscopic Paris that presents a synedoche for the "true" Paris. The topos of the cemetery constitutes a chronotope, which reinvests the landscape with authorial definition, and the bird's-eye view of the writer substitutes for the superior vantage point that was once the king's. And of course, as Balzac makes clear by equating the king's gaze with life and death, the writer aims higher, beyond the king to the deity from whom royal, and narrative, authority derive.

This "urban imagination" is then very much a "synecdochal imagination," defined by the ability simultaneously to conceive the part and the whole. This imaginative power is vital to the urban novel because it alone allows the city to be apprehended beyond the fragmentation implied in the parts that multiply as writers explore the city further. Synecdoche thus bespeaks the aesthetic of integration. *Physiologies* and literary guidebooks disperse energy by dividing Paris into parts. The urban textual equivalent of "divide and conquer" is the "segregate and dismiss" implied by the *physiologies*. Those caricatured are safely Other, they live safely Elsewhere. The urban imagination, however, insists upon the inescapable connections between those parts, not excluding the most extreme. Père-Lachaise is part of the city, so are the sewers; the infamous rue Soly, where the ex-convict Ferragus lives, is contiguous with the rue Menars, which is the home of his eminently respectable and elegant daughter; and the Montagne-Sainte-Geneviève of the scruffy Pension Vauquer is inscribed within the faubourg Saint-Germain of Mme de Beauséant's elegant *hôtel* and vice versa. Balzac never allows the reader to forget or dismiss these connections. Each is a necessary function of the other. Each depends upon the other. The myth of Paris, which crystallizes in the revolutionary energies released by the July Revolution, is in turn a function of the emphasis upon these almost organic attachments.

The personification of Paris, indeed the multiplication of grandiose metaphors of every sort, further attests to this organic conception of the city. Integration overcomes iteration to create the unity that cannot be reproduced because it does not exist. The panorama offers one means of creating unity, global metaphors another. In either case this creation is the vocation of the writer, and the city thus created stands as another in a long line of utopics that allow us to identify with the city, to know it, or to feel that we do. The utopic offers the reader a text, and a tactic, for dealing with the city.

This utopic, properly speaking, is revolutionary. The assimilation of the Revolution into literary France is the task, and the glory, of the writer and the condition of literature. The writer's creation of figurative unity replaces the monarchy but does so only in full acceptance of the consequences of that which destroyed the monarch. The novel makes its distinctive contribution by restoring the human scale of the city through exemplary (not typical) figures, which give the city expression and definition. Rastignac, Quasimodo, Gavroche, Frédéric, Gervaise, Nana . . . are not simply protagonists in novels. They are also actors in a profoundly literary because profoundly revolutionary Paris.

V

Paris est le point vélique de la civilisation.
Victor Hugo, *Paris-Guide*

Paris is the focal point of civilization.

The guidebook, ordinarily, makes few claims to greatness. Its great strength, but also its great limitation, is topicality. If customs change almost weekly, as these works often claim, then they are outdated as soon as they are published. The only answer possible is to put together another guidebook (which, indeed, seems to have been the strategy of choice in the 1830s and 1840s). The novel, on the other hand, proclaims its ambition to understand not the day or the week or the year but the century. The two modes of urban exploration would seem to be irreconcilable. Balzac's incorporation of his occasional pieces into his novels does not fundamentally alter either genre. But when Victor Hugo takes on the introduction of a great collective guide to Paris, the genre virtually splits in two, utterly transformed by virtue of Hugo's reconceptualization of urban discourse.

The fusion of the writer and Paris, Paris and modernity, modernity and revolution, is nowhere more arresting than in the work and the persona of Victor Hugo. And nowhere is Hugo more insistent on making those affinities explicit than in his outsize introduction to *Paris-Guide* (1867). Given his tenacious, vocal, and highly publicized opposition to the Second Empire, Hugo represented a somewhat audacious choice to present a work timed to appear for the World's Fair sponsored by the government. But any work whose title page boasted authorship *par les principaux écrivains et artistes de la France* simply had to include Hugo, so great was his reputation in France and abroad and so strong were his associations with Paris.[19]

The book, like Paris itself, is suffused with light. The title page carries a small seal with a large sun rising over Lutetia (though the buildings mark it as medieval Paris), and Hugo stresses that *Paris-Guide* is an edifice constructed by "a dazzling legion of minds." Further, if all the missing "luminaries" were added, the book "would be Paris itself."[20] Thus Hugo both affirms the writer's right to define the city and attests to the fact of that definition.

Yet, though Hugo speaks for authorial privilege generally, the claims that he makes on and for "Paris itself" are, finally, personal claims. For over thirty years Paris has been Hugo's city, his creation, from *Notre-Dame de Paris* to *Les Misérables*. His identification is total. Paris itself is text and intertext. Old Paris shows up distinctly under the Paris of today "as the old text shows up in between the spaces of the new" (x). So complete is Hugo's assimilation of the city that he conflates his exile with his marginal authorial status: "We are properly on the threshold, almost outside. Absent from the city, absent from the book" (xxxiv).

Hugo's colossal introduction essentially turns *Paris-Guide* into an oxymoron. However brilliant the contributions of the other "luminaries," they supply mere fragments; Hugo provides the only source of light for the City of Lights. He is then in person the guiding light of this work, the sole source of unity. Thus *Paris-Guide* explodes the genre of the literary guidebook. There will be other guides to Paris, of course, and no end of works on one or another aspect of Paris. But

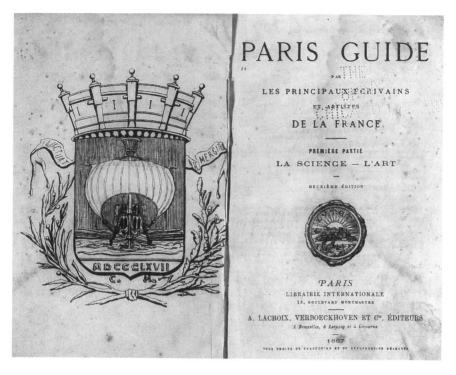

PARIS GUIDE

PAR

LES PRINCIPAUX ÉCRIVAINS

ET ARTISTES

DE LA FRANCE

PREMIÈRE PARTIE

LA SCIENCE — L'ART

DEUXIÈME ÉDITION

PARIS
LIBRAIRIE INTERNATIONALE
15, BOULEVARD MONTMARTRE

A. LACROIX, VERBOECKHOVEN ET Cⁱᵉ, ÉDITEURS
À Bruxelles, à Leipzig et à Livourne

1867

TOUS DROITS DE TRADUCTION ET DE REPRODUCTION RÉSERVÉS

Plate 7. Frontispiece and title page, *Paris-Guide* (1867). The small seal at right shows the sun rising over Lutetia. The seal of the modern city to the left literalizes Hugo's conception of postrevolutionary Paris in a century of progress. In contrast to the official seal, which displays a three-masted ship viewed from the side, this seal exhibits a galley with a single square sail going before the wind with its bank of oars raised. The great billowing sail heading directly toward the reader pictures Hugo's impassioned affirmation in the introduction to this work that "Paris is the center of effort on the sail that represents civilization." Like the winds that converge on a single point of the sail, the currents of modern civilization intersect in Paris. With the crossed olive and oak branches that recall the garlands of the seal of the First Empire, the editors discreetly placed the volume under Napoleonic protection—but that of the first Napoléon not the third. Hugo should have been pleased at the iconographic gymnastics that placed him in the company of the right Napoléon. (Photograph by University of Chicago Medical Center, A.V. Department.)

no other writer lays claim to a vision of Paris anywhere nearly as comprehensive as Hugo's.

Its format places *Paris-Guide* squarely within the tradition of the collaborative, multivolume literary guidebook. The editors of the "encyclopedic enterprise" have the "absolute conviction" that they are publishing "*the most complete* work ever undertaken on Paris" (emphases theirs) (vi). Yet at the very outset Hugo subverts the aesthetic of iteration with his grandiloquent introduction (over forty pages of small type in double columns for the first edition). Hugo pays less attention to the real Paris, its topography or its history, than to the meaning of the city within the progressive development of France and of all western civilization. More than the head of a people, the city is the brain of the universe, indispensable to its life. "The universe without the city would be like a decapitation. One cannot imagine an acephalous civilization" (xxv).

Thus Hugo returns to the very source of unmeaning. Decapitation exemplifies the loss of meaning for monarchical Paris. Hugo's refusal of decapitation accomplishes the impossible. It puts Paris back together again, makes the city whole, and restores its meaning. That meaning has changed. The language through which Hugo accomplishes this miracle has become the language of revolution. The creator of meaning is no longer the monarch but the writer, who achieves thereby something that the man was never able to accomplish. Hugo's vehement opposition to capital punishment from the beginning to the end of his career amounts to an obsession. He presided at two international congresses on the abolition of the death penalty and wrote tirelessly on the topic for over half a century. (It is worth remembering that until France abolished the death penalty in 1981, capital punishment was exactly that, decapitation by the guillotine.)

Clearly, Hugo takes *Paris-Guide* in the higher sense: the book is a guide to Paris, Paris guides humanity. The Paris seal reproduced on the frontispiece shows the traditional ship but now with a great billowing sail that literalizes Hugo's impassioned affirmation that Paris is the point on the sail where all the winds of civilization converge ("le point vélique de la civilisation," xix).

If the history of Paris is a "microcosm of general history" (vi), it is because of the Revolution. The unity of the city whose fragments follow in the table of contents comes from the Revolution. No longer metonymy but metaphor. Not the synecdoche implied by the panoramic view or in the various personifications of the city, Hugo's city is the city of revolution, the city of the Revolution. The Revolution transforms the city into a vast and continually evolving chronotope. Neither the conventional personifications (Paris as hydra, courtesan, queen, monster, bird, colossus, goddess, devil, slave, giant, genius, gladiator) nor the classic metonymies (Paris as head, brain, heart, eye) nor again the familiar topographical comparisons (Paris as forest, volcano, river, ocean, sea, planet, prison, hospital, theater, metropolis, nation, paradise or hell) are able to subsume the fragments that comprise modern, that is, postrevolutionary Paris.[21]

If the most powerful of these figures is insufficient to the writer's task, it is because all of them are essentially static and ahistorical. The city that had been disrupted by the sudden and violent intrusion of historical circumstance and sequence into everyday life, the city that changed continually before the reader's very eyes, the city whose parts multiplied more rapidly with every new regime—that city could be rendered whole only by taking the movement of history into account. That is, the texts of modern Paris had to become the text of revolutionary Paris.

This is Hugo's vital contribution in his introduction to *Paris-Guide*. His assimilation of Paris with the Revolution, and with revolution, alters the very conception of the city. Writing the Revolution entails a revolution in writing. Paris then is the "pivot on which, on a given day, history turned" (xviii). That pivotal date was, of course, 1789, the date that has been the "preoccupation of the human race" for almost a century (xviii). Rome may be more majestic, Venice more beautiful, London richer, but Paris has the Revolution. In an astounding series of comparisons, Hugo endows Paris with the powers of both nature and civilization: "Palermo has Etna, Paris has thought. Constantinople is closer to the sun, Paris is closer to civilization. Athens built the Parthenon, but Paris tore down the Bastille" (xviii).

Revolution gives Hugo the larger figure that he needs to encompass modern Paris. The Revolution both explains and justifies the postrevolutionary city, including the decadent Paris of the Second Empire, to which Hugo gave no quarter. Thus the progressive vision of *Paris-Guide* counters the pessimism of *Notre-Dame de Paris* with its bitter lamentation on the lost unity of medieval civilization. As the medieval world coheres around the Church, so modern society finds its raison d'être in the Revolution: "this powerful nineteenth century, son of the Revolution and father of liberty" (xxxiv). As *Notre-Dame de Paris* signifies medieval Paris, so the Panthéon, "full of great men and useful heros," represents modern, that is, revolutionary Paris. Saint Peter's may be the larger dome, but the Panthéon harbors the more elevated thought (xxviii).

Paris-Revolution—the third term in the equation is Art: "That which completes and crowns Paris" (xxviii) is its literary destiny, a consecration that comes from the "trinity of reason," Rabelais, Molière, and Voltaire (xxvii). In Paris reason and art go together: "Great poetry is the solar specter of human reason." Paris leads humanity, and the poet leads Paris (xxix).

At the very moment that Hugo writes his revolutionary utopic, Haussmann is drastically rewriting the urban text of Paris, creating a very different city from the one that Hugo knew or imagined. Haussmann produces a Paris to be seen and admired, a bourgeois Paris of parks and broad avenues to compete with the royal Paris of the ancien régime. By way of contrast, Hugo is concerned not with the seen but with the seer. His domain is not the material city but the spiritual one. His view of the city takes as its vantage point not the towers of Notre-Dame but rather the dome of the Panthéon, the tomb that radiates above the city like a star. The panorama from which Hugo dominates the city is the sacred place of revolution, the edifice erected for the ancien régime but transformed, like Paris itself, by the Revolution into the very symbol of the new age.

The metaphorization of the city is, of course, made all the easier by Hugo's exile, off the coast of France in British territory, far from the real, confusing, and rapidly changing city of the Second Empire. The Paris of *Notre-Dame de Paris* implies the Revolution of 1789, but Hugo had not yet found in the Revolution the vital synecdoche that so powerfully unifies the introduction to *Paris-Guide* in 1867 and the whole of *Quatrevingt-treize* five years later. That figure is not his invention. As we saw, the collaborative literary guidebooks of the 1830s and 1840s assume the centrality of the Revolution to contemporary literary activity of every sort. But it is in this later work, as the actual Revolution recedes further and further into the past, that Hugo comes to define the city, and the century, in terms of what he views as the fundamental transformation of modern times.

Hugo tells us in the preface to *Notre-Dame de Paris* that he has constructed this novel on a word—"ANAI'KH" (Fatality)—which he found inscribed on a pillar of the cathedral itself. *Notre-Dame de Paris* foretells the fated destruction of a unified civilization: "Ceci tuera cela" ("This will kill that") (bk. 5, chap. 1). The world of the book, of the printing press, destroys the cathedral and the world that it embodies. The mobility of the printed word is bound to shatter the stability that Hugo assigns to the medieval world. This is the original revolution ("la révolution mère") that precedes and prepares the other. The architectural decadence that Hugo denounces so vehemently in *Notre-Dame de Paris* is but the symptom of this fundamental transformation in the mode by which humanity makes itself intelligible. But although *Notre-Dame de Paris* points to the Revolution, the dominant tone is lamentation for the civilization that is no more, that has scattered with the pieces of printed paper and has irremediably fragmented contemporary society. Thirty years and two regimes later, Hugo finds in the Revolution the metaphor that will unify that fragmented civilization and the city that is its center. The introduction to *Paris-Guide* looks forward, not back, to a time when all humanity will have realized the promise of revolutionary Paris.

In due time, Hugo himself will lie in the Panthéon, the sacred place of the Revolution, among the great men and useful heroes of France. For the moment, in 1867, for *Paris-Guide,* he writes from afar, the distance of his exile allowing him to imagine Paris without the encumbrance of visible realities of the bourgeois city. Hugo stakes these claims on the very last page of his introduction to *Paris-Guide* with the name of his home on the Isle of Guernsey. Hauteville House does not simply tell the reader where Hugo lives; it is a sign that designates his relationship to Paris—Hauteville House, high above the city, high within the city. In exile Hugo claims Paris as his own.

It is supremely fitting that Hugo should be so intimately associated with the Republic and that he, in effect, becomes its hero. It is also right and proper that the Third Republic inscribe this metonym for Paris on the cityscape itself. In 1881, to celebrate the beginning of his eightieth year, the street where he lives becomes the avenue Victor Hugo. And it is Hugo's burial in 1885 that definitively transforms the Panthéon into a republican sanctuary, what Hugo himself calls the "tomb star." The city itself confirms what Hugo believes as firmly as Carlyle, namely, that the writer is the hero of postrevolutionary society, for it is through the writer that revolutionary Paris becomes literary France, one more step in the glorification of the writer and of literature that makes genius a national rather than simply individual affair.

VI

Le Tableau de Paris est à refaire!
Jules Vallès, *Le Tableau de Paris*

The Tableau of Paris has to be redone!

One hundred years after Mercier's *Tableau de Paris* first appeared, Jules Vallès began to publish a series of articles that he called *Le Tableau de Paris.*[22] More is at issue than an astute journalist taking advantage of a convenient centennial. Vallès had "dreamed this work for twenty years" (34)—that is, from the middle of the Second Empire when he was a militant republican journalist through the nine years of his exile in London where he fled after the bloody repression of the Commune in 1871. Vallès read his Mercier, and read him well. The *Tableau de Paris* of the 1780s is more than a point of reference, it is a model. The range of sympathies, the outspoken egalitarianism, the resolute commitment to the lived experience of the city in all its diversity, the clear sense of the necessary connections between a new and continually changing city and a new aesthetic that also must change—all of these qualities make Vallès not just a successor to Mercier but the true successor. What *Le Tableau de Paris* has that Mercier's *Tableau* does not, and could not, have is revolution.

Like Hugo, but very differently, Vallès constructs his work on Paris around revolution. But Vallès' conception of the city is not structured by the Revolution as idea, as Hugo's is, so much as it is by revolution as practice—his own and that of his fellow combatants. Whereas Hugo sees in the nineteenth century the fulfillment of the Revolution, Vallès writes from frustration. For the Communard Jules Vallès, revolution represents, and must therefore be represented as, a struggle rather than a victory. If Hugo in 1867 writes revolution out of the triumph of 1789, Vallès in 1882 writes from the failure of 1871. And where *Paris-Guide* calls for contemplation of the victory of the revolutionary spirit, *Le Tableau de Paris* calls to action.

Because he barely knows the Third Republic that is already in its second decade as he begins *Le Tableau,* Vallès in essence writes through his own experience of the Paris that emerged from the political and social cataclysm of the Second Empire, the Paris recounted in his novels *Le Bachelier* (1881) and *L'Insurgé* (1885) and in his journalistic essays. "Poverty, wealth, work, glory, authority, God—nothing walks in the same shoes. . . . hats have changed heads—ideas too! . . . A whole new society has jumped onto center stage!" (29). This is the society, revolutionary in its own way, that Vallès sets out to render.

His immediate predecessors offer no competition. They have, quite simply, missed the point. The superficiality of Edmond Texier's *Tableau de Paris* (1851) and of *Paris-Guide* marks them as inadequate. Texier, maintains Vallès in his introductory article, does not look beyond the facade of the city, and *Paris-Guide* skims over the high points of civilization. Neither work takes the full measure of Paris. Each avoids the inglorious parts and the unfortunate individuals depicted in the works of the Goncourt brothers or Zola. In sum, these two works look at the Paris of the bourgeoisie to which the authors belong. But they do not really *see* the new Paris that lies about them. They do not explore. For Vallès, as for Mercier before him, writing means direct experience, experience not filtered through preconceptions. He "prefers the writer who says only what he has seen" (419). Vallès too rejects every sort of intellectualizing, substituting a camera for Mercier's brush: "The era of philosophical twaddle [*philosophasserie*] is over. That of photography has arrived. The city must be painted as it is" (33). Moreover, he intends *Le Tableau de Paris* to be, like its great predecessor, a "work of action" (28).

In obvious agreement with the hero of his novel *L'Enfant* that "all stones look alike," Vallès dismisses the city in place, the city of monuments and buildings. His is the city of the living, the moving, the Paris of the street, the boulevard, the public promenade, and the open library so hospitable to the writer. But this is also the city of the closed spaces that foreclose action, the asylum, the prison, the scaffold, so many reminders of the continued inequalities of contemporary society that Vallès yearns to combat.

If Vallès' politics are wildly different from Mercier's—the comparison scarcely makes sense—Vallès is closer to the eighteenth-century man of letters than to Hugo, the prophet of the nineteenth century. Vallès' Paris, like Mercier's, is a lived Paris, a chronicle of streets and people, those whom Vallès encountered in the normal course of daily life and those whom he sought out. It is also a chronicle of hardship and misfortune and anguish, both personal and political. But he loves the city not in spite of but because of the suffering he has endured.

"I love this Paris, with all the recognizance of my sorrows." He is so much a part of the city that his very skin has "stuck on the walls of seedy hotels and on the stones in the streets" (34).

For Hugo's transcendent vision of the universe, Vallès substitutes the fraternity of those who work and who have fought to make that fraternity a reality. As will become clearer in the confrontation of Hugo's novel of revolution, *Quatrevingt-treize* (1874), with Vallès' *L'Insurgé*, the politics of the two men, like the aesthetics of the two writers, could scarcely differ more. Vallès' Paris is "the city of combat, which has suffered and bled so much" (420). The whole world listens to the heart of Paris beating and watches it bleed. For the "drops of purple that Paris has sowed on the way" mark the progress of liberty itself (41). But progress is not victory. The commitment to continuing the revolution leads him to reject the association of Paris with intellect and reason. He evokes the conventional synecdoche only to reject it out of hand. Subsuming and thereby justifying the images of blood that recur throughout *Le Tableau*, Vallès speaks in the name of the city: "To those who say that Paris is the head of the world, Paris replies that it is rather the heart of humanity" (389).

Revolutionary politics translate into a revolutionary aesthetics. Vallès gives notice that he will cover the Paris ignored or scorned by *Paris-Guide* and Texier. His city will take its place alongside the Paris and the Parisians of the Goncourts and of Zola, the Paris of the poor, the struggling, the condemned. (One article recounts an execution in considerable detail; several discuss prisons and asylums.) His protagonists are not the great men of public life but the "obscure heroes" of Paris history (420). Should he begin *Le Tableau* at the Church of the Madeleine, in the middle of bourgeois Paris, or at the opposite end of the boulevards, in the working-class Paris indelibly associated with insurrection, at the spot where the Bastille stood? The revolutionary republican naturally opts for the Bastille, taking "the path taken by events that took the route followed by the genius of Paris" (35). Revolution thus provides the starting point of *Le Tableau*. And it is the end point as well, as Vallès evokes "the city of combat" (420).

Vallès is not Mercier, of course, however striking the connections. If one can find hints of the Revolution to come in Mercier's city, Vallès' Paris can scarcely be conceived without revolution. A product of many revolutions, of modernization, of urbanization, the Paris of the late nineteenth century is necessarily larger, more fragmented, more complex than the Paris of the ancien régime. If Mercier's is the stronger because more comprehensive work, Vallès' has the more powerful voice. And it is more powerful because this writer speaks not for himself alone but for revolution, in the past, in the present, and in the future. If, as the very last line of the book asserts, London already has political liberty, Paris for its part wants social equality. The present tense conveys the urgency of the demand. *Le Tableau de Paris* ends with an implicit call to action.

To grasp the intensity of Vallès' appeal we must recognize the significance of his experiences of modernizing Paris, the city of failed revolutions in 1848 and 1871. Vallès, like Mercier, writes from an "aesthetic of the street." But the hundred years between the two Parisian tableaux dramatically alter those streets. The modern city that arises in midcentury turns on the dynamics of urbanization and predicates the deliberate defacement of old Paris. The comprehensive plan for urban renewal directed by Baron Haussmann and Napoléon III construct a new stage for the Parisian tableaux and produce a new drama on that stage. New people and practices, new individuals and institutions, make this another drama of revolution. For a vivid document of that revolution in the making chapter 4 turns to Émile Zola's novel *La Curée* (*The Quarry*). For Zola confirms what Vallès sees, namely, that the Second Empire profoundly transforms not only Parisian topography but the very meaning of urbanity. But the reconfiguration of the city in the 1850s and 1860s also inscribes a failure. When the collapse of the revolution of 1848 ended romantic Paris, the attendant loss of meaning carried over into the writer's ambivalent and ever-changing relation to the city. The *flâneur* is at once the urban personage par excellence and the figure in which the writer projects a sense of self and creative enterprise. It is to this figure that chapter 3 turns.

3

The Flâneur: The City and Its Discontents

Les arts, les sciences, la littérature doivent plus ou moins leurs
progrès au flâneur.

Auguste de Lacroix, *Les Français
peints par eux-mêmes*

Art, science, and literature owe their progress more or less to
the flâneur.

More than any other urban type, the *flâneur* suggests the contradictions of the modern city, caught between the insistent mobility of the
present and the visible weight of the past. *Flânerie,* in conventional
usage, conjures up visions of an urban *far niente,* of ambles through
city streets that offer the fortunate individual the delights of the cityscape and the perhaps even greater pleasures of suspended social
obligation. It is a social state that offers the inestimable, and paradoxical, privilege of moving about the city without losing one's individuality. At once on the street and above the fray, immersed in yet
not absorbed by the city, the flâneur resolves conflict in a seductive
image of independence justified by experience, of a knowledge rendered credible by the self-sufficiency of the knower.

As a practice of the city, and more precisely of the concentrated
urbanization of the nineteenth century, flânerie dramatizes the con-
flicting pressures that beset the individual in a postrevolutionary society. If, as most contemporary observers agree, the flâneur is indelibly Parisian, it is because of the special claims that Paris makes on
our attention and the way that the flâneur resolves those claims. As
the capital of the nineteenth century, in Walter Benjamin's telling
epithet, Paris constituted a veritable laboratory of social change, and
in that laboratory the flâneur served as both an emblem of the city
and a surrogate for the writer in that city. Literally propelled by curiosity to investigate the city whose continual metamorphoses chal-

lenged the very possibility of knowledge, the writer moved through urban society. Could the city be known? By whom? How? Flânerie provided the writer with answers, with material, and with a persona.

The flâneur had to change with the times and with the city that flânerie purported to represent. The debacle of 1848 and the radical disruption of urban renewal in the Second Empire turned the genial ambulatory philosopher of the July Monarchy into a key figure of loss within a larger "discourse of displacement." Baudelaire's ambivalent flâneur already illustrates a significant move from the triumphant Balzacian figure, but it is Flaubert who represents flânerie as a form of dispossession. The displacement of the flâneur within the city translated the writer's own sense of dislocation within bourgeois society. Flânerie ceased to signify freedom and autonomy; it implied instead estrangement and alienation. An urban spectacle that dazed more than it dazzled, a revolution that seemed never to end, converted the flâneur into a figure of exile. The stroller able to quit the city streets at will turned into a drifter. No longer the celebrant of urban enchantments, the flâneur at midcentury confronted not only the alienation and anomie attendant upon life in the modern city but more especially, given the writer's investment in flânerie, the failure that haunts the creative enterprise in contemporary bourgeois society.

Clearly, the flâneur was more than just an especially picturesque subject for the caricatures and the *physiologies* that flourished during the July Monarchy. As Baudelaire and Benjamin understood so well, flânerie posed the fundamental problem of the ways of knowing and being that are possible, even necessary, in the modern city, and only in the modern city.[1] The practice of flânerie turned the artist's unique, and uniquely modern, relationship to that city into a spectacle, a projection of the imperative need to make sense of the city. Ultimately, flânerie was a strategy of representation. The reconfiguration of the flâneur at midcentury exposed the failure of this strategy. Straightforward movement through the city proved inadequate for the city that in slightly over a half a century doubled its population and its territory and repeated its revolution two and three times. Not that the flâneur disappeared. Quite to the contrary, flânerie was everywhere, an urban practice no longer confined to an elite (much less to artists) but open to anyone in the city with a minute or two to spare. Flânerie epitomized "time off" from the real business of life, whatever that might be. Accordingly, the flâneur lost the pretention of comprehending the city as a whole. More than any other factor, this "banalization" of flânerie forced the writer to other strategies and persona to deal with the city and its revolutions.

I

Le flâneur peut naître partout; il ne sait vivre qu'à Paris.
Un Flâneur, *Paris, ou le livre des cent-et-un*

The flâneur can be born anywhere; he can live only in Paris.

The flâneur first appeared in nineteenth-century Paris, an emblem of the changing city and the changing society, a product of urbanization and revolution. The figure takes shape over the first half of the nineteenth century, appearing under the empire, rising to exceptional prominence in the *physiologies* and character sketches that abounded under the July Monarchy, and suffering a radical dislocation at midcentury at the hands of Flaubert and Baudelaire. But the flâneur as we think of the figure today, the flâneur of everyday life, conveys none of the urgency with which writers in early nineteenth-century Paris encountered the city and the society increasingly defined by that city. To recover the flâneur as the urban personage par excellence is to recapture a sense of the powerful tensions that govern the evolving urban context and to mark the writer's changing, ambiguous relationship to that context.

What is so remarkable about this figure is its progressive reevaluation. At the very beginning of the nineteenth century, when the flâneur first surfaces in urban discourse, the connotations are almost entirely negative. The inactivity that the July Monarchy will associate with a superior relationship to society is in the original usage a sign of intolerable laziness. A dictionary of "popular" (i.e., lower class) usage in 1808 defines "un grand flaneur" as "a lazybones, a loafer, man of insufferable idleness, who doesn't know where to take his trouble and his boredom."[2]

This flâneur is clearly Other and manifestly bourgeois, a distant cousin of René, whose insufferable idleness offends and importunes the lower-class speaker. But the term soon climbs the lexicographical and social ladder. The circumflex accent that the word usually acquires signals a redefinition through a change of perspective. Instead of prompting a negative moral judgment, the flâneur's conspicuous inaction comes to be taken as positive evidence of both social status and superior thought. The flâneur grows into the rentier, in whose familiar, comfortable, and unthreatening contours the bourgeoisie can recognize one of its own. Thus solidly ensconced in the bourgeois world, and identified with the city, the flâneur is ready to be taken up and redefined yet again, this time by the writer for whom the flâneur's apparent inoccupation belies his intense intellectual activity.

The bourgeois flâneur does not make his first public appearance where he is usually placed, in Balzac's *Physiologie du mariage* (1826) under the Restoration. In fact, Balzac is already working with a well-established urban personage and practice. The anonymous pamphlet of 1806 that introduces the flâneur seems to have escaped the notice of literary historians and lexicographers alike. The thirty-two-page *Le Flâneur au salon ou Mr Bon-Homme: Examen joyeux des tableaux, mêlé de Vaudevilles* presents Monsieur Bonhomme, better known "in all Paris" as the "Flâneur."[3] The "Historical Preface" detailing M. Bonhomme's daily rounds in Paris is followed by a series of "Petites Réflexions" that pass in review a number of the paintings exhibited in the current Salon held at the Louvre. Nothing hints at the quite extraordinary literary fortune the flâneur was to enjoy thirty years later, and nothing alerts the reader to the emblematic nature that the flâneur would acquire as the urban personage par excellence of the middle third of the nineteenth century.

It is true that M. Bonhomme does not much resemble his successors. He is a dull creature, easily recognizable by his wig, his "Jansenist" style hat (broad-brimmed, plain), and his dark brown suit. A man of the ancien régime (he refers to the Place de la Concorde by the name it carried prior to 1792, Place Louis-XV), M. Bonhomme exhibits none of the intensity that will distinguish the relationship of later flâneurs to the city. In contrast to these "modern" flâneurs, who celebrate the joys of coming upon the unexpected and the untoward, M. Bonhomme makes the same rounds every day and checks in at the same places. Instead of the mysteries of the urban spectacle in which the latter flâneur will revel and the cultivation of the unexpected, M. Bonhomme reassures through the regularity of his routine.

Tedium must have done him in. Despite protestations that "the race of flâneurs shall not perish!" and promises of second, third, and "even 100" sequels, *Le Flâneur au salon* did not meet with the requisite success. The promised sequels apparently did not materialize. A close analogue turned up a few years later with Jouy's immensely popular journalistic Hermit series that inaugurated the vogue of what I have called literary guidebooks. It would not be surprising if Jouy, a well-established and widely published author at the time, was trying out a new formula in the 1806 pamphlet. Certainly, the lineage is there. The article entitled "Le Flâneur" in *Les Français peints par eux-mêmes* does not hesitate to count the Hermit (along with Mercier) among the flâneur's long line of distinguished ancestors.

Nevertheless, M. Bonhomme displays the primary traits of the flâneur, namely, his detachment from the ordinary social world and his association with Paris. The essential egoism of the flâneur requires the first; the variety of his observations dictates the second. Like Jouy's Hermit, the flâneur is solitary by choice, a bachelor or widower (or else, as the flâneur-author for *Paris, ou le Livre des cent-et-un* puts it, he thinks and acts as if he were one or the other). He walks through the city alone and at random. Companionship of any sort is undesirable, and female companionship is especially so. Women, it seems, cannot maintain the detachment that distinguishes the true flâneur.

Later, under the Restoration and the July Monarchy, when commercial arcades (*les passages*) were transforming the practices of the city street, the perils of shopping loomed large, and these arcades were, then as now, inevitably associated with women (*Physiologie du flaneur,* chap. 15). The shopper's (and the seller's) intense engagement in the urban scene, the integration into the commodity exchange, and the consequent inability to maintain the proper distance from the urban scene preclude the neutrality and objectivity cultivated so assiduously by the flâneur. The flâneur desires the city as a whole, not any part of it. No woman can disconnect herself from the city and its seductive spectacle. For she must either desire the objects spread before her or herself be the object of desire, associated with and agent of the infinite seductive capacity of the city. The flâneur's movement within the city, like his solitude, points to a privileged status. But because a woman is defined by the (male) company she keeps, to be alone is to be without station. Mobility renders her suspect. Balzac makes the case eloquently if hyperbolically in *Ferragus,* where the sight of the elegant Mme Jules unattended, and on foot, in a notoriously infamous street immediately compromises her reputation (5:796). Women figure the observed, they cannot possibly reverse roles to join the observers. Women are indispensable to the urban drama that the flâneur observes, to the conjectures he makes, and to the tales that he tells, not the least of these ventures. There are, and can be, no *flâneuses*.[4] The flâneur's constitutive disengagement from the city ties this urban personage to the larger urban discourse, as practiced notably by the literary guidebook. For, like the authors of literary guidebooks, the flâneur strives to describe the city and also to understand how it works. The familiarity with the city that we can see the flâneur acquiring is assumed by the literary guidebook. We should then not be surprised to find a guidebook that appropriates the authority of flâneur. The flâneur's very text inscribes his relationship to the city. The author's random walks in *Le Flaneur* (in two editions, 1825 and 1826) provide the model for the book, composed in the spirit of flânerie "without plan, without order, without method." As it was with Mercier and would be with Vallès in their tableaux of Paris, the writer's own observations—"everything [he has] observed, as objects presented themselves to [his] eyes"—guarantee the authenticity of the text. For this "moral and philosophical exposé," the author of *Le Flaneur* "consulted no work," asked for no advice.

At the same time the flâneur as urban personage becomes one of the arresting phenomena that the literary guidebooks take it upon themselves to discuss. Both *Paris, ou le livre des cent-et-un* (1831) and *Les Français peints par eux-mêmes* (1842) devote chapters to the flâneur, and the craze for *physiologies* produced the inevitable *Physiologie du flaneur* in 1841. Yet none of these fixes the flâneur. Consider the difference between the flâneur and the devil who serves as titular figure of the literary guidebook. As the model taken from Lesage requires and the numerous frontispiece engravings make clear, the devil looks at the urban world from on high. Symptomatically, "Un Flâneur," author of the article "Le Flâneur à Paris" for *Paris, ou le livre des cent-et-un* makes a point of distinguishing himself from Asmodée. He does not practice the "dangerous art" of taking rooftops off houses to reveal the secrets of private life. Rather the flâneur operates in public, outside. For he cannot exist indoors. Like a plant that would be killed in the greenhouse, the flâneur flourishes only in the open air. At the theater, he keeps to the relatively open space of the foyer, preferring not to shut himself up in the "prison" of the theater itself.

Plates 8, 9. Flâneurs from *Les Français peints par eux-mêmes* (1842). These sketches by Henry Monnier (Plate 8) and Gavarni (Plate 9) give two representations of the flâneur, a well-dressed bourgeois, cane in hand ready to set forth in the city. In both renditions, one senses the leisure, the satisfaction, and the spirit of reverie of an individual very much in control of self and setting. (Photographs courtesy of Rare Book and Manuscript Library, Columbia University.)

LE FLANEUR.

Thus does the flâneur urbanize the observer, bringing him down to earth and plunging him into the urban spectacle. The devil looks down upon the city, the flâneur looks up and around and walks endlessly. (Good legs, as the *Physiologie du flaneur* reminds us, are essential equipment.) His field of predilection is the Paris of the arcades, the Paris of restaurants and boulevards and gardens, the Paris of crowds in public places. The reciprocity between the city and the flâneur is complete. "Without the arcades," Louis Huart admits in the *Physiologie du flaneur,* "the flâneur would be unhappy." But the balance tips in the other direction. For "without the flâneur the arcades would not exist" (chap. 13).

Unlike Jouy's Hermits, who themselves become personae in the city they observe—with dates of birth, specified places of habitation, definite habits and tastes—and unlike the dandy whose flamboyant dress sets him apart, the flâneur remains anonymous, devoid of personality, unremarkable in the crowd. It is in fact this undistinctive appearance that allows the necessary social distance. In short, the flâneur sounds very much like an author in search of characters and intrigue. Nights had always been mysterious; the flâneur's stories make days equally intriguing. As Huart reminds us in the *Physiologie du flaneur* (chap. 8), thinking perhaps of Balzac's *Ferragus,* a whole novel can spring from a single encounter observed in the street. There the chance meeting of the young, elegant, and virtuous Mme Jules and her secret admirer in a foul neighborhood leads to "a drama full of blood and love, a drama of the modern school" (5:796).

This bounding of the imagination and the intellect within a street setting both justifies the flâneur's literary claims and sets him apart from the vulgar idlers and gapers (*badauds, musards*) with which the uninitiated might confuse him. Where M. Bonhomme accepted his relationship as "a very distant cousin" of "M. Muzard," the July Monarchy flaneur insists upon the difference. ("The idler apes the flaneur, he caricatures the flaneur and seems made to inspire disgust for flanerie," in the words of the *Physiologie du flaneur,* chap. 15.) He does not look, he observes, he studies, he analyzes. He is in sum a *philosophe sans le savoir.* "Flânerie," emphatically affirms Lacroix in *Les Français peints par eux-mêmes,* "is the distinctive characteristic of the true man of letters."

Nowhere does the flâneur triumph more spectacularly than with Balzac. Although the flâneur's appearance in the very same year,

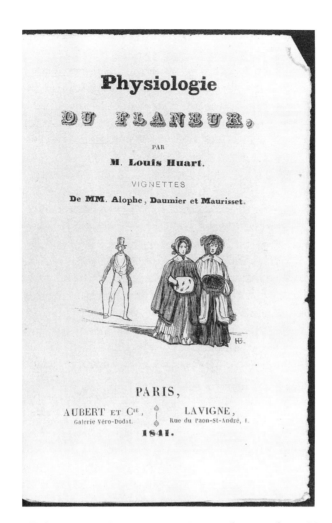

Plate 10.   Title page, Louis Huart, *Physiologie du flaneur* (1841). This incarnation of the flâneur by Daumier emphasizes the importance of the flâneur's gaze—a gaze that begins in the activity of following women. (Photograph courtesy of Special Collections, Butler Library, Columbia University.)

1826, in works as different as *Le Flaneur, galerie pittoresque, philosophique et morale* and the *Physiologie du mariage* testifies to the general familiarity of the figure during the Restoration, the honor of transforming the flâneur into a complete urban personage rightfully goes to Balzac. There will be more elaborate treatments of the flâneur but none more forceful than this first full portrait. Balzac's fervent celebration of the "flâneur artiste" set a model that would control for the next twenty years, not only for Balzac himself but also for the many other writers (and artists) who fixed upon the flâneur as a distinctive feature of modern Paris.

Whereas *Le Flaneur,* as a guidebook, more or less assumes the connections between the flâneur, Paris, and literature, Balzac forcefully articulates the dynamic involved. "To stroll is to vegetate, to *flâner* is to live." "To wander about Paris—adorable and delicious existence!" The artist-flâneur cultivates a "science" of the sensual, a "visual gastronomy" (11:930). The superiority of the flâneur, which will become an article of faith in a very few years, already separates the true from the false flâneur, the true artist from the would-be creator. For like every other type in the *Comédie humaine,* the flâneur admits of more than one exemplar, each of which occupies a particular place within a hierarchy. The artist-flâneur of Balzac's *Physiologie du mariage* belongs to a privileged elite, expression and manifestation of the higher, because intellectual, flânerie.

Other portraits—the vast majority—will at best be ordinary flâneurs, members of a "happy and soft species" (*La Fille aux yeux d'or,* 5:1053) given to random speculations and "silly conjectures" (*Une double famille,* 2:79). These onlookers in the city "savor at every hour its moving poetry" (5:1053) but will invariably be dazzled and bewildered and confused by the "monstrous marvel," "the head of the world." Although these ordinary flâneurs read the text of this "city of a hundred thousand novels" (*Ferragus,* 5:794–95), they are passive readers, taken up and taken in by the surface agitation and turbulence.

The overall distinction between the ordinary flâneur and the artist-flâneur also bespeaks an underlying rationale for the whole category. The highest flâneur understands the city; the ordinary merely experiences it. Here, in other words, is one more indication of the great importance and the even greater difficulty attached to the process of actually comprehending the nature and meaning of modern Paris.

Aesthetically, the movement of the ordinary flâneur duplicates the same quality in nineteenth-century city life. Movement in the artist-flâneur is much more. It is a mode of comprehension, a moving perspective that tallies with the complexity of a situation that defies stasis.

To be sure, ordinary flâneurs are "the only really happy people in Paris" (*La Fille aux yeux d'or*, 5:1053). (The *Physioloqie du flaneur* proclaims the flâneur "the only happy man on earth," since no flâneur has ever been reported to have committed suicide!) Of course, as for the artist-flâneur, that happiness is contingent upon a more intellectual grasp of the incessant movement of the city and its seductions. This flâneur is the great exception to the rules that govern every circle of the Parisian hell that sets the stage for *La Fille aux yeux d'or*. For other figures or types, surrendering to the desires aroused by the city necessarily implicates them in the urban text, which they will not know how to interpret or turn to their advantage. Instead, the expert readers in the *Comédie humaine*—Vautrin, Rastignac, d'Arthez, Mme de Beauséant—owe their skill precisely to their ability and willingness to remain both in and above the inferno. None succeeds entirely.

The walks about Paris that supply the artist-flâneur with material for study may well prove disastrous for the ordinary flâneur unable to maintain distance from the city and hence unable to resist its seductions. The original pejorative connotations of flânerie resurface to characterize the individual at the mercy of the city. Where the ostensible idleness of the artist-flâneur masks the vital intellectual activity of the true artist, the false artist is necessarily a false flâneur, whose inactivity derives from the inability to channel—that is, to use and comprehend—the desires roused by the city. In other words, the false artist lacks the detachment required for creativity. The *Physiologie du flaneur* rails against these loafers who proclaim themselves flâneurs. A policeman on the beat is more deserving of the name than the "incomplete artists" who never finish a painting! (chap. 15).

In Balzac's Paris, seeing is not necessarily believing, and superficial readers do not make good writers. Lucien de Rubempré in *Illusions perdues* quickly surrenders to Parisian brilliance and easy journalistic success. Once Wenceslas Steinbock quits the garret where Cousine Bette keeps him hard at work on his sculpture, he succumbs to the Paris that his success opens to him. Soon, Balzac notes, he joins the lowest order of flâneurs, who let themselves be determined by the city instead of mastering it. His is "the ultimate motto of the flâneur: I'll get right to work!'' Flânerie triumphs over every good intention: "Wenceslas . . . idled [flânait]'' and before long becomes "an artist *in partibus* . . .'' (7:243, 449), thus fulfilling the prediction at the beginning of the novel. Bette knows full well that she must keep her sculptor on a leash, or else he will turn into a flâneur. "And if you only knew what artists call *flâner*!'' her advisor tells her in a telling assimilation of the unproductive artist to the female spendthrift: "Real horrors! A thousand francs in a single day'' (7:116). The true artists of the *Comédie humaine*—the writer Daniel d'Arthez, the painter Joseph Bridau—are anything but indolent. Moreover, Balzac stresses their capacity to withdraw from Paris, their ascetic life, and their absolute commitment to their work. Lucien founders because he is utterly unprepared for the hard work and the many difficult choices that creative work entails.

The artist-flâneur, on the contrary, tempers desire with knowledge. He masters movement after having engaged in it. Whether scholar, thinker, or poet, he is a connoisseur of the "pleasures (*jouissances*)'' of Paris, one of a "small number of amateurs'' who always have their wits about them on their walks, who know how to stroll as they know how to dine and to take their pleasures. In this fusion of science and sensuality lies the key to urban control. Unlike the ordinary flâneur, who is overwhelmed by the appropriately masculine monster (*le monstre*), these "lovers of Paris'' conceive of desire in terms of domination. *Cette* courtisane—or, only somewhat less obviously, a creature (*une* créature) and queen ("this moving queen of cities'')—is logically ("naturally'') subjugated by the (male) artist-flâneur. The conception of Paris as female is hardly new, but Balzac pushes the connection to its extreme by associating flânerie with carnal knowledge. *Jouir* ("to enjoy,'' often with specifically sexual connotations) defines the flâneur's relationship to Paris in terms of desire as he "plunges his gaze into a thousand lives'' (11:930). A manuscript of 1830 makes still more of the sexual resonance of the artist-flâneur's relationship to Paris. The city is "a daughter, a woman friend, a spouse'' whose face always delights because it is always new.[5]

That creativity should be a function of control is evident in the power ascribed to the Balzacian narrator. An observer and also a participant in the city, a reader and also a writer of the urban text, the Balzacian artist-flâneur adroitly maneuvers distance and assimilation. Like the detective whom he resembles in so many respects, Balzac's artist-flâneur situates individuals within the city. More significantly still, individual destinies lead to the city itself. "Every man, every fraction of a house" is a "lobe of the cellular tissue" of this "creature" whom the artist-flâneur alone knows so well (5:795). Here as in the birds'-eye views of Paris so popular in the 1840s, an "aesthetic of integration" bespeaks the strong narrative control for which synecdoche supplies the characteristic trope. The impossibility for any individual to take account of the multiplication of urban space is refuted by the artist-flâneur, the surrogate author who takes that unknowability and makes it a condition of creativity.[6] Nowhere is Balzac's fundamentally romantic conception of the genius more evident than in the flâneur turned narrator, a voice imposing his will on the city and its texts.

II

Flâner—Se promener en musant, perdre son temps à des bagatelles.

> *Dictionnaire de l'Académie française*
> (1879)

Flâner—to dawdle about, to waste one's time on trifles.

The urban discourse secured in the texts of Balzac and his contemporaries is a discourse of placement, of exploration and explanation. Narrative control is a function of urban possession. This discourse of placement acknowledges the diversity, the mystery, and even the danger of the city, but it also assumes control of risk by unraveling each mystery before the reader's very eyes. By midcentury flânerie becomes altogether more problematic, the flâneur a suspicious character. The Revolution of 1848—the hopes raised and then dashed—divides more than the century; among other things, as Roland Barthes would later point out in *Le Degré zéro de l'écriture,* it is the crucial factor separating Balzac from Flaubert. The Second Empire that arose out of the coup d'état of Louis-Napoléon Bonaparte in 1851 staged both a new politics and a new urban text, and the Paris that we know today is largely the city torn down and rebuilt in the 1850s and 1860s under the aegis of the prefect Haussmann. A program of drastic urban renewal propelled Paris into the present. Necessarily, the flâneur performs very differently in the assertively modernizing city of broad boulevards and expansive parks, of fashionable promenades and race-tracks, of new apartment buildings, a city made over for and in the image of the grande bourgeoisie.

In the radically different urban setting made by haussmannization, the flâneur embodied a new, and disquieting, relation to the city, one that held special meaning for the artist. Despite Balzac's early classification of the artist-flâneur, Baudelaire's recasting set the archetype of the flâneur as modern artist and the artist of modernity. Baudelairean flânerie offers the key to Baudelaire's conception of the artist and his tortured relationship to society. And, however different from his predecessor, Baudelaire's flâneur in search of modernity claims as his ancestor the paradigmatic artist-flâneur of the July Monarchy investigating the city.[7]

Like Balzac's artist-flâneur, Baudelaire's painter of modern life aims "higher" than the "pure flâneur." But those heights are defined differently. The city is no longer reflected in the puzzles resolved by the detective but by the mysteries confronted and savored and, for that matter, created by the artist. The flâneur has become "L'Étranger" (1862), the opening poem in *Le Spleen de Paris* that transforms the observer into the "enigmatic man," the "extraordinary" foreigner-stranger who loves "the clouds that pass . . . , the marvelous clouds," the painter of modern life who proposes to "extract the eternal from the transitory." Balzac's controlling narrator gives way to Baudelaire's anguished poet, for whom exploration of the city is a pretext for the exploration of self. He seeks not society, and not the city, but modernity. The locus of personal misery, the city is also the site of creativity, the place of "Idéal" as well as of "spleen." The realm of pure art, this Paris is also the empire of prostitution, but it is, as Baudelaire has it for his poet-man of the crowd in "Les Foules," "the sacred prostitution of the soul." The flâneur's ambivalent, and ambiguous, relationship to the city now enters and defines the very condition of creativity.

The recasting of flânerie is not Baudelaire's alone, and his is not the only flâneur in Paris at midcentury. The malaise of the artist to which his work bore witness was social, not individual. The other great universe of flânerie in nineteenth-century literature, an urban universe contemporaneous with that of *Le Spleen de Paris,* is that created by Gustave Flaubert. In 1869, the same year that *Le Spleen de Paris* was published, *L'Éducation sentimentale* ushered in another world in which the flâneur plays an exemplary role. Flaubert's flâneur is nei-

ther Balzac's triumphant artist nor again the detached onlooker of
the July Monarchy. He does not even attain the intermittent creativity
of Baudelaire's tortured artist. He is, rather, a figure of failure, of the
impossibility of placing oneself in the city so emphatically producing
the space of modernity. Balzac's ordinary flâneur from the July Monarchy turns into the hapless soul of the Second Empire, overwhelmed
by the city that refuses security. Far from empowering the walker in
the street, the altered urban context disables the individual and dev-
astates the collectivity. Distance and inactivity no longer connote superiority but rather estrangement, alienation, anomie. Moreover, it
is not the creative estrangement that sets the condition of Baudelaire's poetry but an alienation that paralyzes the will.

There are, to be sure, earlier hints of the darker side of flânerie.
Startling images of failure develop in Balzac's later work—Lucien de
Rubempré's disastrous first sojourn in Paris in *Un Grand Homme de
province à Paris* of 1839, the feckless Wenceslas Steinbock's decline in
La Cousine Bette of 1846. In *César Birotteau* (1844) Balzac warns us that
the Parisian flâneur is just as often a desperate man as an idler (6:63).
Yet Balzac's own work affirms that the artist-flâneur remains a possibility. Balzac's romanticized, essentially aristocratic producer of the urban text has no station in the relentlessly bourgeois city depicted by
Flaubert. The new Paris of squandered opportunities utterly lacks the
dramatic derelictions and successes depicted by Balzac, Hugo, and
other urban novelist-adventurers like Eugène Sue or by their successors
like Zola and Maupassant. The flânerie that undermines the resolve of
Wenceslas Steinbock and Lucien de Rubempré governs Flaubert's entire universe. The artist-flâneur has become extinct. Productivity of any
sort is not even a remote possibility in Flaubert's world because the
artist-flâneur at midcentury stands for anomie and alienation.

Unlike Balzac or Baudelaire or others, Flaubert says relatively little
about the flâneur or flânerie. Nowhere does he call Frédéric Moreau
a flâneur.[8] Nevertheless, Frédéric is a flâneur, and even though the
novel takes place during the July Monarchy, Frédéric is a flâneur for
the Second Empire during which Flaubert wrote the novel. Frédéric
is a flâneur who does not possess the city so much as he is possessed
by it. Flânerie defines his world and his being. Most obviously, Frédéric and his friends (including his beloved Mme Arnoux) spend an
impressive amount of time moving about the streets of Paris, back
and forth across the Seine, up to Montmartre, over to Saint-Augustin,
down to the Quartier Latin, and back again. The chance meetings on

those streets that play so conspicuous a role in the novel bear further witness to the role flânerie plays in defining the novel, and surely it is fitting that Frédéric and Mme Arnoux mark their final encounter with a walk through the streets of the city that has both favored and frustrated their liaison. Paris has provided space for their meetings, but the city affords no place for their love.

The aimlessness of Frédéric's meanderings, in particular, contrasts sharply with the energy that dispatches the characters of Balzac and Hugo from one place to another. Place still signifies for the older generation of romantics. For Balzac, who writes in the July Monarchy about the Restoration, Eugène de Rastignac's route from the Montagne-Sainte-Geneviève to the faubourg Saint-Germain in *Le Père Goriot* and Lucien de Rubempré's movements from one *quartier* to another in *Illusions perdues* are charged with symbolic significance. Streets exist as places, each endowed with a particular character—as in the meditation on la rue Soly that opens *Ferragus* or the entire section, "L'Idylle rue Plumet et l'Épopée rue Saint-Denis," that Hugo places in *Les Misérables*. Because Balzac and Hugo equate Paris with history, the monuments, streets, and neighborhoods speak eloquently about the past and portentously about the present. For Flaubert, writing about the July Monarchy and the Revolution of 1848 from the vantage point of the Second Empire, the demonstration at the Panthéon, like the destruction of the Louvre during the February days of 1848, mirrors the degradation, the confusion, and the loss of meaning in Paris as a whole.[9]

Notwithstanding the evident difference of these many urban landscapes of *L'Éducation sentimentale*, flânerie constitutes an exceptionally appropriate image for a man distanced from his surroundings. Walking alone at night after quitting Mme Arnoux, Frédéric "was no longer conscious of the milieu, of space, of anything" (99). Walking heightens this insensibility because it is associated with intoxication (*ivresse*). The night that he walks the streets "the movement of his walking kept up the intoxication" (129). Incapable of concentrating on any task in the absence of Mme Arnoux, he spends hours on his balcony contemplating the Seine (116); on the first day of the Revolution of 1848, he and Rosanette spend the afternoon on the balcony looking at the crowd in the street (352, *cf.* 429). When he comes into closer contact with the insurrection, events scarcely touch him. The wounded "did not seem like real wounded men, the dead did not seem like real dead men. It seemed to him that he was watching a performance [*un spectacle*] " (357). Some time later on "his promenade" (389) on the boulevards in search of something to do, Frédéric finds the agitated crowd of workers, policemen, and bourgeois bystanders "a very amusing sight [*un spectacle*]" (390). The detailed presentation of events of 1848 only makes more obvious the essential absence of the revolution.

Frédéric's inability to direct his steps—his existential flânerie—signals his inability to conduct either his career or his emotions. He has little attachment to society despite his many ineffectual attempts to participate fully therein. Frédéric has no effective ties to the numerous and diverse milieux that he frequents. His many undertakings are so incompatible that he executes none of them. His abortive candidacy at the Club de l'Intelligence, like his consideration of M. Dambreuse's proposition to be general secretary of a new corporation and his scheme for a wealthy marriage, not to mention the great works he thinks about painting or writing, all come to naught. Frédéric is suspended in the city and in society at large, but this suspension is the consequence less of choice than of a marked aversion to the responsibilities that choice demands. Not surprisingly, his most important resolutions appear negative—not to accept M. Dambreuse's offer, not to run for office, not to seduce Mme Arnoux, not to marry Mme Dambreuse, and so on.

Paris cannot be conquered because it is a utopia, an elsewhere forever beyond reach, another creation of Frédéric's imagination. However much time he spends contemplating the city, Frédéric never perceives it clearly. Thus, in the first scene he is leaving Paris. Its buildings recede in the distance, obscured by the smoke and the cloud of steam emitted by the boat, and by the fog (47). Returning to the capital a richer man a few years later, he watches factories "smoking" and the sun shining "through the haze" (156–7). The pervasive rain, fog, and mist all blur the line between reality and reverie. All in all, it is no wonder that the city remains unfocused, particularly given the frequent association of Frédéric with one or another variant of intoxication, dizziness, or bedazzlement (*ivresse, étourdissement, éblouissement*).

For all of Flaubert's sociological and historical acuity, the Paris of *L'Éducation sentimentale* is filtered through the stereotypical exoticism of his protagonist's febrile imagination. As Frédéric quits the city in the opening scene, he daydreams about what he will do when he takes up residence there two months hence. Yet once in Paris Frédéric almost immediately sees himself elsewhere. Settling into his rooms on the quai Napoléon conjures up visions of furnishing a Moorish palace (104). His career plans resemble grandiose fictions of a place in Parisian society—in the courtroom and the Assemblée Nationale (139), in the diplomatic corps (152), in the Conseil d'État (152, 214, 220). Deslauriers urges Frédéric to turn to fiction for his models: "Remember Rastignac in the *Comédie humaine!*" (65). But unlike those of his Balzacian model, Frédéric's innumerable trips about Paris prove as meaningless as his imaginary dislocations in time and space. In a suitable irony, Frédéric finds his space in Paris only when away from the city. At his mother's in Nogent-sur-Seine, he "plays the Parisian," creating a fictive capital for the locals in compensation for his disappointments in the real Paris. Once again Frédéric fails to rise above mediocrity. His knowledge turns out to be gossip about the theater and high society that he has culled from magazine accounts (308).

Frédéric can no more depict Mme Arnoux than he can define the city, and this is true despite the considerable detail given to each— on the one hand, Mme Arnoux's dress, her hair, her beauty mark, and especially her possessions, and on the other, the scrupulously delineated topography of Paris, its different *quartiers,* and its institutions. For the one as for the other, detail distracts. It diffuses attention instead of focusing desire. The "rapture of his whole being" propels Frédéric toward Mme Arnoux (441), but that rapture impedes action. As he tells her on their last meeting, she affected him like "moonlight on a summer's night, when everything is perfume, soft shadows, whiteness, infinity" (503). Her very dress appears "infinite" (261). Mme Arnoux fades into the pervasive unreality of Frédéric's life, scarcely more real than the revolution that he also observes through the prism of reverie.

The city and the woman, in loose equation, are as limitless and as elusive as the air that Frédéric breathes. They compose his milieu in the physiological sense of the term, for they supply the medium within which he evolves. The possibility of frequenting the Arnoux household holds the promise of "living in [Mme Arnoux's] atmosphere," the very thought of which sends Frédéric through the deserted streets "at random, lost, carried away," until he finds himself on the quais, where the lights "vacillated in the depths of the water," a "luminous fog floated above the roof tops," and all the noises "melted into a single hum" (99–100).

Ultimately, Paris, like Mme Arnoux, is not so much unconquerable as evanescent. Flaubert takes such care to join the two because Frédéric views each in much the same light. Everything about Paris "related to her" (120), and Frédéric's conviction that "any attempt to make her his mistress would be in vain" (120) applies equally to his perception of Paris. The city too is the "sphinx" (261) whose enigma Frédéric never solves. His halfhearted attempts to conquer the one and the other, the woman and the city, succumb to the inertia induced by reverie. It is not by accident that here as elsewhere Flaubert takes the Balzacian model only to reverse it. Both writers associate Paris with a woman and the flâneur with male desire. But the correspondence of the trope only highlights the difference between these worlds. The metaphor that Balzac uses to imply possession is used by Flaubert to signify precisely the opposite. In *L'Éducation sentimentale* desire is dreamed, never realized.

Unlike Balzac or Hugo, Flaubert calls on no outsize, controlling metaphor to subsume the many parts of the city into a powerful, unitary definition. For Balzac's personification of Paris as *créature, courtisane*, queen, or monster, or Hugo's portrayal of a leviathan ("L'Intestin de Léviathan" in *Les Misérables*), Flaubert substitutes the elusive Seine, which connects Frédéric to Paris and to Mme Arnoux, to his home in Nogent-sur-Seine and his mother. Paradoxically, the very mobility of the flâneur precludes effective—that is, directed—movement, and the river joins the omnipresent drizzle, showers, vapor, and human tears in a universal aqueous medium that dissipates Frédéric's ambition, dilutes his desires, and dissolves his will. In contrast to Balzac's conquering aristocratic flâneur who seduces the city-as-woman to engender the urban text, Flaubert's bourgeois flâneur idles to no effect. Frédéric does not seduce; he is seduced, by the city to which he remains almost literally enthralled. He slides through the social hierarchy as he roams about the streets. Aristocratic inclinations and artistic tastes notwithstanding, Frédéric is neither aristocrat nor artist. The text, like the city and the woman, remains out of reach. At every turn the city frustrates desire, baffles intelligence, and resists control.

III

L'errance que multiplie et rassemble la ville en fait une immense expérience sociale de la privation de lieu.
                    Michel de Certeau, *L'Invention du quotidien*

The moving about that the city multiplies and concentrates
makes the city itself an immense social experience of lacking
a place.

In this period of almost incalculable change for the country and
for its capital, the novel came of age and sociology was born. More
than coincidence connects the two. From Balzac, Auguste Comte, and
Alexis de Tocqueville in the 1830s and 1840s through Flaubert and
Marx from the 1850s through the 1870s to Émile Zola, Maurice
Barrès, and Émile Durkheim in the 1880s and 1890s, to take only the
most obvious candidates, the literary and the sociological imagination
worked with shared perceptions and concerns as they confronted a
society that resisted conventional modes of representation. If Flaubert
strikes a discordant note within this sociological tradition, it is because
he has, in a very decisive sense, been taken at his word. Obdurate
aestheticism and adamantly apolitical politics have obscured the profound sense of a century out of joint that Flaubert shares with writers
like Balzac and Zola, who made a point of articulating the sociological
relevance of their work.

Like the sociologist, Flaubert consistently frames the individual in
terms of the collective. Despite the singular connotations of the subtitle of *L'Éducation sentimentale—Story of a Young Man*—Flaubert specified that the novel had greater ambitions. It was a "novel of modern
mores." More specifically, his announced goal was to write the "moral
history" of an entire generation—his own—and to analyze the historical conditions responsible for its lack of accomplishment. This
novel, he noted, was to be a story of love and of passion, but "passion
as it can exist today, that is, inactive" (letter to Mlle Leroyer de Chan-
tepie, 6 October 1864). For Flaubert as for Balzac, as for any sociologist, the most intimate of emotions is also and at the same time the
most social. Flaubert's first book shows a similar split between the
individual focus of the title, *Madame Bovary,* and the social milieu of
the subtitle, *Moeurs de province.*

What secures Flaubert's place on the sociological agenda of the
nineteenth century is his evident preoccupation with the deteriora-

tion of contemporary society. Emma Bovary and Frédéric Moreau do not reflect the sorry state of nineteenth-century France, they are themselves agents of that decline. Flaubert's indictment in 1857 for "outrage to public morality" in *Madame Bovary* offers clear testimony to the relevance of a sociological reading of the novel. The author may have inhabited an ivory tower; his readers most assuredly did not. They saw and insisted upon precisely that which Flaubert shrouded in his aesthetic pronouncements, namely, the forceful social subtext of his work.

This subtext places Flaubert's novels, and *L'Éducation sentimentale* in particular, not only between the works of Balzac and Zola, where they have long had a place, but also between those of Karl Marx and Émile Durkheim. Although Marx and Durkheim are more often set in opposition than in tandem, the Marxian category of alienation offers more than one parallel with Durkheimian anomie, and both are relevant to the Paris of *L'Éducation sentimentale*. Each theoretical construct points to an aspect of the modern city around which Flaubert constructs his novel.

Anomie is the term that Durkheim resurrected from the fifteenth century (from Greek) to characterize a society that fails to anchor the individual in significant social groups. In addition to its specific philosophical heritage through Hegel and Feuerbach, alienation resonates with the usage in both Roman law and contemporary psychiatric discourse to identify a society that dispossesses the individual of both work and worth. Durkheim uses suicide much as Marx uses fetishism, as a sign of futility and, hence, of social pathology. Intended as an affirmation of the individual choice, retreat into death, like escape into materialism, surrenders control to encompassing social forces.

In very different, possibly antagonistic theoretical systems, anomie and alienation designate a social structure marked by the radical disjuncture between the whole and its constituent parts. Both concepts belong within the larger discourse of displacement that becomes increasingly strident as the century progresses—precisely that discourse in which the flâneur figures so prominently as the urban personage par excellence. Differences between the analytic and narrative practice of social representation only accentuate the commonality of the problem. The claim here is not one of influence. Marx passionately admired Balzac's work, but he said nothing of Flaubert; and Durkheim never accorded literature and the arts more than cursory notice. But Marx and Durkheim share with Flaubert a common culture of concern. The discourse of dislocation that Flaubert narrates and dramatizes, they articulate and theorize.

The same division of labor (Durkheim's first book, in 1893, is the *Division du travail social*), the same rampant individualism, and the same consequent splintering of society that are the target of Durkheimian sociology also structure Flaubert's novels. Indeed, Flaubert's world of flânerie, so notable for the absence of stable social relations, could serve as a model for Durkheim's vision of modern society. Of Durkheim's major works, *Le Suicide* (1897) evidences the strongest connection to Flaubert's texts of displacement. In this pioneering work, notable for its synthesis of statistical and theoretical analysis, Durkheim argues that suicide should be considered a social rather than individual phenomenon. As such, it requires a sociological, not a psychological, model of explanation. Accordingly, Durkheim approaches suicide by classifying suicidal behavior in terms of varying relationships between the individual and society. The disjuncture between the two determines what Durkheim points to as the prevailing forms of suicide in contemporary society: "egoistic" suicide signifying insufficient attachment to society and "anomic" suicide resulting from inadequate regulation of desire.

In conjunction and separately, anomie and egoism detach the individual from society much as flânerie disconnects the flâneur from effective social activity. Each designates the erosion of social bonds and the loss of social integration. To complete the logical possibilities, Durkheim posits "altruistic suicide," which originates in excessive attachment to the collectivity, and "fatalistic suicide," which results from overregulation of the passions. But these last categories are of less moment. (Fatalistic suicide, which Durkheim ascribes to slaves in antiquity, gets no more than a footnote.) Like so many others in the nineteenth century (and here lies the connection to Balzac), Durkheim believed modern society should worry about weak rather than strong social bonds and concern itself with the excesses of passion rather than its repression.

Behavior that can be classified as suicidal may or may not actually end in death. In any case, what matters to Durkheim is not the individual act of suicide but what that act reveals about society. Similarly, as his determination to focus on his generation indicates, Flaubert is concerned less with Frédéric or the others as individuals than with what their fates reveal about their generation and the absence of meaningful affective bonds and social ties. Durkheim, like Flaubert, considers individual acts—suicide, passion—so many private manifestations of a social state that comprehends but also transcends the individual.

Frédéric Moreau does not commit suicide. He is tempted, but on the evening that he contemplates throwing himself into the Seine, the parapet on the bridge seems a bit too wide and "lassitude" wins out (129). Nevertheless, Frédéric greatly resembles Emma Bovary, who does kill herself. Both exhibit the particular blend of egoism (weak social bonds) and anomie (unregulated passion) that Durkheim judges characteristic of certain cases. The close relationship of these two social states is borne out by the examples that Durkheim calls up to illustrate the psychological manifestations of a social state. Like Lamartine's egoistic Raphaël lost in "the infinity of dream," Frédéric misdirects his ambitions; like Goethe's Werther and like Chateaubriand's René, lost in "the infinity of desire," he wallows in his love for Mme Arnoux.[10] Disillusionment is inevitable because the most boundless passion inevitably comes up short against the real world. "The boundaries encountered by the dissatisfied individual can lead him . . . to seek distraction from disappointed passions in an inner life. But since he finds nothing there . . . he can only flee once again." As Frédéric's successive enthusiasms repeatedly demonstrate, such flight only increases "disquietude and dissatisfaction." The cycle perpetuates frustration, with the result that "despondency alternates with agitation, dream with action, transports of desire with melancholy meditations."

Durkheim also recognizes that, despite apparent differences, egoism and altruism are really two aspects of the same social state, and, hence, may work together to produce a maladjustment on the part of the individual. Frédéric's allegiance to Mme Arnoux, like the fervent zeal with which Sénécal serves the republic, illustrates the distinctive fusion of selfishness and devotion that Durkheim finds in modern, "disaggregated society." When society itself cannot serve as a goal for individual activities, individuals or groups look for something else "to which they can attach themselves and which gives a sense to their life." Reality being of no use, these individuals elect an "ideal reality, . . . an imaginary being whom they serve all the more exclusively for being out of sorts with everything else, themselves included." "Hence," Durkheim concludes, "they live a double and contradictory existence: individualists for everything in the real world, they turn into immoderate altruists for everything that touches the ideal object."

Thus Frédéric justifies every selfish action with the thought of his ideal love. In hopes of becoming closer to Mme Arnoux, he reneges on his promise of money to Deslauriers and gives the money instead to her husband; subsequently, for much the same reason he slanders his friend Dussardier in order to justify borrowing a substantial sum from his fiancée, Mme Dambreuse, to pay Mme Arnoux's debts. The most striking instance of the association of altruism and egoism occurs during the coup d'état of 1851 when the one-time republican militant Sénécal, for whom the ideal state apparently excuses every excess, turns policeman for Louis-Napoléon Bonaparte and shoots Dussardier, once his republican comrade.

This social fragmentation, which *L'Éducation sentimentale* enacts and with which Durkheimian sociology contends, also links Flaubert to Marx. Marx and Flaubert were exact contemporaries, and Marx spent important years in Paris and wrote about the July Monarchy and the Second Republic. Here, once again, and for both writers, Paris is the essence of the modern condition. Where Durkheim renders the division of labor and excessive individualism responsible for the crisis in which modern society finds itself, Marx indicts the division of property and the class society. Where Durkheim takes his model from disease, talking of "pathology" and of society as an "organism," Marx thinks in terms of materialism. The cornerstone of Marxian theory is also basic to *L'Éducation sentimentale*, a setting dominated by the commodification of human relations, love, art, and politics. Frédéric's almost obsessive furnishing of his *hôtel particulier* implies the debasement of art into merchandise that is writ large not only in Arnoux's trajectory from editing the journal *L'Art industriel* to selling religious objects but also in the sordid negotiations over Rosanette's portrait (itself a hodgepodge of stylistic references that defy the very notion of authenticity). The engravings of Venice, Naples, and Constantinople that Frédéric rushes to hang in his first rooms, like the travel accounts and the atlas he purchases subsequently, substitute for the trips he does not take. When he finally quits France and travels to exotic lands, the voyage seems to be out of an album filled with visual clichés ("the melancholy of steamer ships, the awakenings on cold mornings in a tent, the dizziness of landscapes and ruins, the bitterness of interrupted companionship" [500]).

The promiscuity dictated by the market begins, and ends, at home. The most arresting of the many objects that give so much material weight to the novel, and certainly the most evident both thematically and structurally, relate to the Arnoux household(s). A surprising number of items circulate between spouse and mistress in an apparently endless exchange. The silver casket that Arnoux gives his wife reappears throughout the novel, a "relic" of Frédéric's devotion, but the devotion is more than a little ambiguous because the relic is shared by both of Frédéric's mistresses. Rosanette (also Arnoux's mistress) has the casket for a time, and Mme Dambreuse later buys it at auction. By propelling the private into the public domain, the auction puts Mme Arnoux herself into circulation, like every other woman in the novel, like every other man. Mme Arnoux is effectively "sold off" at auction. The passing about of her personal effects, her furs, her dresses, her boots, her hats, her gloves, and especially her petticoats and shifts transforms the room into a bordello (the bedroom furniture is prominently on display) and confirms suspicions that no dream can resist circulation in the Paris market.

The drama of the auction arises from its public, that is, indiscriminant nature. It forces Mme Arnoux onto the open market, as opposed to the restricted, "local" market within which she had circulated until then. Mme Dambreuse's purchase of the iconical casket is the sentimental equivalent of Sénécal's shooting of Dussardier the next day during the coup d'état. The conversion of this last "treasure" into the debased common coin punctures Frédéric's dream as surely as the coup d'état liquidates the republican ideal embodied by Dussardier.

The auction stages the process of commodification that has directed the novel from the beginning. However much "the force of [Frédéric's] dreams" places Mme Arnoux "outside human conditions" from the first apparition to the last rendezvous, Flaubert persistently brings her back in (230). The association with objects is not limited to those she actually possesses. Frédéric sees Mme Arnoux in every shop window, imagines her in the displayed cashmere shawls, lace, earrings, and satin slippers. This propensity to see Mme Arnoux everywhere, and especially in objects that are for sale, subjects her to the implacable logic of substitutability that applies to people as well as to things. "All women reminded him of her," prostitutes, middle-class women, working-class girls, as well as the women in the paintings at the Louvre for whom he "substituted" her image (119–20).

Frédéric copies Arnoux in associating Mme Arnoux with Rosa-nette, but goes one better by adding Mme Dambreuse. Moreover, Arnoux's outspoken admiration of his wife's physical attributes, like Cisy's insult that provokes the duel with Frédéric, intimates that Mme Arnoux is not as different from other women as Frédéric would like to believe. Then too, Mme Arnoux herself visits Frédéric to solicit financial assistance, and although she speaks in her husband's name and is accompanied by her child and his maid, the situation, as Fré-déric cannot help realizing, raises questions about her motives. Not the least ambiguous aspect of the final encounter between Frédéric and Mme Arnoux is the financial transaction that prompts a visit after more than fifteen years (repayment of a debt long outstanding). Fré-déric suspects that Mme Arnoux has come to give herself to him, but she instead presents the sum in a small wallet that she has embroi-dered with golden palms. This wallet, along with the long lock of hair that she cuts for him, is all that Frédéric will ever possess of her. From beginning to end, from the shawl that Frédéric hands back to her at their first meeting to the purse that she returns to him more than a quarter century later, Flaubert ties Mme Arnoux to the material world.

That material world, the novel makes abundantly clear, is totally illusory. It is incapable of fixing Frédéric, who is condemned to wan-der through life as he roams about Paris. The city, love, politics—all in *L'Éducation sentimentale* are an experience of absence. The travels that Frédéric embarks upon following Mme Arnoux's departure and the coup d'état are as desultory as his walks about Paris. These travels to exotic places amplify the basic model of flânerie. In the city or in the world at large, the encounter with place produces an absence. In contrast to the flâneur-artist of Balzac or Baudelaire, who is very much tied to place, Flaubert's flâneur has no space. His is very much the world of anomie and alienation, of social fragmentation and the il-lusion of presence. Flaubertian flânerie transposes the social and po-litical crises of the nineteenth century onto the city. Where Durkheim and Marx analyze modern society, Flaubert narrates the contempo-rary city, the revolutionary Paris where revolution too had become an absence.

IV

Le regard que le génie allégorique plonge dans la ville trahit
... le sentiment d'une profonde aliénation. C'est là le regard
d'un flâneur.
                Walter Benjamin, "Paris, Capitale du XIXᵉ siècle"

The look that allegory plunges in the city . . . betrays a profound alienation. It's the look of a flâneur.

Reading Flaubert through Durkheim and Marx suggests a type of
interpretation that might fuse the imaginative mode of literature and
the analytical method of social science—precisely the kind of history
it was Walter Benjamin's ambition to write. Benjamin's work on
nineteenth-century Paris is a mine of information, of literary and historical analysis, and of meditations on just what it is that ties the nineteenth century to the present. Benjamin sought the congruence of
the apparently incongruent, the immaterial embedded in the material. Behind "the facts fixed in the form of things" he looked to the
illusions around which those facts and those things cohered.[11] Not
accidentally, the subject demanding this integration was, once again,
Paris. In "Paris, Capitale du XIXᵉ siècle," the second of the two introductions that he wrote for his unfinished project on nineteenth-
century civilization, he circles around the Marxist notion of fetishism.
But Benjamin sees Paris as much through the lenses of Baudelaire's
poetics as through the lenses supplied by Marxian theory. He parts
company with orthodox Marxism when he singles out the illusions
produced by a materialistic civilization. In this short summary of his
intended great work on Paris, Benjamin points to a universe of illusions that brings us back to Flaubert's Paris and its flâneurs.

Benjamin seized upon the flâneur as an exemplary character type
produced by the nineteenth-century city. Working largely from Baudelaire's conceptions of the modern artist and the flâneur, Benjamin
elaborated a vision of a city of revolution, but a revolution that somewhere, somehow went wrong. So remarkable are the correlations with
L'Éducation sentimentale that the novel seems almost a blueprint for
the Benjaminian vision of history. For before Benjamin and contem-
poraneously with Baudelaire, Flaubert uses flânerie to represent the
modern city and the illusions that it sustains. But the differences are
instructive and suggest why Benjamin paid little attention to Flau-

bert's flâneurs and their world of dislocation. The flâneur that Baudelaire allegorizes, Flaubert represents. The archetypical modern urban
landscape of *Le Spleen de Paris* contrasts with the scrupulously delineated topographical and historical Paris of *L'Éducation sentimentale*.
The fascination with the allegories of modern life that drew Benjamin
to Baudelaire suggests that his inattention to Flaubert may be explained by the very different, realistic mode in which the novelist
necessarily operated. Flaubert's flâneurs are Parisian in ways that
Baudelaire's, and Benjamin's, are not.

Yet despite the evident difference in mode, Flaubert very clearly
renders the kind of spectacle for which Benjamin appropriated the
term *phantasmagoria*. (The term, which originated in popular enter-
tainments that used optical illusions to produce shadows or *fantômes*,
was appropriated by Marx to designate the illusory, reified nature of
personal relationships under capitalism.) Benjamin outlines the
phantasmagoria in tantalizing brevity. Against the public illusions of
the market place, which find their privileged expression first in the
arcades and subsequently in the World's Fairs and the department
store, he sets the private illusions of the collector who endeavors to
abstract objects from the market by idealizing them. In the Paris reconstructed by Haussmann, Benjamin uncovers the mask that society
has composed for itself. The new Paris is "phantasmagoria turned
into stone." All of these elements together disguise the primary transformation of nineteenth-century society in the reduction of objects
to their exchange value, that is, their commercialization. There remains only the illusion of freedom and security, which coexists in the
anxiety of those living the illusion. Modernity, as Benjamin concludes
citing Baudelaire, is the world dominated by its phantasmagoria.

Benjamin traces these phantasmagoria through their material
manifestations—a logical enough approach given the weight that fetishism bears in the Marxist model and his own vision of a material
history, a "thing-oriented representation of civilization." But Benjamin's notion of materialism is singular. It is not dialectical, and if it
is passionately historical, the history in question remains a quirky one.
Still, if we can talk about Flaubert's materialism, it is through just this
sort of twist. Flaubertian materialism does not issue solely from the
oppressive presence of objects in these novels or the innumerable
lists of almost every sort. Were that the case, almost any realist novel
would do (and the naturalist Zola would presumably provide an even

more telling model). Flaubert's "historical materialism," like Benjamin's, takes a specific turn. It resides in his insistence that desired objects are illusory, and it places its stress upon the fact and importance of illusion as such. Frédéric illustrates to perfection Benjamin's notion of the collector who accumulates possessions in order to make a place in a world in which, in truth, he has no place.

In this world of phantasmagoria, Frédéric and everyone else in the novel exchange roles, ideologies, politics, lovers, and governments as easily as objects change hands. The exchange-value of objects and people everywhere supersedes their use-value. *L'Éducation sentimentale* portrays a reified world, where Benjamin's arcades have been elaborated into a metonymy for the city and the society beyond, where the market solicits through the illusions it sustains. Frédéric meanders about Paris like the flâneur passing through an arcade, giving himself over to the illusions of the material. The bumbling protagonists in the unfinished, posthumously published *Bouvard et Pécuchet* (1880) similarly pass from one illusion to another as they meander through the facts and fads of the nineteenth century, unable to find a place or a text that fits. More radically than *L'Éducation sentimentale*, *Bouvard et Pécuchet* stages the drama of intellectual and social dispossession. Displacement has been redefined from a matter of individual disposition (and election) to a question of social (dis)organization. In sum, the flâneur's temporary suspension from society has become the urban condition. No longer one of many social roles that the urban dweller may adopt from time to time, the flâneur occupies a full-fledged social status that defines and confines existence itself—a negative construct of truly modernist proportions.

Between the vibrant city of Balzac and Hugo and the haunting, strangely empty metropolis of Flaubert and Baudelaire loom the Paris of Haussmann and the France of Napoléon III. This city and this society furnish the sociological intertext for *L'Éducation sentimentale*, one that intervenes between the action of the novel (1840–51) and the presumed narration (1867). The text of Paris (re)written by Haussmann, like the rules of government redrafted by Napoléon III, does not efface the past so much as it inexorably marks off the present. Frédéric's consternation at seeing Mme Arnoux's white hair renders the shock provoked by the confrontation with the new Paris and the consequent realization that the old is irretrievable. The "adorations" that Frédéric directs to "the woman she was no longer" (503) echo the laments for *le vieux Paris* that grew louder and louder as *le Paris nouveau* took shape. Flaubert does not even specify where this last meeting takes place, surely a significant absence in a novel notable for topographical specificity. The rue Rumford where Frédéric has his *hôtel particulier* in the late July Monarchy disappeared into the new boulevard Malesherbes between 1855 and 1860, so it cannot be there that Mme Arnoux comes in 1869. Frédéric's last apartment exists in something of a non-place, just like his great love affair that does not so much end as dissolve into the city lights reflected on the shiny, wet streets of their last walk together. Once again the urban topography supplies a basic figure for the narrative at large. Haussmannized Paris is not merely the setting for Frédéric's nonexistence from 1852 to 1869, summarized in two paragraphs, it is the necessary figure for that nonexistence.

Unlike Balzac and unlike Baudelaire, Flaubert offers no artist-flâneur to make sense of this universe, to retrieve the past by refashioning it. Flaubert in the Second Empire can only come up with idlers whose constitutional *dés-oeuvrement* (idleness) must be understood as *dés-oeuvrement*, as "un-working." Of the eight instances of "désoeuvrement" and the five that concern Frédéric, four are explicitly related to the absence of work (69, 72, 116, 500), once in direct reference to the novel that Frédéric never finishes (72). Flaubert achieved the paradoxical construction of a work (*oeuvre*) out of idleness (*dés-oeuvrement*) in a latter-day equivalent of creation from the void. Accordingly, *L'Éducation sentimentale* is an oxymoron. The very existence of the work refutes the conclusions reached by the text. As Georg Lukács noted in *The Theory of the Novel,* the achievement of *L'Éducation sentimentale* contests the default of the artist and the degradation of art that the novel performs so vividly.

Frédéric "sustained the idleness [*désoeuvrement*] of his intellect" (500) during the decade and a half that followed Louis-Napoléon's coup d'état of 1851. But those were the years of the Second Empire during which Flaubert became a writer, the years of *Madame Bovary,* of *Salammbô,* of *L'Éducation sentimentale* itself. He took to heart the advice he gave Louise Colet in 1852. From the top of his ivory tower, Flaubert could see the Second Empire and the transformed Paris, but he rendered them by their absence. The "blank" space of the novel —from 1851, when the sentimental and political drama ends, to 1867, when the novel ends—was filled by Flaubert's hard work. History is dislodged but also filled by art. The discourse of displacement becomes, in a final paradox, the means of creation.

The infinite emptiness with which *L'Éducation sentimentale* has so often been taxed derives not from the loss of illusions but, quite the contrary, from their persistence. Like Bouvard and Pécuchet, Frédéric and Deslauriers end up exactly where they started out, older to be sure, sadder certainly, but scarcely wiser. The final scene reveals the illusion in which the novel originated—that is, the time before either came to Paris—which Frédéric and Deslauriers agree was "the best that we have had"(510). But the novel begins after this time, and it begins, as it ends, in Paris, though once again in a non-place. At the very heart of flânerie, as Benjamin understands, lies an "anguished phantasmagoria," the anguish of the citizen reduced to one of many in a crowd. Such is also the artist's anxiety as he faces the "crowd" of competitors in the expanding literary market of the nineteenth century and the resulting degradation of both art and society.

The social space of failure analyzed by Durkheim and Marx is imagined, peopled, and narrated by Flaubert. The Paris of *L'Éducation sentimentale,* then, is a dystopia. Only by removing himself from the city, at his home near Rouen, could Flaubert write about the flâneur and the phantasmagorical city. "Let the Empire go its own way," he exhorted his mistress Louise Colet (she was also a writer) in November 1852 barely two weeks before Louis-Bonaparte officially became Napoléon III, "let's close our door and climb to the top of our ivory tower."[12] For Flaubert, the flâneur's disengagement from society defines at once the dilemma of the artist and the solution that is art.

In its overwhelming complexity, the modern city defies description. The metaphors by which it is conveyed engage through simplification. Whether of a woman to be known or of a woman who cannot be known, whether of a panorama to be dominated or of a scene lost in the reflections of the viewer—these tropes all work through simplification. But they do work, and the consequence is that observers of the city hold onto them for explanations. The problem of knowledge becomes an insuperable one, and yet every urban dweller must create a city that can be known and with which it is possible to cope. Hence the flâneur epitomizes a general predicament, and the discourse of disruption that surrounds the figure concerns every reader. For this reason, the links between Balzac, Flaubert, Durkheim, and Marx are neither fortuitous nor superfluous. Each observer constructs a narrative to control proliferating meaning, and each succeeds through personal creativity but also through the knowledge and authority of linkages perceived and accepted. The flâneur is one of those links, a vital mechanism in the course of understanding. No wonder understanding the understander is as much a matter of sociological analysis as of literary creativity.

It was not by chance that the flâneur appeared on the streets and in the narratives of early nineteenth-century Paris. The postrevolutionary city both invited and required new urban practices. The disarray engendered by continually shifting political and social bases, like the incertitude fostered by a constantly fluctuating population, undermined the sense of the city as a whole. The narratives of a ubiquitous flâneur joined otherwise separate parts.

The intrinsic surety of this relationship to the city, the authority confidently assumed by the flâneur-writer to define the city, is one manifestation of the myth of Paris as the paradigmatic modern city, Benjamin's capital of the nineteenth century. Like the namings of one and another part of the city itself and along with the directions to the altered social and cultural urban landscape offered by guidebooks, the urban narratives of the flâneur produced what I have called a "discourse of placement." These mappings of revolutionary Paris controlled, and thereby produced, the city. Yet, because the modern city in particular necessarily escapes any narrative, the discourse of placement turned into a discourse of displacement. The conspicuously unproductive flâneur at midcentury pointed to the plight of the individual now overwhelmed by those very processes of change that had once seemed so exhilarating. Revolution exemplified not opportunity but loss.

Flânerie lost its authorial connections. With flânerie disconnected from narration, the flâneur once again became the ordinary stroller, temporarily disengaged from urban woes, with no thoughts of turning flânerie to productive account. A democratized flânerie opened the city to anyone with a bit of leisure time at his (and now also her) disposal. Flânerie returned to its original sense of "insufferable idleness," inactivity unredeemed by creativity of any sort. The 1879 edition of the dictionary of the Académie française puts flânerie beyond the pale of bourgeois society, in the realm of "dawdling," "wasting one's time on trifles." The final blow to the flâneur-writer received what must have been a final confirmation in the term *flâneuse*. The feminine substantive appeared in 1877—to designate a type of chaise lounge! Sturdy legs were no longer needed to take one about the city! For that matter, scarcely more than daydreaming, flânerie lost its connection with the city. In the twentieth century, anyone can be a flâneur almost anywhere and anytime that nothing is happening. Passive, solipsistic, the ordinary flâneur turned into the ultimate consumer. Not surprisingly, this paradigmatic urban personage moved inside, away from the now disquieting city toward the comforting interior, the enclosed structure of social control.

By the last third of the nineteenth century the semipublic, semiprivate space of the arcades had been taken over by the department store. Women entered the public sphere as consumers, in the self-sufficient social microcosm of the department store that kept the city outside, at safe remove. "Window shopping" was not random flânerie but directed toward consumption. Feminine flânerie became another mode of shopping, thus realizing the fears expressed by the artist-flâneur early in the century.[13] This final twist, the metamorphosis of the flâneur into the flâneuse and the consequent banalization of flânerie, effectively ended the flâneur's special relationship with the city. There will be flâneurs in the twentieth century, many of a literary inclination. Apollinaire will call one of his works *Le Flâneur des deux rives*. But the connection has become incidental to the conception of the city and to urban discourse.

In bringing about the urban revolution that would produce modern Paris, the failure of 1848 cuts across the philosophical and sociological value of the flâneur as definitive subject and controlling perceiver. The new landscape of power and the new practices of Paris at midcentury required another kind of character, another kind of perception, and, above all, another kind of movement *within* movement. For a vision of that complex revolution in the making, no work offers a clearer vision of the new ties between the sociological work of modernization and the aesthetic vision of modernity than Émile Zola's novel *La Curée*. No work is further from the universe of flânerie. Zola's characters are frenetically and absolutely engaged in the city. His Paris is no place for the idle or detached observer, and something more murderous also has entered the urban dynamic. Whichever translation of *La Curée* one decides to use—*The Hunt, The Kill, The Quarry*—the world of Paris is now divided between the hunter and the hunted. Movement is much more than movement. Midcentury transmutes movement into direct conflict. The writer must devise a new strategy to deal with the city of revolution.

4

Haussmann's Paris and the Revolution of Representation

Le vieux Paris n'est plus (la forme d'une ville / Change plus
vite, hélas! que le coeur d'un mortel).
> Baudelaire, "Le Cygne"

Old Paris is no more (the form of a city, alas, changes faster
than the human heart).

On 24 November 1853, the city of Paris received a new seal. Most of
the elements from the traditional emblem remained in place—the
château-crown at the top, the fleurs-de-lys against a blue field to signal
the monarchy, and, naturally, the three-masted ship in full sail against
a red field. But the ship is no longer the proud man-of-war familiar
from previous insignia. The new model displays a simpler merchant
vessel reminiscent of the small boat that figured on the earliest seal
of 1215, and there is a notable addition: the motto. Although *Fluctuat
nec mergitur*—It Floats and Sinks Not—can be found in one form and
another as early as the late sixteenth century, it first appears on the
official city seal in 1853.

The individual who decreed the new city seal was Baron Georges-
Eugène Haussmann (1809–91), the prefect of the department of the
Seine, and his symbolic reconfiguration came just in time to mark
the first anniversary of Louis-Napoléon Bonaparte's proclamations of
the Second Empire and himself as emperor (it was also the second
anniversary of the coup d'état that began the dissolution of the Second Republic). Haussmann thus signaled an authority over the city
roughly equivalent to the Second Empire itself, from his appointment
by the emperor in June of 1853, when the empire was barely six
months old, to his dismissal in January 1870, only a few months before
the ignominious defeat by the Prussians in September and the proclamation of the Third Republic.

Even as Haussmann launched the program of metamorphosis that
would eventually bear his name, he chose to represent the city not

Plate 11.   Seal of Paris, 1853. Just in time to celebrate the first anniversary
of the proclamation of the Second Empire and signaling his takeover of the
urban renewal that would bear his name, Prefect Georges-Eugène Haussmann
proclaimed a new seal for the city of Paris. In a significant gesture of reconciliation he retained most of the elements from earlier emblems—the gold
château-crown at the top and the gold fleurs-de-lys against a blue field, to
signal the monarchy, as well as the silver three-masted ship in full sail on silver
waves against a red field. But Haussmann replaced the man-of-war familiar
from many of the insignia of the ancien régime and the Restoration with a
much simpler vessel, a merchant vessel that harks back to the boat that figured
on the earliest seal of 1215. There is a notable addition: the motto. Although
Fluctuat nec mergitur—"It Floats and Sinks Not"—is found in one form and
another on coins and maps and various seals as early as the late sixteenth
century, 1853 marks its first official appearance on the city seal. Are the waters
choppier than on earlier seals? Perhaps not, but Parisians who lived through
the period of drastic and often ruthless urban modernization during the Second Empire certainly must have thought so. (Photograph by the University
of Chicago Medical Center, A.V. Department.)

with a symbol or sign of modernity but rather with an emblem that drew upon the very oldest iconographical traditions.[1] Urban renewal at midcentury began, then, with a deliberate link to the old. With this gesture, Haussmann himself posed the problem of representation of authority that "haussmannization" would pose over and over again for his contemporaries. How to represent a city that was changing before one's very eyes? A city that was no longer recognizable? A city that defied definition as it was producing new definitions of urban life and society?

Haussmann wrote his answers to the problems of modernization in the streets. Parisians had to learn to read those answers in the city, and for many, it was a disconcerting process. The new text of the city brought traditional models of interpretation into question. Constructing modern representations of Paris required coming to terms with the new spaces and the new society signaled by those spaces. A whole new literature of articulation was a necessity. What I call a "discourse of haussmannization" attests to the pervasive sense of disruption in Paris and of the life lived there. For a writer like Flaubert, this discourse of displacement encountered the problem of representation by absence. But the fact of absence is unsettling, and ultimately, it is an impossible stance. The Paris Flaubert depicted in *L'Éducation sentimentale* was disappearing as he wrote in the 1860s; he opted to fix his new literature in the past.

The next generation could not so readily elide either the Second Empire or haussmannization. Zola, twenty years younger than Flaubert, confronts the problem of haussmannization directly, and he does so by making change the subject as well as the object of his novel. If Flaubert places *L'Éducation sentimentale* under the sign of the past —"the best that we have had" in Deslaurier's final comment to Frédéric—Zola dennes *La Curée* (1872) by and for the future. Frenetic activity governs Zola's Paris. Where Flaubert writes back from the Second Empire to the July Monarchy, Zola writes forward, to the Third Republic and to the Paris that Haussmann built. *La Curée* focuses neither on Paris past nor yet on Paris present or future but on Paris in the making, on a Paris becoming. More than any other literary text, perhaps more than any other text altogether, *La Curée* represents Paris in the throes of transformations as revolutionary as any the city would know.

I

C'est Haussmann qui a lancé Paris dans le tourbillon des
grandes dépenses. Les villes ont imité Paris, les particuliers
ont imité Paris.

                                    Zola, Notes for *La Curée*

Haussmann launched Paris into the whirlwind of great ex-
penses. Cities imitated Paris, individuals imitated Paris.

Haussmannization is used very loosely, to designate virtually every
topographical alteration or social change that marked Paris during
Haussmann's tenure as prefect of the Seine. The word itself has come
to signify in shorthand any radical topographical modernization of
any city. The verb appeared in 1892, and the substantive in 1926;
each gave linguistic presence to a phenomenon that was recognized
if not baptized by Haussmann's contemporaries. The uniform facades
and long, straight avenues of the new city led Verlaine to complain
about "the long boredom of your *haussmanneries*" (*Sagesse,* III, xix,
1880). Like any abstraction, haussmannization is an umbrella concept, with a variety and number of elements that can be crowded
under its reach. For many observers haussmannization came to stand
for everything that fit under the still more comprehensive category
of urbanization, itself to be found under the most capacious classification of all—modernization. Haussmannization certainly partakes
of these phenomena. But the enterprise of urban renewal on which
Haussmann and others embarked in the nineteenth century is by no
means equivalent to urbanization and still less to modernization. On
the contrary, its advocates invariably present urban planning as an
antidote to the chaos attendant upon urbanization. The model urban
planner attempts to impose order on the disorder that is the inevitable consequence of dramatic social change.

Haussmannization has the further advantage of designating agency
and therefore assigning responsibility for otherwise incomprehensi-
ble large-scale social phenomena. Individuals, discrete actions, and
particular circumstances render the vagaries, the complexities, and
the conundrums of social change more comprehensible. At the same
time, attribution to an individual of that which reaches well beyond
the scope of any individual risks the fallacy of misplaced concreteness.
Why, as well, should one speak of "haussmannization" instead of

"napoleonization"? Why should one focus on Haussmann, the administrator, rather than on the emperor, the individual most responsible for the transformation of Paris? Napoléon III dismissed Berger, Haussmann's predecessor as prefect of the Seine, because he seemed incapable of executing the grandiose plans that the emperor had for Paris. Haussmann recounts in his *Mémoires* that, on his first day in office, Napoléon III presented him with a map marked in red for the new streets to be constructed. To be sure Haussmann added much, and the water supply and sewer systems were understandably his special pride. (He lamented in his *Mémoires* that his sewer systems went unappreciated because unseen.)

The focus on any one individual, prefect or emperor, is probably misguided. Urban renewal did not commence with Haussmann or the Second Empire. It was the Second Republic that began work on the rue de Rivoli, and earlier prefects, such as Chabrol under the Restoration and Rambuteau during the early part of the July Monarchy, had sought to modernize the city.[2] Then too, the remodeling of Paris undertaken by Napoléon III and Haussmann fits within the tradition of urban planning that began in the Renaissance and was realized in a number of eighteenth-century cities (including Bordeaux, where Haussmann spent several years as prefect). But where Versailles, for example, was built entirely according to plan from almost the very beginning, the nineteenth-century city had to dislodge centuries of the old before it could install the new.

Every attempt to redo a city is fraught with both anxiety and adventure. Descartes' scorn for the patently irrational layout of the medieval city carried an assumption of potential mastery. Utopian notions of a rationally organized urban environment made that assumption explicit throughout the Enlightenment. There is more than a little justification in reading the reworking of nineteenth-century Paris as an amazing, and ultimately futile, attempt to impose Cartesian France on the unruly France of the romantics and the Revolution.[3] Such an ambitious enterprise had to fall short, for these visions of a reconfigured Paris demanded actual control over urban phenomena that seemed to elude human authority. But in every instance, the dream of definition also raised the specter of meaning lost in complexity, confusion, and change.

The program for the new, modernized Paris of the Second Empire differed from urban renewal plans elsewhere in the self-confidence and the practicality that lay behind the dream of definition. The age of Haussmann trusted its ability to adapt an old urban infrastructure to new demands upon space and authority. Then it did so. In imposing a new order on itself, Paris after 1850 stood out in the scope, in the centralized execution, and in the identification with a single figure that lay behind the enterprise of change. Compared to Haussmann, predecessors and successors in urban planning were timid— both in Paris and elsewhere. Of course, they also lacked the unconditional support to meet pressing new demands that Napoléon III gave his prefect.[4] Like the seal itself, Haussmann's plans tied the city to both past and future in a consciousness of overall grandiosity. The majestic spaces and broad avenues belong to a long tradition of urban planning. Haussmann's politics of nomination were calculatedly familiar in pushing his own agenda. The empire made sure to mark urban space, new and old, as its own. Just as the ancien régime named the new streets of the new Quartier Dauphine after members of the royal family, the empire baptized the splendid new boulevards with the names of the imperial family: 1854, only a year after Haussmann's appointment, saw the opening of the avenue de l'Impératrice (currently the avenue Foch), the avenue Joséphine for Napoléon III's grandmother (now the avenue Marceau), the avenue de la Reine-Hortense for his mother (avenue Hoche), and the avenue du Prince-Jérôme for his cousin (avenue MacMahon); 1857 celebrated the birth of the imperial prince the year before with the boulevard Prince-Eugène (boulevard Voltaire); and 1858 gave the boulevard along the right bank of the Seine to the emperor (now the avenues Henri-Martin, Georges-Mandel, du Président-Wilson). With the exception of the avenue du Prince-Eugène, all of these new streets lead either to the Arc de Triomphe or to the imperial playground, the Bois de Boulogne. In 1857, as Haussmann recounts it, instead of the title of duke that he did not want, the emperor accorded Haussmann the even greater consideration of his own boulevard (which crosses the site where he was born).

Contemporaries quite naturally experienced these changes as inescapable dislocation. If Descartes despaired over the jumble of the premodern city, small as it was, how much more disorderly, how much more distressing, was the European capital of 1850 that had doubled its population in only fifty years. Or the city of 1860 that had incorporated the immediate suburbs into the city proper, doubling its area, increasing its population by one-third, and moving from the twelve arrondissements or administrative subdivisions that it had maintained since the early eighteenth century to the twenty that Paris has still today. By 1870 great numbers of apartment buildings had been torn down and replaced, and broad new thoroughfares like the boulevard Saint-Germain in the Latin Quarter had cut through the labyrinth of criss-crossing, narrow, crooked streets of old Paris. The confident discourse of placement so prominent in the works of the July Monarchy soon gave way to a discourse of displacement. Balzac's intensely creative and authoritative flâneur turned into Flaubert's bewildered artist and failed revolutionary who wanders the city with no more than idle thoughts about making it his own. If Baudelaire's flâneur was a successful artist, he was ambivalent about the city that supplied the very conditions of his creativity. This ambivalence within dislocation was a constant theme. The sense of the city as the site of the pathology of modern life was not born in Paris or in the middle of the nineteenth century, but it was there and then that the city became indissolubly associated with a pathological state.

The sense of dislocation focused on the transformations engineered by Haussmann. Not that the dislocation began or ended with the empire. From the beginning of the Arc du Carrousel in 1806 to the completion of the Eiffel Tower in 1889, Paris added monuments. The destruction of medieval Paris began early in the century. Napoléon determined to complete the Louvre early on in the First Empire and initiated numerous building projects in central Paris. One of the sites that the original *Flâneur,* M. Bonhomme, took in on his daily rounds was the Arc de Triomphe. But if construction on the monument began in 1806, shortly after the resounding victory over the Prussians at Austerlitz, it was not inaugurated until 1836, two regimes and thirty years after the scaffolding first went up.

Given the time that these many projects took to complete, many Parisians were well aware that they were witnessing the end of one world and the birth of another. In a note that he added to the definitive edition of *Notre-Dame de Paris* in 1832, Victor Hugo protested vehemently against the "vandalism" that deprived the city of many of its most admirable medieval and renaissance buildings. A decade later, in 1844, Balzac evoked the end of the old central market. It would thereafter exist only in the work of those novelists "courageous enough to describe faithfully the last vestiges of the architecture of our forefathers."[5] Two years later in *La Cousine Bette,* and at a length that is exceptional even for him, Balzac painted a somber picture of the insalubrious and dangerous quarter surrounding the Louvre (where the glass pyramid of the Grand Louvre stands today). "Our nephews," he noted, "who will undoubtedly see the Louvre finished, will refuse to believe" that such a shameful, "barbarous" place actually existed in the heart of Paris, right under the windows of the royal palace (7:99).[6]

Balzac was right. His "nephews" did see the completion of the Louvre. The *quartier* that Balzac portrayed in such vivid detail disappeared without a trace, swallowed up by the magnificent rue de Rivoli in Haussmann's vast urban enterprise. At midcentury the pace and scope of urban transformation accelerated perceptibly. Demolition was not confined to one area; it occurred everywhere and over almost the entire city. Destruction and construction dominated experience of the city as never before.

So strong was the sense of a new city that Émile de Labédollière entitled his history-cum-guide book of 1860 *Le Nouveau Paris.* Yet another work on Paris? The author answered his own question by insisting on the absolute necessity of this one: "Paris is transfigured." Much has been done, but—and here the present tense is especially striking—"great highways are opening every day."[7] The detailed maps of every arrondissement that accompanied each section of *Le Nouveau Paris* used dotted lines to indicate projected new streets. Labédollière equated all of this construction with progress. The frontispiece of *Le Nouveau Paris* shows the towers of medieval Paris being carted away to the cheers of the workers standing by.

Others, predictably, were more reticent. The clearing of the area around the Arc du Carrousel preparatory to the completion of the Louvre moved Baudelaire to a poignant portrayal of exile. In one of his most celebrated poems, "Le Cygne" (1860), the poet mourned that "old Paris is no more (the form of a city, alas, changes faster than the human heart)." The swan that he later remembered had escaped from its cage in search of water. Flopping about miserably in the dust, the awkward bird presents the very image of exile, just as

Plate 12.   Frontispiece by Gustave Doré to Émile de Labédollière, *Le Nouveau Paris* (1860). Gustave Doré's engraving shows old Paris being carted away past a crowd of cheering workers. Meanwhile, the devil looks on from above at the latest transformations of the city. His gaze focuses on the map of the new Paris held in place by the bespectacled author. (Photography courtesy of the Houghton Library, Harvard University.)

the building blocks and the debris lying about are so many signs of rupture with the past. In this poem dedicated to Victor Hugo (who had recently refused to accept the amnesty that would permit him to return from exile) the newly completed Louvre reminds Baudelaire of the disconsolate bird and "anyone who has lost that which can never be recovered."[8] However divergent their interests and their goals, both Labédollière and Baudelaire, writing in the same year, translated the drama of haussmannization. That drama of urban transformation was all the more intense, and haussmannization all the more disruptive, because they were part of the larger, still more intense drama of the economic and social transformations of the Second Empire. A "whole new society," as Jules Vallès later put it in *Le Tableau de Paris,* "jumped onto the stage." Paris of the Second Empire was at once product and producer of haussmannization. Like many of his contemporaries, Vallès denounced this society and criticized the Second Empire for its authoritarian government, dissolute social elite, and corrupt politics. It was the coup d'état of 2 December 1851, from which the empire emerged a year later, that prompted Marx (in the opening paragraph of *The Eighteenth Brumaire of Louis Napoleon*) to make the celebrated observation that when history repeats itself, the first time is tragedy, the second is farce. For other critics as well, of almost every persuasion, although for different reasons, the Second Empire labored under the great disadvantage of not being the First. Victor Hugo never tired of pointing out that Napoléon the Little was not Napoléon, whatever the apparent lineage.

The discourse of haussmannization participated in a more comprehensive discourse of the Second Empire and in the transformations of French society encouraged by the government. (The Second Empire is generally identified as the "take-off" period for the modern French economy.) In a regime with minimal parliamentary politics and where the censors were ever vigilant, criticism was likely to be indirect. So much is true of any authoritarian regime. Haussmann, in the context, was an ideal target of indirection. Haussmann and haussmannization could be attacked, criticized, or simply discussed in terms distanced from but obviously related to the emperor and his regime. In a very short time, haussmannization became a recognizable metaphor for the Second Empire itself.

II

Mon Aristide, c'est le spéculateur né des bouleversements de
Paris.

Zola, 6 November 1871, Letter to Louis Ulbach

My Aristide is the speculator born of the upheaval in Paris.

No literary work takes on the discourse of haussmannization more
directly than Zola's *La Curée*. That *La Curée* (1872) does not figure
among the central texts of the nineteenth-century novel alongside
L'Assommoir (1877) and *Germinal* (1885) or among the best known
works in the Rougon-Macquart series—*Le Ventre de Paris* (1873), *Nana*
(1880), *Au Bonheur des dames* (1883), and *L'Oeuvre* (1886)—is only
partially imputable to the somewhat scattered nature of the novel. *La
Curée* is an ambiguous work—an ambiguity that derives ideologically
from Zola's ambivalence. As in his journalistic pieces at the time, Zola
condemns the Second Empire without reserve and without rest. The
title announces the judgment: *la curée* signified the mad scramble for
booty and political spoils.[9] Yet Zola simultaneously celebrates the new
Paris, the beautiful city that serves as backdrop for the corrupt society
he denounces. He celebrates as well, almost against his better judgment, the unscrupulous financier whose phantasmagoric speculations define the novel. Aristide Saccard reaps a fortune from his in-
sider's knowledge of the plans for the reconstruction of the city (he
has worked to effect in city hall). Notably, this consummate speculator
shows no more compunction in fleecing his wife than in swindling
the state. Domestic and public corruption merge in the speculator as
agent of modernity.

The phenomenon of *la curée* is not an individual enterprise. Saccard's fraud mirrors the thorough corruption of postrevolutionary
society. "My novel would have been impossible before '89."[10] By abol-
ishing the barriers erected by caste and tradition, in Zola's view, the
Revolution legitimated every ambition, sanctioned every appetite,
and is ultimately answerable for the decadent society that the novelist
depicts in *La Curée* and the other novels that take the Second Empire
as their setting. Notwithstanding his unrelenting denunciation of that
society, Zola cannot help admiring his protagonist's phenomenal energy and acuity. Renée Saccard, when she finally recognizes how
abominably she has been used by her husband, stands in awe of the

man who is the very incarnation of willpower. He is not so much immoral as amoral, almost a force of nature, grand by his very excesses. Aristide Saccard bespeaks the contradiction and the conscious tension between the collective project of *La Curée* and the individual who both realizes that project and escapes it. This ambivalence captures the ambiguity of haussmannization, caught as it is between the old and the new, at once destructive and constructive, the name of a single individual and the dehumanized statement of a process.

Zola's first mention of the novel appears in 1869, when he promises his publisher a work on the "shady and unbridled speculations of the Second Empire . . . determined by the demolitions and constructions of M. Haussmann" (353). It is the moment when Haussmann's manipulation of credit and debit financing of the great works of Paris comes under increasing criticism. Zola actually starts writing a year or so later, in the spring of 1870, after Haussmann's dismissal as prefect of the Seine and just before the disastrous rout at Sedan that ends the empire in September. "The Terrible Year"—Victor Hugo's epithet for the period that extends from the declaration of war in July 1870 to the suppression of the Commune in June 1871 —intervenes and turns a work conceived as a novel of contemporary society into a historical novel. As Zola indicates in the preface to *La Fortune des Rougon* (1871), work on the series began well before the defeat of the empire. But the logic of the work requires that defeat, "the terrible and necessary denouement of my work." *La Curée*, in consequence, becomes "the tableau of a dead reign, of a strange era of madness and shame."[11]

La Curée finally appears in serial form in November 1871. If one takes an admittedly rare but logical sense of the term *monument*—"that which serves as a document or archive"—*La Curée* becomes a literary monument to an old regime, an essential document in the archive on which future generations will draw for their history.[12] Zola's larger project of the social and natural history of a family under the Second Empire aims at constituting just such an archive of the parallel destinies in family and regime.

The terrible year of 1870–71 turns the urban renewal of Paris—haussmannization—into history, ties the renewal to a particular regime and a certain individual, both safely in the past. In the event, there is considerable continuity. Although Haussmann was dismissed before the end of the Second Empire, the projects that he initiated were long-term enterprises, and many were not completed until well into the Third Republic. Garnier's splendiferous Opéra, for one striking example, was opened to the public only in 1875. Still, the Paris that took shape over the Second Empire, which is in large measure the Paris of today, was the city envisioned by Napoléon III and realized by Haussmann. It too is a monument as well as a record.

But if they are monuments, *La Curée* and remodeled Paris are very equivocal ones. Beyond the question of what, precisely, the monuments are to recall, there is the incongruity of a moving and dynamic monument—something of a contradiction in terms. For where monuments are (usually) stationary, these urban texts definitely are not. *La Curée* assumes movement—the furious rush for self-advancement. Haussmannization too, as the suffix signals, is a process—of destruction or construction, as the case may be—and, consequently, movement. Moreover, Zola like Haussmann is very much concerned with change—social, political, economic, scientific—and specifically with the emergence of a modern society. Paradoxically, the novel as monument welcomes movement of every sort, destructive as well as constructive. The one cannot be construed without the other. The marked ambivalence of contemporary as well as latter-day assessments of haussmannization has a great deal to do with whether the point of reference is the past or the future, the destruction of old Paris or the construction of the modern city.

The paradox sharpens when the text makes clear that the structuring mobility of *La Curée* is a function of the immobile, the stationary—namely, *l'immobilier,* property or real estate. Indeed, the mobilization of the immobile (the destruction of buildings, the reapportionment of property) and also the reverse, the compensatory immobilization of the mobile (that is, the translation back into real estate of the speculative profits realized from the original destruction) are what haussmannization is all about. Zola's title suggests what the novel demonstrates, namely, that this mobility concerns individuals less than it does the pattern of social practices within which those individuals necessarily operate. In every domain the fixed yields to fluctuation. *L'immobilier* becomes *le mobilier.*

Here is the significance of the speculative fever that dominates the novel. Investment in real estate (*l'immobilier*), once the most conservative of investments, becomes extraordinarily volatile and immensely profitable for those able to manipulate the system (rather like investments in junk bonds in the 1980s). For the novelist this is the very stuff of drama. The government floats bonds to finance the public works, and deficit spending becomes the order of the day. In a much discussed pamphlet, "Les Comptes fantastiques d'Haussmann" ("The Fantastic Accounts of Haussmann," 1867–68, in *Le Temps*), Jules Ferry plays off Offenbach's recent operetta, *Les Contes d'Hoffmann* (*The Tales of Hoffmann*), to denounce the financial manipulations of haussmannization. With the substitution of "Saccard" for "Haussmann," the title could serve as a subtitle to *La Curée*.

Saccard is not Haussmann. The prefect is a shadow presence in the novel; he never appears directly (though his boulevard is mentioned). Historically, the prefect defended himself vigorously against charges of personal profiteering, and subsequent commentators concur in this assessment. But the practices that he set in motion fostered speculation on a grand scale. As Zola sees it, "other cities imitated Paris, and individuals imitated these cities."[13] Yet if Saccard is not Haussmann, he assuredly is the projection of haussmannization. The very name suggests depredation, with its resonance of *saccager* ("to sack") and *gens de sac et de corde* ("cutthroats"), quite as much as the money bags that Aristide himself has in mind when he takes the name. In contrast to Haussmann, whose static patronymic fixes him as "man of the house," the man who presides over the construction of the new Paris without partaking of it, Saccard's name conjures up movement. However ignoble the character, Saccard's dynamism places him on the side of modernity and, for Zola, on the side of genius. In the city and in the novel the massive manipulation of texts engenders the prevailing sense of unreality. Exploitation in turn reinforces the connections between the written texts of the city and the city-text itself. A *ville-texte* under construction, Haussmann's Paris engenders a *ville-fiction* in Zola's novel.

A metaphor, an image, and the ubiquitous symbol of mobility, money figures the tension between the stable and the speculative that governs the novel. Money reifies the mobility that it both signifies and makes possible. Money is, first of all, in the usage that dates from the nineteenth century, a *liquid* asset.[14] It literally flows through the novel: a "mounting wave of speculation whose foam was going to cover all Paris . . . the hot rain of coins falling straight on the roofs of the city" (109); "the rain of gold" (111); "the streaming of the cash register" (164); "this river of gold" (165). However, liquidity has its dangers. Ready money is not capital and too easily flows through one's fingers.

Zola's appraisal of Saccard's assets elaborates the contradiction inherent in the metaphor: "The river of gold finally had a spring. [Saccard has just sold property to the state at a monumental profit.] But it was not yet a solid fortune, dammed up, flowing in an even and continuous stream" (324). As his less wealthy but more prudent accomplice Larsonneau points out, Saccard is much better at producing money than he is at holding onto it (326).

In Zola's imagery, money is as solid as it is liquid. Zola invokes the traditional solidity of the gold coin: "the handful of guineas" ("les poignées de louis," 164) and "the real money that he threw by the shovelful on the shelves of his iron safe" ("les vrais écus," 325). The traditional forms of money like the *écu* and the *louis* (neither current in mid-nineteenth-century France, though *louis* was used to designate the twenty-franc coin) reach to the ancien régime and to a long line of literary misers that stretches from Molière's Harpagon in *L'Avare,* compulsively clutching his purse (*cassette*), to Balzac's Old Grandet of *Eugénie Grandet* in his obsession with the gold coins that he doles out to his daughter one by one. Zola makes it clear that this "real money" is for show, and more precisely, for the *tableau vivant* at the costume ball, where the riches of the earth are represented by piles of twenty-franc coins, "coins spread out, coins piled up, a multitude of coins. . . . a modern strongbox . . . in the middle of Greek mythology" (284). The more solid the money, the more allegorical, as the audience is well aware. This *tableau vivant* plays out Zola's allegory of haussmannization.[15]

Even more than the liquidity, the textuality of money makes wealth ephemeral in *La Curée*. Money, in this world of frenetic speculation, partakes at once of the materiality of an artifact that stands on its own and the immateriality of a text that must be read. Zola departs from the familiar metaphors of liquidity and materiality in his insistence on the absolutely conventional nature of money; that is, there is no necessary relation between the possession of gold or property—the solid, material assets by which a fortune is customarily gauged—and wealth. Convention and convenience determine which goods are designated as *immobilier* and which as *mobilier*. Property bought on credit is far more the latter than the former, and the banker decides. Against the standard invocations of the solidity of "real money," Zola sets the rampant textuality of modern banking paraphernalia and practices —bank notes, stock titles, promissory notes, paper sales under real and false names, evaluations of property, even marriage contracts. To be sure, Zola is not the first novelist to deal with speculation. Balzac in fact predicts the frenzied speculation in Parisian real estate in *César Birotteau* (1838), which he defines succinctly as an "abstract business, . . . whereby a man skims off revenues before they exist, . . . a new Kabbala!" (6:241–42). The difference is that, for Zola, a whole society practices what the Baron Nucingen alone ("the Napoléon of finance," 6:241) could manage forty or fifty years previously.

Its "authentic" organic origin in nature reinforces the value of gold. Because gold is irreducible to any other element (and no element is reducible to it), the value of gold is maintained by the limited nature of the substance. (The Eldorado into which Voltaire sends Candide dramatizes the destruction of that value by abundance.) Paper, however, is a composite substance, the components of which vary with the producer. Its value has no requisite connection to its composition. Paper has only the value assigned to it by use. Moreover, it can be produced at will. Saccard's genius lies in his ability to convince all of Paris that his speculations are "as good as gold." But this is precisely the fiction of all paper money. Going off the gold standard is so traumatic a move for so many in the twentieth century for the very good reason that it removes the correlation between resources in kind (gold) and national wealth.

Because Saccard's is a paper fortune ("In truth no one knew whether he had solid, clear capital assets," 163), he must turn himself into an alchemist. He must transform one substance into another, entirely different and unrelated substance. Saccard himself, more modern, likens the projected transformations to chemistry: "You'd say that the whole quartier is bubbling in some chemist's beaker" (113). Saccard must turn a manufactured product into a natural substance. Paper, itself a product of human ingenuity, is far less substantial than gold, a product of nature. Yet Zola contends in *La Curée* that this is the competition by which contemporary society is determined. Saccard's success tells us that, contrary to traditional economic as well as literary expectations, paper wins out.

Like the text of the novel, indeed of any work, the authority of these papers must be guaranteed. The issuing institution in mid-nineteenth-century France—the state—stands at the center of the corruption in *La Curée*. The preoccupation of Aristide's sister, Sidonie, with the recovery of the English debt pushes this contradiction to the extreme. The issuing institution—the Stuart monarchy—is as bankrupt as the France of Napoléon III after September 1870.

Sidonie and Aristide are two of a kind. Brother and sister alike work to convert paper into money. He succeeds where she fails, but the fixation is exactly the same. Sidonie's investment (she spends two months and ten thousand francs on research in British libraries) does not pay off, and the seventeenth-century certificates that she holds turn out to be worth no more than the paper on which they are printed. Aristide's speculations pay off because the government writes, that is, issues, the texts in question. It acts as both author and authority to legitimate the conversion of paper into money.

La Curée vividly demonstrates that the paper revolution is not the least of the revolutions of the mid- and late nineteenth century. The modern system of banking, based on credit and investment, is put in place at this time. The Société Générale du Crédit Industriel et Commercial in 1859 and the Crédit Lyonnais in 1863 are intended to provide capital for commercial development. The Crédit Foncier de France in 1852 provides the necessary momentum for the Parisian real estate market. The whole system is not unlike an elaborate fiction in which people must believe for it to work. (Haussmann becomes a political liability for the emperor when the failures of the Crédit Mobilier and the Compagnie Immobilière in 1867 bring to light the rampant corruption on which Zola draws for *La Curée*.) Aristide banks on the future, Sidonie on the past. There is no question who will win.

There is another paper revolution, one that directly concerns Zola and every writer. The discovery of a process for making paper out of cheap wood pulp cuts the cost of publication and opens the way for a vast increase in the production of books of every sort. In 1889 the *Bibliographie de la France* registers some fifteen thousand new book titles, almost double the seventy-six hundred titles registered in 1850. And books are only part of this paper revolution—journals and mass-circulation newspapers flood the market. The overproduction intensifies the competition among writers and engenders an anxiety of failure. Octave Mirbeau, a follower of Zola, sees literary production as "more threatening" every day:

> Books rise, overflow, spread; it's an inundation. From overcrowded bookstores breaks a torrent of yellow, blue, green, and red cascading from displays that make you dizzy. You have no idea of all the names torn from the depths of the unknown which this floodtide throws up for a moment on the crest of its waves, rolls about pell-mell, and then flings away onto a forgotten corner of the beach, where no one passes, not even beachcombers.[16]

Like every writer in this ongoing and increasingly aggressive paper revolution, Zola is a speculator. Like Saccard, Zola has a paper fortune, which he works to translate into capital assets. A few years after the publication of *La Curée*, the runaway success of *L'Assommoir* would make Zola close to a millionaire. In a classic move of the translation of *valeurs mobilières* into *valeurs immobilières*, with his royalties from *L'Assommoir*, Zola buys property. The house at Médan that becomes the meeting place of Zola and his disciples in the 1880s is the unequivocal sign of success in convincing readers of the authority of certain kinds of paper and the peculiar alchemy involved in writing.

Zola is and is not Saccard. Despite the condemnation of the regime, he clearly identifies with the "artist's love" that propels his creature into one deal after another and turns the simplest matter into a "gothic drama" (251). The Aristide Rougon who could not quite figure things out in *La Fortune des Rougon*, the first novel in the Rougon-Macquart series published just before *La Curée*, comes to Paris and transforms himself into Aristide Saccard, thanks to the opportunities offered by the new Paris in the making. The parallels with Zola are striking. Both Saccard and Zola come from Provence to lay siege to Paris. Like Saccard who learns about the city through a minor but key post in the municipal administration, Zola enters literary life in a subordinate position in the Hachette publishing firm. Zola too transforms himself by dint of hard work and genius from the unsuccessful student, hard-pressed journalist, and struggling author into the writer who laid claim to the legacy of Balzac.

Finally, quite as much as Saccard, Zola needed the Second Empire, and, like Saccard, he profited by its corruption, by its venality, by its immorality. "The Rougon-Macquart," he tells us in the preface to *La Fortune des Rougon*, "tell the story of the Second Empire through their individual dramas, from the ambush of the coup d'état to the betrayal of Sedan." Without the end that brought the fervently anticipated Third Republic but also without the beginning that established the despised empire, Zola would not have had the twenty volumes of the Rougon-Macquart cycle. Without the depredations of haussmannization and the corruption of Saccard, there would have been no *La Curée*. The creator's fascination with his character and beyond, with the urbanist, gives to this novel an ambiguity that belies the explicit moral and political condemnation.[17]

III

Paris est comme la statue de Nabucodonosor, en partie or et
en partie fange.
        Voltaire, to the comte de Caylus, January 1739

Paris is like the statue of Nebuchadnezzar, part gold and part
filth.

The physical remodeling of the city topography—the buildings
torn down and rebuilt, the grand boulevards cut across the maze of
streets—are only the most visible manifestations of a more profound
transformation of urban society. Haussmann's Paris is revolutionary
because it is modern, and it is modern because, with individuals continually crossing geographical and social boundaries and with the
boundaries themselves shifting, it requires movement on so many
levels. Modernizing society breaks down customs and practices of
every sort. If it does not eliminate social barriers altogether, it certainly obscures the familiar boundaries between one domain and another. The greater the movement across boundaries, the less fixed,
the less defined those boundaries seem. Continual movement, or mobility, necessarily brings a crisis of identification for the individuals
concerned and also for the collectivity. What is the city in an urban
society defined by movement and flux? Such are the questions posed
in and by the Paris constructed by Haussmann and the haussmannized Paris represented by Zola. Topographical transfigurations in Zola's descriptions intersect on every level with social transformations
in his plot. Furthermore, the vitality of this nexus owes everything to
the essence of haussmannization at work in the actual city, in the
continuous erasure and remarking of spatial and social boundaries.
Zola's novel and Paris meet over streets where none previously existed, over easier circulation across the wide boulevards that replace
the convoluted, narrow streets of the past, and over a general destruction of the past that enables the future to dominate the present.

Perhaps the most striking example of the obliteration of boundaries in the city itself comes more subtly with the annexation of the
immediate suburbs in 1860. The pen, in the redistricting, proved as
mighty as the bulldozer. An administrative decree more than doubled
the area of the city and increased its population by one-third.

That population was itself changing. The reconstruction of Paris
needed workers, and those workers came from the provinces. The

migration of unskilled and semiskilled labor into Paris augmented the lower-class population. These inhabitants were concentrated in certain *quartiers,* and notably in the faubourgs. When Zola chose la Goutte d'or in Belleville as the setting for *L'Asssommoir,* he had just these social differences in mind. When Gervaise Macquart and Lantier arrive from Provence in the early 1850s, they settle in Belleville, which was then outside the city proper. For Gervaise and the whole neighborhood (with the exception of one bourgeois), Paris looms in the distance, "over there" ("là-bas"), definitely foreign territory. Zola enacts the correlation of physical distance and social distance in the trip of Gervaise's wedding party into central Paris. Not only do the *faubouriens* get lost in the Louvre, they themselves become the spectacle for the bourgeois habitués of the museum. When the group climbs the column in the Place Vendôme, their bird's-eye view reveals nothing except their own neighborhood, which they locate only with considerable difficulty, outside the city. As Zola makes clear, the integration of Belleville into the city proper can only intensify the already dramatic contrasts within Paris.

La Curée stages the topographical and demographic mobility of Second Empire Paris. The mobility encouraged by the transformation of the city governs Saccard and provides the model for relations in every domain. The multiple mobilities of the novel blur boundaries of every sort—sexual, social, and spatial. Zola's moral geography, in sum, equates mobility with transgression.

The most fundamental of these transgressions is sexual. Sexual license defines the novel—the ubiquity of shady financial practices tolerated by the state is mirrored in the promiscuity of Second Empire elite society, where the reader can hardly keep track of all the liaisons in the making and unmaking. The reader is unsure how many lovers to attribute to Renée Saccard. The "whirlwind of expenditures" that Haussmann unleashes on Paris is personified, dramatized, and amplified by this rampant promiscuity. This novel, as Zola indicated in the preface with an image to which he would return more than once, showed "this life of excess" ("la vie à outrance"), which converted the whole regime into a bawdy house ("mauvais lieu").

But Paris goes beyond that bawdy house. The sexuality that pervades the novel signals a more fundamental perversion, a corruption of nature. Mobility in the realm of sexuality can only mean sexual ambiguity. The degeneration of the entire Rougon-Macquart family, and of the society that they incarnate, is rooted in the physiological degeneration of "a race that has lived too fast and which ends in the man-woman of corrupt societies." Sexual ambiguity pervades the entire novel. Maxime, Saccard's son from his first marriage, is a "strange hermaphrodite . . . in a society that was rotting" (152). If Maxime is the "man-woman" with "a temperament of a courtesan" (269), with the "indulgences of a neuter being" (211), Renée is his counterpart. For Zola their liaison is not just incestuous, but profoundly unnatural in the reversal of the most basic roles that nature creates. At the Café Riche, the scene of the seduction, Maxime finds Renée "original. At times he wasn't really sure of her sex; the great wrinkle that crossed her forehead, the pouting of her lips, her indecisive nearsightedness, made her a tall young man" (184). Appropriately, Renée seduces Maxime and continues to dominate him until the stronger force of his father prevails.

And theirs is not by any means the only such instance of sexual mobility. Zola marks the blatant lesbianism of "the Inseparables," Mme d'Espanet and Mme Haffner, Renée's two friends from the convent, and the homosexuality of Baptiste, Saccard's valet, as further symptoms of a society so confused that it no longer recognizes the most elementary classifications. And lest we forget the necessary connection between these sexual deviations and the financial mobility, Zola shows us "the Inseparables" at the costume ball: "Gold and Silver [their costumes] were dancing together, lovingly" (317). In Second Empire Paris, Zola tells us, deviation is the norm. It is also completely reified in the ubiquitous social construct of money as gold and silver intertwine in full public view.

So great is the force that mobility exerts on sexuality that Aristide Saccard himself puts all his energy into his speculations, taking mistresses primarily because spending money on women is part of his plan of conspicuous consumption. But Aristide prefers money (156) and intrigue. Similarly, Sidonie has invested all her sexual energy in myriad transactions, deals, trades: "The woman was dying in her; she was no longer anything but a broker" (95). Aristide recognizes her "appetite for money" as his own. But in her case "the common temperament" had produced "this strange hermaphrodism of a woman who had become neuter, all at once businessman and procuress" (96).

The incest of Renée and Maxime that directs the novel provides a striking illustration of the pervading sexual license while offering the most flagrant manifestation of the breakdown of the family. This disintegration in turn, in the customary synecdoche, signals as it produces the disintegration of society. Marriage becomes one more speculation, and family ties offer little more than a privileged access to potentially profitable connections. Both brothers plan to change their names, Aristide after some prodding by Eugène: "We will bother each other less" (87). (Eugène Rougon in fact keeps his name.) Elsewhere, the relations between father and son depend on the use each can make of the other. Ever the speculator, Saccard "couldn't for long be near a thing or a person without wanting to sell it, somehow to profit by it. His son wasn't yet twenty before he thought about how to use him" (160).

Zola invokes commercial practices to characterize the deviant family unit formed by Aristide, Renée, and Maxime. They are not a family at all but Saccard Ltd—a company of limited responsibility, Saccard et Cie S.R.L. (*Société à responsabilité limitée*): "The idea of a family was replaced for them by the notion of a sort of investment company where the profits are shared equally" (152). Renée finally realizes just how limited that responsibility is. She is herself one more element in Saccard's financial strategies: "Saccard had thrown her down like a bet, like an investment. . . . She was a stock in her husband's portfolio" (312). The ending of the novel, which sees the reconciliation of Saccard and Maxime over a financial transaction and the elimination of Renée, can be reconstrued in financial terms as the reassertion of patriarchy with the transformation of Saccard et Cie into Saccard Père et fils, following nineteenth-century commercial custom.

Symptomatic of the general decadence is the absence of a mother worthy of the name to anchor the family. Saccard's first wife Angèle dies at an opportune moment and in any case was never a significant figure. Not surprisingly in a novel that dramatizes the tension between the *immobilier* and the *mobilier*, she is likened to "a troublesome piece of furniture" (82). Angèle and Aristide's little daughter, Clotilde, is shipped off to her uncle in Plassans as soon as her mother dies. Saccard accepts Renée's unborn illegitimate child as his for a fee—her dowry and for the step up the social ladder he takes by marrying into the solidly established Parisian upper bourgeoisie. Further, his "honor" remains intact, since Renée, as predicted by Sidonie (100, 111), has a well-timed miscarriage. Renée's maternal solicitude for Maxime (230–31) is a denatured love. The only true nurturance comes from the Seine, the mother substitute for the orphaned Renée and her sister Christine: "The Seine, the giant . . . [Renée] remembered their tenderness for the river; their love of its colossal flow . . . opening around them . . . in two arms . . . whose great and pure caress they could still feel" (338). But the river offers no real refuge, contributing instead to the symbolism of movement and mobility that structures the novel as a whole. The image of the Seine that dominates the novel comes earlier: "And it seemed, at night . . . that the Seine was carrying, in the middle of the sleeping city, the filth of the city" (162).

As no mother nurtures in *La Curée,* no father governs. Aristide seems totally unaware of the customary bond between father and son. The authority that he exercises derives from the power of his purse. Maxime is an associate; he and Maxime are comrades, united by "a familiarity, an abandon" (156) that leads them to frequent the same *demi-mondain* milieu, to share the same pleasures and the same women—and this well before Renée takes up with her stepson. Vice is "the persistent perfume of this singular home" (158). Renée, abandoned by Maxime, cannot stand to see father and son together. She takes revenge by forcing Saccard to acknowledge the incest: "Now she would no longer see them making fun of her, arm in arm, like comrades" (327). But the final image of them in the novel brings father and son together again, in the Bois de Boulogne as the emperor passes, smiling at Aristide's "Vive l'empereur!" The relationship is more depraved still since the "man-woman" Maxime is "a kept man" ("entretenu," 312), and he is kept by his father. Zola had not read Marx, but Maxime's status recalls the end of *The Eighteenth Brumaire,* where Marx cites Delphine de Girardin's quip that France, for the first time, has a government of "kept men" ("hommes entretenus").

The blurring of boundaries, the confusion of identities, and the transgressions of norms that preside over the moral economy of the novel are at once sign and symptom of a complex interplay between moral and physical space. From the omnipresent mirrors to the *tableaux vivants* at the end, the theatricality of the novel dramatizes the confusion between public and private. The obscuring, to the point of obliteration, of the boundaries between inside and outside has significant moral implications. The Bois de Boulogne is a boudoir, the Saccard apartment an extension of the rue de Rivoli. "The street came up into the apartment, with its rumbling carriages, its jostling strangers, its permissive language" (153). Given the promiscuity that attends its transformation, Haussmann's Paris is an active agent in Renée's degradation, madness, and death; and this same "complicitous city" (338) is also the necessary setting for the corruption of the Second Empire. The merging of outside and inside is symptomatic of the larger ideological confusion between public and private. The society of *La Curée,* Saccard in the lead, can make no distinction between the two. Typically, Saccard manages to get himself named to the commission d'enquête charged with evaluating property to be expropriated by the state for the city, in which capacity he is able to give his own property (owned under a fictitious name) an astronomical assessment.

La Curée scarcely mentions old Paris. The Second Empire redefines the royal palace by completing the Louvre. The Communards who burn the Tuileries in 1871 attack not the bastion of the monarchy and vestige of the ancien régime but the new Louvre, the work of the Second Empire. But the true monument to this regime and to this city, the true repository of their archives, is the extravagantly sumptuous home that Saccard builds off the Parc Monceau, constructed on property "stolen from the city" (163). This *hôtel* is notable for more than the highly eclectic architecture and the incredibly lavish furnishings that have all Paris agog. The same identification with the regime that leads Saccard to acclaim the emperor in the Bois de Boulogne leads him to turn his own home into a "small version of the new Louvre" (53). The extravagance and the excess deployed in this construction preside over the regime itself.

The nouveau Louvre and Saccard's *hôtel* raise equivalent monuments to the Second Empire. Both represent the public as private— Saccard's theft of his property from the city, the financial dealings that take place at the dinners he gives—but also the private as so very public. All of Paris—*le tout Paris* in any case—knows virtually everything about the Saccard *hôtel,* from the salons and the traditionally public rooms to Renée's bedroom, her dressing room, and even her bathtub. "People spoke about 'the beautiful Madame Saccard's dressing room' just the way they speak about 'The Hall of Mirrors, at Ver-

sailes'" (209). Zola faces the problem of any historical novelist—
how to deal with the necessary famous personages—by turning the
Saccard *hôtel* into the Louvre in miniature. He does not need to show
us the court around Napoléon III (he will do so a few years later in
Son Excellence Eugène Rougon); the goings-on in and around the Saccard *hôtel* convey by metonymy the depravation of the regime as a
whole. Like the ruins of the *petites maisons* that serviced Louis XV's
sexual appetites, the Saccard *hôtel* will one day stand as a reminder of
a society that is no longer. Of the one and the other, distant observers
will say, following the respectable businessman looking at what is left
of the *petites maisons*, "What odd times those were" (325).

The new city under construction makes the public so very private.
Like all the other couples in the novel, Renée and Maxime live their
liaison in public. The seduction occurs half in public, in a private
room ("cabinet particulier") in the Café Riche. More generally the
lovers had the "love of the new Paris" (228), which they turned into
their personal—but scarcely private—space. Their "carriage seemed
to be rolling over a rug. . . . Every boulevard became a corridor of
their hôtel" (229); "the Bois de Boulogne was their garden" (332).
The Parc Monceau next to the Hôtel Saccard is "the necessary flower
bed of this new Paris" (229), Renée's special domain to which she
has her own key. The greenhouse (*la serre*) in the *hôtel* itself offers the
ideal site for Renée and Maxime's adulterous affair, a cross between
a bordello and a hothouse. The strangely beautiful but also fright-
eningly exotic flowers exist only to mimic and stimulate desire (76–
80, 218–20). Renée herself becomes the most exotic flower in the
greenhouse (80) and in the city that the greenhouse recalls. If the
greenhouse evokes a bordello, the city—the bawdy house—reaches
back to the hothouse. Renée is the "strange, voluptuous flower" that
could grow only in this city under this regime (205–6).

Tradition survives in one place only, in the Hôtel Béraud on the
Ile Saint-Louis. But this part of the city is of another time, placed
under the sign of Henri IV, not Napoléon III. The ile, like the Hôtel
Béraud, is a product of Henri IV's first Parisian urban renewal at the
beginning of the seventeenth century. As Saccard's *hôtel* reproduces
the new Louvre, the courtyard of the Hôtel Béraud presents a smaller
version of the Place Royale, the center of court life under Henri IV
(125). No wonder that Renée and Saccard find it "a dead house"

(126) in "a dead city" (124), "a thousand leagues away" from their promiscuous new Paris of light and noise and warmth.

No wonder either that Renée's father complains that "the city is no longer made for him" (234). His rare ventures off the ile take him to the Jardin des Plantes (another creation of the ancien régime), which, topographically and socially as well as horticulturally, lies at virtually the opposite end of Paris from the stifling greenhouse of the Hôtel Saccard, the Parc Monceau, and the new boulevards that demarcate the Paris of his daughter and son-in-law. M. Béraud Du Châtel's refusal to visit the Parc Monceau strikes the one note of political opposition in the entire novel. And it is, as it must be, altogether ineffectual. Renée's father offers silent opposition that holds out no alternative. After the death of his sister, he walls himself off—"cloistered" is Zola's term (336)—from any human contact. For if the new Paris is associated with vice, Zola's images, his similes and metaphors, again and again also associate this city with light, with the sun, with flames, heat, and color, with the din of incessant activity, in a word, with life.

Fueled by the heat of these images, Zola's modern Paris must expand, and life must win. The Hôtel Béraud and the Ile Saint-Louis may provide the geographical and moral center of the city; they could not be further from the social and political center. The Hôtel Béraud conveys a vision of the past, and Monsieur Béraud Du Châtel is a man marked for another age, by his rectitude, by his austerity, and above all by the privacy that he guards so zealously.

IV

L'habit ne fait pas le moine.
French proverb

For the apparel oft proclaims the man.
Hamlet (I, iii, 72)

The success of the new Paris, the exploits of Saccard and the society that he keeps in constant turmoil, are condensed during Renée's last promenade in the Bois de Boulogne in Saccard's cry of "Vive l'empereur!" as Napoléon III passes in "a triumphal parade" (336). That triumph has its costs in the maladies that are on public view. The sickness of the emperor, seen twice, each time weaker, is the obvious exteriorization of the illness that will bring down the regime. The emperor who ages noticeably over the two years of *La Curée* will turn into the totally bewildered old man facing certain defeat at the hands of the Prussians whom Zola portrays in *La Débâcle* (1892). But Renée's own disease, her vice, and her crime center the novel. If the emperor manifests the sickness that saps the Second Empire, Renée brings that disease to the city itself. Her beautiful shoulders are twice characterized as the pillars on which the empire rests: "Admit outright," Maxime tells her, "that you are one of the pillars of the Second Empire" (45, *cf.* 205). Her malady and her fever will be its malady and its fever. But the same scene immediately ties Renée to the city. Those bared shoulders and décolletage so impress the public officials in attendance at the ball that Eugène Rougon knows he will have little trouble the next day voting another loan for the city.

With Renée, Zola elaborates two familiar images of Paris: the city as woman (and particularly as courtesan) and the city as the head, *le cerveau, l'intelligence, la tête du monde*. From the beginning to the end of the novel Renée is characterized as an intelligence gone awry. Her nervous disposition will easily turn into madness. And so it does. "La folie" becomes an ever more frequent notation as the novel progresses. This insanity implicates the city as a whole: "Maxime himself was beginning to be frightened by this head where madness was spreading, and where he thought he could hear at night, on the pillow, all the uproar of the city lusting after pleasure" (241).[18] When, predictably, Renée dies, her illness is acute meningitis—that is, brain fever, which once again stands for the madness of the city itself: "In the feverish sleep of Paris, one could sense the breakdown of the brain, the golden and voluptuous nightmare of a city crazed by gold and flesh" (163). Paris realizes the predictions of Saccard, "pure madness, the infernal gallop of millions, Paris intoxicated and knocked out flat" (114).

This is the Paris of the hunt, and more precisely of *la curée*, that is, the most dramatic moment in the very public spectacle of the hunt. Although the figurative sense of his title dominates (the race for political spoils), its literal meaning invariably brings the original sense of the hunt into play. Zola takes care to specify that the wedding of Aristide and Renée occurs at a time when "the passionate rush for spoils [*la curée*] filled a corner of the forest with the yelping of the hounds, the cracking of the whips, the flaming of the torches" (162).

Plate 13. *La Curée* by Gustave Courbet (1856). The hunt was a favorite subject for Courbet. Here the painter focuses on the final moment, when the entrails of the quarry are to be thrown to the hounds. The hunter leaning against the tree is curiously detached from the death he has caused, quite as Aristide Saccard in Zola's novel *La Curée* dissociates himself from his wife's descent into madness and eventual death even though he too has loosed the hounds on the victim. The painting would have been familiar to many readers through the lithographic reproduction that appeared in the literary review *L'Artiste.* (Photograph courtesy of the Henry Lillie Pierce Fund, the Museum of Fine Arts, Boston.)

The hunt provides both a general image for the novel and one specific to Renée. The associations with animality throughout the novel—her hair, the fur and velvet skating outfit, the bearskins on which she and Maxime make love, the fur wrap with which she covers herself at the ball, and especially the dress embroidered with all the motifs of a deer hunt—turn her into the quarry (*la curée*) in the original sense of the term, the part of the animal fed to the hounds that have run it to the ground.[19] The image would have been familiar to contemporaries from Courbet's painting of *La Curée*, exhibited in the Salon of 1857 and reproduced in a lithograph in *L'Artiste* the following year.[20] When Renée finally "sees" herself naked, she understands that she is trapped and that Saccard has directed the hunt from the beginning, putting out his traps "with the refinements of a hunter who prides himself on capturing his prey with style" (251). One might further connect Courbet's strangely passive and detached pipe-smoking hunter-artist and the piping huntsman to Saccard and Maxime strolling in the Bois de Boulogne at the end of the novel, puffing on their cigars, altogether as indifferent to Renée's plight as Courbet's huntsmen are to the dead roebuck hanging in the opposite corner of the painting.

Saccard has despoiled Renée of her entire fortune and thrown her to the hounds just as he has attacked Paris. In a key scene early in the novel, Saccard surveys the city from the heights of Montmartre, and "with his outstretched hand, open and sharp like a cutlass," he sketches in the air the projected transformations of the city (113). Saccard later recalls his prediction with great satisfaction: "There lay his fortune, in those famous slashes that his hand had made in the heart of Paris . . . a slash here, then on this side, another slash, a third slash in this direction, another in that . . . slashes everywhere" (113–14)—all in all a very apt description of Saccard's calculated attack on Renée. His was not the original rape of Renée, and his was not the idea for the transformation of Paris. It was the emperor who traced the original plan on the city map. When Saccard surreptitiously consults the famous map marked up by the emperor for the prefect, he sees that "these bloody lines of a pen slashed Paris even more deeply" than had his own hand (116). But Saccard, not Haussmann, is everywhere at once. Saccard rushes in the same day from the construction site of the Arc de Triomphe to that of the boulevard Saint-Michel, from the excavations on the boulevard Malesherbes to the embankment work at Chaillot. "The central city was being slashed all over, and [Saccard] had a hand in all the slashes, in all the wounds" (142). The Crédit Viticole founded by Saccard—his "purest glory" (143)—"held the City of Paris by the throat" (276).

The clear connection between Renée and Paris, the responsibility that Saccard bears for Renée's debasement, his parallel responsibility for the "disemboweling" of Paris, would seem to constitute an unequivocal condemnation of Saccard and by extension of Haussmann and his great works. But the novel is nowhere nearly that simple. If Renée dies, Paris lives on in the Third Republic from which Zola writes, having recovered from its "fever," its "wounds" having healed. What then of the denunciation of *la curée* and of the transformations of the city that let loose the hounds? The contradiction is only apparent. Renée is not a Balzacian metaphor of the city as woman, but an exemplum of a very particular society. The associations Zola establishes with Paris are with a Paris that disappears, the Paris of the Second Empire, which dies along with, if somewhat later than, Renée. The moment of *la curée*, we must remember, signals the end of the hunt.

Renée is, for that matter, rather too obviously the incarnation of that society. Her sickness—"her sick heart" (47), her "morbid air" (49), her "madness" (56)—does not end the novel but begins it, and the explicit association that Renée herself makes with *Phèdre* brings to mind Racine's opening description of his heroine, "a dying woman seeking death" ("une femme mourante, et qui cherche à mourir"). Renée's other associations are with the artificial. At one point she is likened to "an adorable and astonishing machine that is breaking down" (247). At several other instances her image is of a statue, as she poses at Worms' studio (139), in the *tableaux vivants* at the costume ball, and elsewhere (206, 270, 308). Similarly the connection with dolls. In the mirror she sees a "strange woman in pink silk . . . [who] seemed made for the love affairs of marionettes and dolls. She had come to this, a big doll whose torn chest only lets out a stream of sawdust" (311); and when she finds one of her old dolls in the attic of the Hôtel Béraud, the body limp from all the lost sawdust, the painted head still smiling, she bursts into sobs.

Paradoxically, Renée is most fully herself as the nymph Echo in the *tableaux vivants* staged during an evening at the Hôtel Saccard. For she is the Echo of the Second Empire. Her unsatisfied desires are those of all the other characters; in her malady resonates the madness of the Second Empire. As Echo she acts out her desire for Maxime-Narcissus. Rejected by Narcissus as she will be by Maxime, Renée stages her own death. Powdered from head to toe, as one of the spectators rather maliciously observes, she looks dead. The insatiable desires of the Second Empire will lead to its downfall as Renée's ever greater desires will lead to her death. Understandably, the audience does not much like the final *tableau*, which depicts the deaths of Echo and Narcissus. Although the audience cannot appreciate the complexities of the allegory, the identification with the wealth in the earlier *tableau* has been too strong for them not to reject the depressing denouement.

This "textuality" sets Renée apart and makes her a product of this society rather than of a Paris for all time. Renée's texts are, indisputably, her dresses, her "rags" ("chiffons"), as Saccard calls them (117). The continually changing outfits that astound all Paris situate Renée within the same economy of mobility and ephemera that governs Saccard. Moreover, the debts that she accumulates for the clothes that allow the perpetual transformations of self, the vast sums that she owes the great designer Worms, offer an exact parallel of the debts incurred by the city for its continual transformations. In both cases the solid bourgeoisie pays: Renée's father, not her husband, pays Worms' bill of 257,000 francs just as the run of ordinary citizens ultimately will finance the loans floated by the city.

Beyond the overwhelming extravagance that they proclaim, the individual outfits are virtually the only manifestation of Renée as an individual, which is also her definition by society. Clothes, in this instance, express and make the woman. Just as Saccard would not exist without his masses of papers, so too Renée has no social existence apart from her closets full of "rags." Hence the burden borne in the novel by the particular ensembles. What distinguishes Zola's descriptions from the fashion reporting on which he drew for these descriptions is, paradoxically perhaps, their significance. These clothes signify Renée, and beyond Renée they signify the Second Empire. The two most striking examples are the costumes that Renée wears for the *tableaux vivants*—an allegory within the larger allegory of the performance: "The nymph Echo's dress was a complete allegory all by itself" (280) and the ball dress, "that famous satin dress the color of bushes on which a complete deer hunt was embroidered, with all its features, powder horns, hunting horns, broad blade knives'' (226). Her very dress identifies Renée as the quarry, *la curée.*

The factitiousness of Renée's wardrobe that marks her as uniquely a product of society contrasts with the garb of the Seine. The river not the woman wears the most beautiful dress in the novel, a dress that owes nothing to Worms (but everything to Zola): ''The Seine had put on its beautiful dress of green silk flecked with white flames; and the currents where the water eddied added satin ruffs to the dress, while in the distance, beyond the belt made by the bridges, streaks of lights spread out panels of material the color of the sun'' (338). The ''changing dresses'' of the Seine ''went from blue to green, with a thousand hues of infinite delicacy'' and from afar resembled ''the enchanted gauze of a fairy's tunic'' (128). The view from the turret of the Hôtel Béraud reveals a Paris outside fashion and outside history, a mythic Paris whose ''soul'' is the Seine, ''the living river'' that flows ''in tranquil majesty'' (128). As a young girl Renée easily tires of this immense horizon; as a woman, sick unto death, she comes too late to prize this ''old friend'' (338), this Paris far from the frenetic new Paris of the boulevards and the Bois de Boulogne. Unlike Renée, caught in the maelstrom of a particular historical period whose movement she is unable to discern (her myopia is telling in this regard), this eternal Paris, nourished by the Seine, will recover from the ''fevers'' of the Second Empire.

V

Saccard montrait, dans toute cette affaire, un amour d'artiste.
Zola, *La Curée*

In all this business Saccard showed an artist's love.

But the Paris that survives will be the legacy of the Second Empire, Haussmann's Paris, Saccard's Paris—and Zola's Paris. *La Curée* offers Zola's solution to the representation of the modernizing city. The portrayal of haussmannization partakes of a larger effort to convey the essence of contemporary society in the making. In the Paris of *La Curée,* Zola proclaims his aesthetics—the aesthetics of modernization. Saccard, in effect, stands as the greatest artist of the novel because he most fully realizes the force and the vision of modern life. That this vision comprehends material destruction and social disorder and the accompanying sickness, madness, and immorality gives Zola's measure of modernity. The Saccard who plunges Paris into disarray constructs that modernity, or more accurately for Zola, writes it. For "in all this business Saccard showed an artist's love" (251), he creates movement and, like Zola in this novel, creates life out of destruction.

Other artists in *La Curée* amplify the definition of revolutionary art, of a modern art, by which Zola creates the Paris of the Second Empire. The most obvious representative of art in the novel is the great couturier Worms. Almost a caricature of the romantic artist, Worms keeps all the women in thrall, makes his customers wait for hours, and produces an outfit only when truly inspired. Contemplating his client, "he reflected further, seemed to descend to the very depths of his genius, and, with the triumphant grimace of a Pythian oracle . . . , finished [his pronouncement]" (139). Yet the ideas come from Renée—the "prodigiously original and graceful dress" that she wears to the Tuileries is *her* "real discovery" that comes to her one sleepless night (166), just as her "daring imagination" leads her to "risk" the "famous" hunting scene gown.

In this partnership, Worms is the artist who offers Renée, and the society of which she is part, a privileged means of expression and Zola a privileged mode of characterization. Her dresses put Renée on display: her excess (the Tahitian tunic that leaves her virtually nude), her plight (the dress embroidered with the deer hunt), her fragility (the black and white dress she wears for her first visit to the Tuileries turns her into "a flower for the picking, a mysterious white and black carnation," 168), her growing disequilibrium (her "crazy outfits," 217), and her increasing ignominy ("the nymph Echo's dress . . . spoke of the game that she had accepted, for the singularity of offering herself to Maxime in public," 313).

Clothes both make and express the woman and, beyond the woman, the society. Worms is the representative artist of the Second Empire because his medium so perfectly captures its frivolity, its excess, its extravagance—and also its mobility and impermanence. Like Saccard's account books that appear and disappear throughout the novel, Worms' outfits make up the archives of the Second Empire. Renée's deer hunt gown plays on the double sense of *la curée*, since it figures her own situation as quarry and also the larger hunt that designates the regime as a whole. Then too, Worms, like Saccard though without specific intention, is responsible for Renée's downfall—his bills and they alone push her into ever greater debt. Artist to the hunt, Worms takes his place in the pack of hounds that Saccard unleashes against Renée.

There is one more artist in *La Curée,* a slightly ridiculous figure all too easily dismissed by his contemporaries in the novel and most likely by readers as well. Yet, still more directly than Worms' creations Hupel de la Noue's *tableaux vivants* figure this society and the woman who is at once its quarry and its model. A prefect in the provinces who manages to spend eight months of the year in Paris, where he likes to tell scabrous stories and seduce women as much as anyone else, M. Hupel de la Noue is very much a man of this world. And the man of this world achieves his art. The election that this prefect orchestrates in the provinces is "a veritable heroic-comic poem" (246). But his finest moment is the staging of the *tableaux vivants,* "The Love of Handsome Narcissus and the Nymph Echo," at the costume ball given by the Saccards. He writes his poem not with words but "with ingenious combinations of fabrics and poses chosen from among the most beautiful" (273). All the women have appropriate roles, from the "Inseparables" as "a reminder of Lesbos" (279) in one corner of the first *tableau,* to Renée as Echo and Maxime as Narcissus in all three *tableaux.* Hupel de la Noue intends Echo's pose to show "the sorrow of unsatisfied desire" (280), and the nymph dies of those unsatisfied desires.

The second *tableau* presents the other side of the Second Empire, Saccard's side: "After the temptation of flesh, the temptation of gold." The ploy is classic, as one of the men remarks, adding the ultimate compliment, "You know your times, Monsieur le Préfet" (283). The "Inseparables" costumed as Gold and Silver and clothed in real gold and silver, the other women covered with the precious stones that they at once embody and represent, and especially the great pile of twenty-franc pieces spilling all over the stage—these elements overwhelm the drama of Echo and Narcissus in the foreground much as *la curée* obscures the drama of Renée and Maxime.

The conversations in the audience between scenes, which are all about the financing of the new Paris, replay the work taking place on the stage. The two industrialists need no tutoring in the classics to read the allegorical *tableau* with absolute accuracy: to them, the money on stage suggests all the money necessary to tear down the city and build it up again. The parallel does not escape Saccard's brother the minister Eugène Rougon: "We would do great things if M. Hupel de la Noue minted currency for us" (286). The complicated allusions in the *tableaux* to Ovid's *Metamorphoses* and to classical mythology, which Hupel de la Noue tries to explain at length, are beyond the audience, their competence and their interest. If these sensible and essentially practical men and women (290) instinctively reject the final *tableau* that portrays the death of Echo and Narcissus, they respond enthusiastically to the first two *tableaux,* effortlessly recognizing their world in the reality of the scene as well as in the temptation that scene represents.

The final transformation of this society will not come for some time. But it will come. For Zola, finishing *La Curée* under the Republic, it had come. Hupel de la Noue, like Zola, takes the measure of his time. But the prefect-poet is, as Zola is not, the prisoner of this society. He can only proceed by allegory, whereas Zola, as he tells us, adopts "the realist's lens," "a simple window pane that claims to be so perfectly transparent that the images go through it and are then produced in all their reality."[21] Zola refuses the distancing classical allegory. He takes reality not at one remove but directly. Zola, the text tells us again and again, is the greatest artist of the Second Empire. The classics in *La Curée* serve as the sublime backdrop from the past against which the present is measured and found wanting: Racine's *Phèdre* consciously replayed by Renée and Maxime, Ovid's *Metamorphoses* translated by Hupel de la Noue for modern times in the *tableaux vivants,* the Pythian oracle turning up as Worms, Renée as a "gigantic Messalina" (220), the vulgar *demi-mondaine* Blanche Müller as the heroine in Offenbach's operetta *La Belle Hélène,* itself a semiparodic appropriation of classical models for modern times. If Marx saw in the Second Empire history replayed as farce, Zola saw literature replayed as parody. Yet that parody serves Zola well, for it supplies the foundation on which he builds his history and his novel.

Saccard is the greatest artist in *La Curée* because he is on Zola's side, on the side of energy, of creation, of mobility, in a word, of modernity. Zola's modern art moves, and he, the omnipresent artist, moves with it. The protean writer encompasses every artistic role— architect, couturier, stage designer, interior decorator—and master of the new city. Zola well recognizes the costs of that modernity— Renée's fate is exemplary—but he squarely faces the challenge and accepts those costs. Renée herself has to acknowledge her husband's superiority as an agent of a new world. He is less an individual than a will to power; he is totally oblivious of personal danger, at work in a forge, indeed practically a forge unto himself (he is the "color of iron," his laugh is like "a pair of tongs") (311). How could Zola not be drawn to the winner of this arduous steeplechase, "chewing on his 20-franc pieces as he runs" (312)? For Saccard has brought forth a new city and a tomorrow that will long outlive the individual.

So too Zola. "We are the men of tomorrow, our day is coming," Zola wrote his friend and disciple Paul Alexis in February 1871. Haussmannization and the Second Empire itself have taken necessary steps in the march of progress. With this perspective of the past as the future in the making, Zola joins the Victor Hugo of *Paris-Guide* discussed in chapter 2. Written just three years before *La Curée,* this introduction to the collective work on Paris collapses the whole of the nineteenth century into the movement of revolution. Zola wrote a very different nineteenth century, but he too wrote the revolution, the revolution of modern urban society. For this reason Haussmann presides over *La Curée,* his hand everywhere. The evident depravity of the emperor, the corruption of the regime, and the dissoluteness of its subjects condemn this society. But Zola faces the future. The preface to the Rougon-Macquart, written in 1871, relegates the Second Empire to "a dead reign, a strange era of shame and madness." Yet from that dead reign Zola will bring a living literature; from that era of shame and madness, he will create a scientific analysis, the literature of tomorrow, the literature of the republic. If haussmannization was a moment to be denounced, the city that emerged from that moment yet raised a monument to the eternal city of light, the capital of the world. Another revolution that made the world we live in.

Revolution has become permanently inscribed on the modern landscape. But it never entirely escapes the ambiguity of the relationship with tradition, with the past. This tension, between past and present, between fixity and movement, quite as much as any particular phenomenon, conveys the sense of modernity, the sense of great social movement—modernization—for which, to all intents and purposes, one can posit no end. To see oneself as "modern" means to

see oneself as "revolutionary," to recognize the continuing significance of disruption in everyday life. Modernity forces the connection
between the ever-changing material conditions of postrevolutionary
society and the consciousness of change. The particular bent of modernity, the explanations of change, will naturally vary. Where Zola
fixed on haussmannization as the paradigmatic manifestation of this
postrevolutionary society, Marx indicted capitalism. Yet the two contemporaries were not as far apart as their divergent political agendas
might lead one to assume. Their imaginations occupied similar terrain. The purpose of interpretation differs greatly, but surely Zola
would have recognized his own imaginative context, including the
vision of *La Curée,* in Marx's contention that, with the advent of modern industry, "all bounds of morals and nature, of age and sex, of
day and night, were broken down. Capital celebrated its orgies."[22]

Zola worked with and from this understanding of revolution as
change, to the straining toward the new and the destruction of every
boundary. At the same time, his novel, like every interpretation, aims
at fixing experience, at arresting movement, at making connections
to the known, to the familiar, to the past. As Haussmann reached to
the past for the seal of Paris, so Zola wove his work about revolutionary
change around interpretive devices from the past—the somewhat
forced invocation of *Phèdre,* the association of woman and city, the
dense metaphorical structures, and most strikingly, the image of the
hunt. But revolution is a process and, like the other social processes
of mid-nineteenth-century Paris, urbanization and modernization, it
cannot so easily be contained. The modern condition speaks to just
this acute sense of the ambiguity and ultimately to the impossibility
of containment.

5

The Terrible Years

Depuis 89, il y a toujours eu un roi de France, et il n'y en a
eu qu'un seul: c'est Paris.
                    Louis Veuillot, *Paris pendant les deux sièges*

Since 89, France has always had a king and only one: Paris.

On 4 September 1870, the newly constituted Government of National
Defense proclaimed France's Third Republic. It was a date that echoed back across the century both to the fall of one earlier regime and
to the beginning of another. Whatever hopes the proclamation contained, the blue, white, and red tricolor waved in bitter victory. The
most fervent Republican could take little joy in a triumph born of
dishonor and defeat. On 2 September, after the disastrous rout by
the Prussian troops at Sedan and barely six weeks after the French
declaration of war, Napoléon III capitulated to the Prussians at Sedan.
The humiliation was all the greater and the irony all the crueler because this war, which sent the French empire down to defeat, wit-
nessed the (re)birth of an arch rival. On 18 January 1871, Bismarck
and William II announced the establishment of the German empire
from the same Hall of Mirrors at Versailles in which the new republican government was negotiating the official capitulation of France.

Yet the Treaty of Versailles that ended the five-month siege of Paris
and imposed such harsh terms on the country—notably, the payment
of significant indemnities, the surrender of Alsace-Lorraine, and the
occupation of Paris by the German army—played out only the second
act of the tragedy that Victor Hugo called "The Terrible Year." The
Third Republic received its true baptism in the desperate civil war
that followed Sedan in the fighting of French against French. The
Terrible Year saw France oppose and then conquer Paris. On 28
March 1871, four weeks after Prussian troops finally entered the city
after a siege of several months, its duly elected members proclaimed
the Commune of Paris, signaling its rejection of the armistice that
had been negotiated by the fledgling republican government. Two

152

months later the final battle for the city of Paris pitted the woefully outnumbered Communards against veteran troops dispatched by the new government at Versailles. At the end of the "Bloody Week," significant portions of Paris lay smoldering in ruins, and more than twenty thousand Parisians lay dead, the immense majority not killed in actual combat but summarily executed under orders by the French army. To gauge the dimensions of the slaughter, we need only note that the army lost just 877 men.[1]

The long shadow cast by the Commune over the Third Republic looked all the darker by virtue of insistent, inescapable parallels with 1793. That, too, was a Terrible Year. Then, too, foreign armies threatened the integrity of the country; civil war tore the country apart; and a republican government exterminated its enemies in the name of justice. Just as much separated the First and the Third Republics. Instead of the glorious French victories that repulsed the coalition of Prussians, Austrians, British, and Russians in the 1790s, the war of 1870–71 brought ignominious submission and occupation by Prussian troops. In 1793 Paris and the new revolutionary government held the key to victory and to the new society while a counterrevolutionary alliance of peasants and royalists worked from a territorial base in the far reaches of western France. In 1871, Parisians were the rebels to be crushed. Even before the declaration of the Commune, the republican government had "decapitalized" Paris by electing Versailles as its headquarters. In 1789 ordinary Parisians marched to Versailles demanding that the king come to the city; 1871 saw the invasion of the city by republican troops sent from Versailles. In 1793 the republic executed the king and ratified the new sovereign. "Since 1789," as the monarchist critic Louis Veuillot so aptly observed, "France has always had a king and only one: Paris."[2] In a twist of irony that can have escaped none, in 1871 the army from Versailles executed Paris and decapitated France.

The Third was manifestly not the First Republic. The very limits of the monarchical analogy point to the great disparity between the two. Modern Paris could not so easily be vanquished. Paris—the capital of the nineteenth century—spoke to the future, not the past. This monarch could not so easily be executed. Yet the blow dealt to the city created an untenable situation. If the defeat of France devastated the country, the defeat of Paris called into question the legitimacy of the government. The opposition of Paris and the provinces was not new, but the Terrible Year gave it new vitality and jeopardized the claims to progress made for Paris since the beginning of the century.[3] This dilemma required an entire cultural reconfiguration of the city.

If the city could not be overthrown, it could be, and had to be, redefined. Just as the execution of Louis XVI in January 1793 required the reconceptualization of the royal topography, so the "decapitation" of Paris in 1871 severely compromised the understanding of the modern city and especially its claims to world leadership. Where was Balzac's queen of cities, monstrous marvel, and courtesan? An even more devastating sign of loss, where was Hugo's luminous city, the "head" of France and even, in Hugo's grandiose conception, the leader of the whole world? Events forced Hugo to think the unthinkable and to pose the awful question: "Can the human species be decapitated?"[4] By way of answer to that question, the Third Republic diligently rewrote Paris. It compelled a new city, new urban practices, and these in turn demanded a new urban poetics. Once again, new texts were in order to enable the city to be read in a new way.

Victor Hugo and Jules Vallès supplied some of the most striking of these new texts. In very different modes, each writer offered a model of and for the changed city. Each spoke for, and to, a Paris that could recover from the shame of defeat and regain its sovereignty. Each author undertook to rewrite revolutionary Paris for what turned out to be a postrevolutionary age. That neither succeeded in imposing his vision on French culture is telling. Ultimately, their failures testify to the ideological impasse of the Revolution as the nineteenth century drew to a close. The catastrophe of 1871 and, even more, the politics of the Third Republic drastically undermined the revolutionary vocation of Paris. Despite Hugo, despite Vallès, revolution no longer served as an interpretive model for urban space.

I

Je vis dans l'exil; là je perds le caractère de l'homme pour prendre celui de l'apôtre et du prêtre.
                                    Victor Hugo, *Journal d'Adèle Hugo*

I live in exile; there I am losing the character of a man to take on that of the apostle and the priest.

No writer, before or after 1871, was more forcefully identified with Paris than Victor Hugo, and few celebrated the city as passionately or as constantly as he. From Quasimodo's defense of the cathedral and the celebrated bird's-eye view of medieval Paris in *Notre-Dame de Paris* of 1831 to Jean Valjean's dramatic escape through the sewers in *Les Misérables* of 1862, from the 1827 "Ode à la Colonne Vendôme" of the young liberal royalist to the introduction to *Paris-Guide* of 1867 by the fervent quasi-socialist republican and to the poems in *L'Année terrible*, Hugo obsessively returned to Paris again and again.[5] The city was at once his subject and his object. One caricature of 1841 shows him dominating the cityscape, astride the Seine, a pile of (his own) books at his side. In the background appear all the places Hugo had either written about or been associated with in the city, from the cathedral of Notre-Dame to the theaters where his plays had resounding success to the Académie française to which he had recently been elected.

Paris, Hugo never tired of repeating in one colossal form or another, guided the universe. It was, as he proclaimed in the introduction to *Paris-Guide*, the "focal point of civilization" (XIX) and its history was a "microcosm of general history" (VI). Moreover, Paris owed this centrality to the Revolution. He wrote, "1789. For close to a century, this number has preoccupied the human race. It contains the whole of phenomenon of modernity" (XVIII). Naturally, Hugo took this revolutionary modernity as his own and, sometimes, as himself! The often cited definition of romanticism from the preface to *Hernani* (1830) — "romanticism, all things considered, . . . is only liberalism in literature" — emphatically proclaimed the connection between the literary and the political that would define the writer's career over the next half century, his politics no less than his literary production. Hugo's pact with Paris was a true covenant, both the product and the sign of his belief in the pivotal role played by the Revolution of 1789 for all of human history.

These associations with the Revolution were clear well before Hugo went into exile in December 1851, immediately after the coup d'état of Louis-Napoléon Bonaparte reversed the Second Republic and led, a year later, to the proclamation of the Second Empire. Revolution pervades Hugo's work. Take, for example, *Notre-Dame de Paris*. Notwithstanding the subtitle of 1482, this is manifestly a novel of 1830. Beyond the chronicle of 1482, beyond the melodrama of love and lust that opposes Quasimodo the hunchback, Claude Frollo the priest, and Esmeralda the gypsy, beyond the recreation of the late medieval city, *Notre-Dame de Paris* inscribes the present. Of course, this work has all the trappings of the historical novels made so popular in the 1820s by the many translations of Scott. Although Hugo undertook serious historical preparation for the work, he does not write historical novels. That is, he does not construct a past that exists on anything resembling its own terms. Nor does he claim to do so. Quite to the contrary, and throughout the novel,1 he insists upon the living present. "We, men of 1830" is a constant refrain, and Hugo continually opposes fragmented modern Paris with its motley architecture and the organic Paris of the late Middle Ages, which finds its highest expression in the cathedral of Notre-Dame.

Of course, 1830 is not just any year. It is the year of the July Revolution, which erupted just as Hugo began to write *Notre-Dame de Paris*. The very first lines of the novel situate the writer very specifically in the revolutionary present: "Three hundred forty-eight years six months and nineteen days ago today. . . ." A count forward from the date given later in the paragraph leads the reader to 25 July 1830, that is, two days before the July Revolution broke out. Yet *Notre-Dame de Paris* represents neither the present, 1830, nor the past, 1482, so much as it reconfigures 1789. As Hugo reaches back to the waning Middle Ages, he looks forward to the Revolution of 1789. The unsuccessful revolt of 1482 represented in the novel, like the successful revolution of 1830 alluded to in the text, makes sense only in reference to 1789, which is the realization of the one and the origin of the other. These explicit references, like Hugo's editorializing more generally, are only superficial symptoms of a more constitutive rationale. The Revolution of 1789 dominates the entire novel, its images, its metaphors. The Bastille looms so large in the novel because its future destruction will commence the Revolution. If Louis XI successfully puts down the Parisians' revolt in 1482, readers of 1830 are never allowed to forget that some three hundred years later, Louis XVI will not be so lucky. Typically the confidence of Hugo's king in the capacity of "my good Bastille" to withstand an uprising forces the revolutionary intertext upon the most obtuse reader.

In keeping with *Notre-Dame de Paris* and the many dramas written in the late Restoration and the early July Monarchy, Hugo's exile during the whole of the Second Empire put into practice the revolutionary identification that he had long preached. "Romanticism and democracy are the same thing," he declared in 1854, carrying

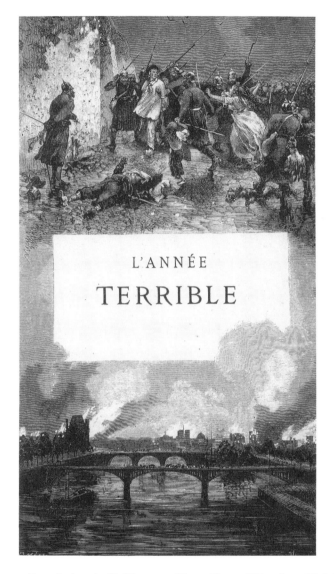

Plate 14.   Frontispiece by D. Vierge to Victor Hugo, *L'Année terrible* (1874).
The first illustrated edition of Hugo's collection of poems on 1870–71. The
year is encapsulated by the German siege at top and the burning of Paris at
bottom. (Photograph courtesy of the Library of Congress.)

his earlier definition of romanticism one step further.[6] No public figure defied the Empire of Napoléon III with greater vehemence or greater personal drama. For eighteen and a half years, from Brussels, from the Channel islands of Jersey and later Guernsey, his diatribes against the man whom he baptized "Napoléon the Little" made him the most visible of those who fled or opposed the Second Empire. Hugo's scorn for the amnesty offered by the emperor in 1859 magnified the original act of exile a hundredfold. In ostracizing "ideas, reason, progress, light," Napoléon III sent "France itself" into exile. "The day that all that comes back," Hugo notes in his diary (19 August 1859), then and only then will he return. From that moment and that decision onward, Hugo's exile was entirely a matter of principle. Although he gave up writing for the theater after the failure of *Les Burgraves* in 1843, Hugo never gave up drama. He staged and performed his exile. Arguably, it was his best drama—certainly the one with the longest run and with the greatest effect.[7]

The theatrical gestures in which Hugo excelled did not simply publicize an existing or precisely formulated political position. They belonged inherently to a politics of performance. Performance formulated the position. Hugo was, arguably, France's first modern media hero for whom the medium was the message. A famous, widely diffused photograph shows the writer on a rocky promontory above the sea sternly facing France. In 1854, after only three years in exile, he already saw himself "losing the character of a man to take on that of the apostle and the priest."[8]

Hugo's return to France, on 5 September 1870, the day after the proclamation of the republic, resurrects the man in the apostle and the priest. The whole event is a good measure of the successful (re)constitution and manifestation of self as a political symbol. When Hugo's train passed through the Normandy countryside, people lined the train tracks to cheer the returning hero. So dense was the crowd waiting at the Gare du Nord that his party took over two hours to traverse Paris to where he was staying near the Étoile. As Hugo recounts the day in his journal, he had to speak four times. This tumultuous welcome in turn merged into the Hugo legend, thanks to the wide diffusion through newspaper reproductions. In this moment Hugo *was* Paris. So intense, so passionate, was the conjunction of the writer and the city that it seems perfectly natural that the Société des Gens de Lettres should request Hugo's authorization for a public

Plate 15.   Victor Hugo in exile. Hugo, in a carefully staged photograph, appears perched on the "rock of the banned" ("rocher des proscrits") on the
Isle of Jersey, where he spent the first years of his exile before settling on the
neighboring island of Guernsey until the Second Empire came to an end in
1870. Not until "ideas, reason, progress, light" returned to France would he
return, he vowed, refusing the amnesty offered by Napoléon III in 1859. He
had to wait over a decade. On 11 September 1870, barely a week after the
proclamation of the Third Republic, Hugo entered Paris in triumph. It took
two hours and four speeches for the returning hero of republican resistance
and symbol of Paris to make his way from the Gare du Nord to his lodgings
near the Étoile. (Photograph by Charles Hugo-Auguste Vacquerie from the
Musée Victor Hugo, © 1993 ARS, N.Y./SPADEM, Paris.)

reading of *Les Châtiments,* the poems written against the Empire, the proceeds of which would purchase a cannon to defend Paris against the Prussians. And nothing could be more logical than naming the cannon in question the *Victor Hugo.*[9]

The politics of performance ill serve the practice of everyday politics. Hugo's political career, taken in narrow terms, could not be called a success. Theatricality did not play well within the (comparatively) narrow confines of the Assemblée Nationale to which Hugo was elected in 1848 and again in 1871. The eloquent speeches before the Assemblée Nationale reached no effective audience. In fact, scarcely a month after his election in 1871, he resigned. A bid for reelection later that same year failed miserably. He was vilified, and his house attacked, for opening his home in Brussels to Communards escaping France. He had stood against—against the Empire, against Napoléon III—and from afar. When it came to maneuvering in the arena of practical politics, in the corridors of the Assemblée Nationale, Hugo was at a loss. His grandiloquence moved hearts; it did not pass laws or engineer the programs of a new society.

It is no wonder, then, that Hugo dwells so exclusively within a symbolics of protest over one of explicit social reform. His central symbol is the Bastille, though not the Bastille placed or remembered as much as the Bastille destroyed. The fall of the prison that symbolized every injustice is the equivalent of many another cultural birth. "Athens built the Parthenon, but Paris tore down the Bastille," Hugo writes, fully confident that the negative juxtaposition makes a triumphant claim. That he makes such a contention in the introduction to *Paris-Guide* (XVIII) testifies to the centrality of a revolutionary politics in his conception of the city. These politics center on a spatial absence, on the place where the Bastille no longer stands, in a city where Hugo, in exile, no longer lives.

This conundrum of absence also suggests the problem of a politics of performance geared entirely to protest. What could come after successful remonstration in 1870? Hugo, though not his fellow deputies in the Assemblée Nationale, found the answer in his own stupendous identification with Paris. Just as he remained the quintessential Parisian through every moment of exile, so every Parisian could know the glory of the Revolution through the empty space of the Bastille. It was the radical idea of Paris and not the social agenda to be performed there that drew Victor Hugo and sustained his work.

Yet the politics of performance served Hugo, and the republic, well. His inability to cope with practical politics, his ineffectiveness in parliamentary maneuvers—paradoxically, these failings made him an even more powerful symbolic figure. Hugo had stood against the empire. Hence he stood for the republic. Which republic? Whose republic? Hugo stood for the broadest ideology of the republic. Precisely because he could not be restricted to any particular political party or program, he could be appropriated by a Third Republic that had begun under such inauspicious circumstances and that needed legitimacy in a continuing context with both the right and the left. The now legendary Hugo, with republican credentials that none could contest, provided an alibi for those who squabbled over the new political directions to be taken. As on the rock at Jersey, Hugo could be seen from afar. Physical distance, translated into psychic terms, defined Hugo within the contemporary society. The same prophetic stance of *Notre-Dame de Paris,* which foresaw 1789 from 1482, turned the older writer into the patriarch of the Third Republic, one who viewed contemporary events from above and beyond immediate context.

The sense of remoteness from the present came all the more easily in the striking contrast between the Paris that Hugo left in 1851 and the aggressively modernizing city to which he returned twenty years later. The Paris to which Hugo returned in 1870 was a city transformed. At issue, beyond the comparatively simple matter of moving stones and streets, was a whole new relationship of self and space. Much of the topography would have been unrecognizable. Stranger still, no doubt, was the urgency of change. Haussmannization had recast the city into a dazzling modern and markedly different form. The metropolis of the Second Empire, the frenetic city of *La Curée,* had replaced the city of *L'Éducation sentimentale* and Hugo's own *Les Misérables,* the Paris of the July Monarchy that Hugo knew so well.

Especially in light of Hugo's convictions concerning the inextricability of the political and the literary, it was inevitable that the politics of performance would inform his later writing as well as his public persona. Moreover, it is symptomatic that in none of the major novels about Paris—*Notre-Dame de Paris* (1831), *Les Misérables* (1862), and *Quatrevingt-treize (Ninety-three)* (1874)—does Hugo deal with contemporary Paris directly. In each case Hugo reads the contemporary city through a vision of the absent city of the past. ''The outline of old

Paris shows up under the Paris of today," he writes in *Paris-Guide*, "like an old text in between the lines of the new" (x). More succinctly than any other single statement, this definition of urban intertextuality correlates text and topography.

Paradoxically, the intertext, old Paris, offers a more powerful means of comprehending the current text, the Paris of the present. As *Notre-Dame de Paris* fashioned a Paris for the July Monarchy, and *Les Misérables* for the Second Empire, so *Quatrevingt-treize* would construct a city for the Third Republic. As the first novel integrated the Revolution of 1830 into Parisian history and the second made a July Monarchy for the Second Empire, so *Quatrevingt-treize* produced a scenario incorporating the Terrible Year of 1871 into the Third Republic. In this novel the politics of distance performed a revolution made to measure for the Third Republic, a revolution that belonged to a Paris triumphant, a Paris that could keep as its motto the "Fluctuat nec mergitur" that Haussmann had bestowed on it. Hugo's Paris refuted the Commune and at the same time reaffirmed the Revolution. The writer offered a city that harmonized the contradictions of the new republic. "Madness on both sides," Hugo pronounced in April 1871, well before the final disaster. "But France, Paris and the Republic will come out alright."[10] *Quatrevingt-treize* takes on an impossible task. It seeks to reconcile the irreconcilable by turning the Terrible Year to positive account. With a gesture more audacious still, Hugo restores the monarch deposed by 1871—the Paris created and crowned by the Revolution.

II

L'histoire a sa vérité, la légende a la sienne.
Hugo, *Quatrevingt-treize*

History has its truth; legend has its own.

The dilemma posed by the excesses of 1793 had long concerned Hugo. As early as 1841, in his speech upon entering the Académie française, Hugo painted a positive portrait of the Convention Nationale, the legislative assembly that condemned the king to death in January 1793 and authorized the Terror in the months that followed. He began gathering material for *Quatrevingt-treize* as early as 1863, well before the Terrible Year. Yet *Quatrevingt-treize* is very much a novel of the moment. Hugo scrupulously notes in his diary the date he began writing: 21 November 1872. Ironically, this novel too was a work of absence, written at Hauteville House, that is, the home on Guernsey in which the writer had spent most of his years of exile, where he had written, among many other works, *Les Misérables,* his novel of the Restoration and the July Revolution. Here as before, Hugo seems to have been able to conceive Paris best by removing himself from the complexities, and the distractions, of the contemporary city.

The challenge of 1793 for any appreciation of the Revolution is to account for the founding event of modern France by accepting its least acceptable moment. To define the Revolution by and through 1789, as Hugo did in *Notre-Dame de Paris* and in the introduction to *Paris-Guide,* raised few problems, certainly not for Hugo, who never wavered in his belief that Paris owed its place in history to the destruction of the Bastille. Clearly, though, the year of 1793 required different tactics; violence on all sides sullied the ideal of the revolution. The execution of the king that opened the year ("the legend of the 21st of January seemed tied to all of its acts," as Hugo would note in *Quatrevingt-treize*),[11] the governance of the Committee of Public Safety, the summary justice dispensed during the Terror, the war against the Allied forces in the east, and the civil war in western France—altogether these events constitute a year fully as "terrible" as any Hugo had lived through, including 1871.

The novelist needed to refurbish the ideal of the Revolution, and in order to do so, he needed an interpretation that would transcend the ideological divisions of the present and provide common ground on which the republic could build. Translated into his writings, the politics of performance showed up in the novel as a politics of transcendence: "Above revolutions truth and justice remain like the starry sky above the storm" (171). "Above" was Hugo's preferred point of vision; his was the eye of the bird in flight that moved across space, the vision of the prophet who ranged across time. At issue are the points of intersection between the political and the literary. *Quatrevingt-treize* fulfills the dual political and literary engagement that drove Hugo's entire career. This novel is, in sum, Hugo's legacy of the Revolution to the republic. Once again Hugo consolidates existing political equations into a re-vision of the political landscape.

Quatrevingt-treize recounts the dramatic tale of the Vendée, the metonymy that then, as now, designates the counterrevolution of the 1790s fought by an alliance of royalists and peasants in western France in the Vendée and in Brittainy just to the north. For Hugo, writing from the vantage point of 1872, the revolt was a lost cause that provoked ferocious cruelty on both sides, "savagery against barbarity" (177). At the same time, the Vendée was "a prodigious phenomenon," another example of the union of contraries "so stupid and so splendid, abominable and magnificent" (181). Hugo personifies the epic confrontation of the royalist Whites, led by the marquis de Lantenac, against the republican Blues, led by his grandnephew, the ex-vicomte Gauvain. The Blues carry the tricolor flag and swear allegiance to France and to the republic. The Whites and the ignorant Breton peasants remain faithful to the king, to the church, in a word, to the past. "To understand the Vendée, one must imagine this antagonism: on the one side, the French Revolution, and on the other, the Breton peasant. . . . Can this blindman accept this light?" (181–82). The fundamental problem is one of vision. The Revolution literally lights up the dark forests in which the peasants live almost like animals, in caves, in the bush, in one instance in the hollow of a dead tree.

The Revolution also carries this light forward in time from the Enlightenment (the "Age of Lights" for the French language) and outward from Paris (the "City of Lights," as French culture has conceived it). Although almost four-fifths of the book takes place in Brittainy, part 2 ("In Paris") occupies a pivotal place in the novel because Paris determines the course of the Revolution and, hence, contains the future. What is 1793?, Hugo asks in his usual grand rhetorical style: "'93 is the war of Europe against France and France against Paris" (118). One could scarcely imagine a more succinct definition of 1870–71. Hugo continues with the question that figures the entire book, "And what is the Revolution?" The answer Hugo gives to this constitutive question makes it clear that the present—1871—contradicts the past: "It is the victory of France over Europe and of Paris over France," a conquest that explains "the immensity of this terrible minute, '93, greater than all the rest of the century" (118).

Despite the relatively few pages taken up by events in the capital, the opposition Paris-France structures the entire novel. Hugo's summary highlights both the double generic reach of *Quatrevingt-treize*, which comprehends epic as well as tragedy, and its dual periodicity, which includes the subtext of 1871 as well as the text of 1793. "Nothing more tragic," Hugo notes early on in the novel, "Europe attacking France and France attacking Paris. A drama that has the stature of an epic" (118). Once again, Hugo's visionary sense reveals to him the palimpsest of history. No writer is more conscious that every text is simultaneously an intertext that makes sense only within the larger network. So too every regime reaches backward and forward to other regimes. Hugo's distinctive vision of history is precisely that history is a vision. In the introduction to *Paris-Guide,* Hugo the historian reads backward, from the contemporary city to the old. In *Notre-Dame de Paris* and *Quatrevingt-treize,* Hugo the prophet reads and writes forward, from the old city, and the old regime, to the new. But Hugo's novel, like history, like the city, like the Revolution that it produces, holds both the old and the new.

The metaphors and images that carry the novel leave no doubt of the victor in this monumental battle of light against darkness, good against evil, and, more curiously, compassion against the exigencies of revolutionary justice. The present will necessarily triumph over the past. The only question is how to represent the struggle so that the necessary outcome also appears as the right outcome. *Quatrevingt-treize* makes yet another gesture in a politics of transcendence. Hugo attains the necessary distance from the quotidian by constructing the novel around the dramatic confrontation of contraries, by "sublimating" the individual into the cosmos, and by "naturalizing" social and political phenomena. All three strategies are characteristic Hugolian modes of textuality. Here, in the context of the Terrible Year, each operates to produce a politics, and a text, of transcendence that sets the Revolution back on course and on site, in Paris.

Perhaps the most striking example in *Quatrevingt-treize* is the treatment of the Convention Nationale, the legislative assembly that governed France from 1792 to 1795. It is for Hugo the "visible envelope" for the revolutionary idea, through which materializes "the immense profile of the French Revolution." Too long, Hugo asserts, has this key moment in the Revolution been misunderstood by "myopic" judges, who can see the "abyss" and "the monster" of the Terror but not the "sublimity" of the "prodigious phenomenon" that founded the First Republic. It is, once again, a question of perspective (150–51). It was also the stage for the Revolution. "Whoever saw the drama [of the Convention] thought no more about the theater" (157). There was "nothing more deformed, nothing more sublime" (157), in the judgment that echoed the prescriptions Hugo had offered for romantic drama over forty years earlier, "a pile of heros, a herd of cowards" (157). Hugo depicts the workings of the Convention as a battle of words as "violent and savage" as the war being waged in Brittainy (156). The epic combat between right and left pits a "legion of thinkers" against a "group of athletes" (157).

Hugo builds his own drama from just such antitheses, which contend only to create a higher synthesis. "Antithesis," he argues, "is the great organ of synthesis; it is antithesis that makes light." In Enlightenment terms, that light is not an artificial creation of the intellect but a product of nature.[12] The Convention produced the revolutionary synthesis effected by the confrontation of opposites. "Even as it was bringing forth the revolution, this assembly was producing civilization. A furnace, but also a forge. In this cauldron where terror was boiling, progress was fermenting" (167). The mechanical metaphors are hardly accidental. Friction and combustion produce light, enabling a revolution on the technological no less than on the political plane. The alibi and the justification of the Convention and, by extension, of its acts, always come back to its place in history as an agent of progress. To substantiate the association of the Convention with modernity Hugo lists its many decrees, from the abolition of slavery and the establishment of free public education to the new codes of uniform weights and measures and the Institut de France. Of the 11,210 decrees of the Convention, Hugo proudly reports, two-thirds had a humane rather than a narrowly political goal.

As in *Notre-Dame de Paris,* Hugo operates within a visionary mode of history. To convey the immensity of the revolutionary phenomenon he frequently reaches beyond history to myth. The Convention is a combatant in the eternal war of light against darkness as it struggles against the "hydra" of the Vendée that it carries in its entrails and the heap of royal tigers on its shoulders (168). Yet, because this myth plays out in specific historical circumstances, it is, properly speaking, neither myth nor history but legend. For his novel Hugo claims this truth of legend. "History has its truth, legend has its own" (181).

The rhetoric in which Hugo indulges—the great use he makes of antitheses, the outsize, even grotesque images, the litanies of names and events—is the linguistic resource by which he recasts history into legend. The dramatization of the Convention, the synthesis of opposing ideologies, the dissolution of ideological contraries into a larger, comprehensive whole, have the effect of depoliticizing this most political of institutions. The litany of names ends up obscuring their differences. The product—modern France and the civilization that it incarnates—justifies the production; the end justifies the means.

The political is depoliticized still further by the transformation of individuals into types whose archetypical status is stressed by continual reference to classical heroes. The youthful, wise, and brave Gauvain is likened to Hercules (204), to both Alcibiades and Socrates (205), to Achilles (219), and to Orestes (227). In a mother seeking her kidnapped children, Hugo sees Hecuba. And so on. The even more forceful Christian model moves the individual still further beyond the narrowly historical. Gauvain is patently the christological martyr who sacrifices himself to save humanity and, here, to redeem the Revolution. Plainly not entirely of this world, Gauvain acts as the agent of a superior force. His followers see him as a Saint Michael who, as in all the images of this local Breton saint, will triumph over the hydra of the Vendée (168, 345). The scaffold frames a veritable apotheosis in the "vision" that transforms Gauvain into an archangel surrounded by a halo (379). In Hugo's eschatology, Gauvain's sacrifice enables the Revolution to move beyond 1793, beyond the deadly strife incarnated by the marquis de Lantenac, on the one side, and Cimourdain, the emissary of the Committee of Public Safety, on the other.

The Christian model, in turn, is sublimated into a vision that encompasses all of nature. The insistent comparisons between the individual and the natural, between the social and the cosmic, assimilate the quotidian into the cosmic, into nature itself. The Convention is a mountain top, a Himalaya (150), a wind, an ocean wave (170–71). The most striking example of this naturalization of the political and the historical is the extended confrontation of La Tourgue, the medieval tower that is the ancestral Breton home of Lantenac and Gauvain, and the guillotine, the efficient modern machine of death that has been transported from Paris. The one is the emblem of feudalism, the other of the Revolution; the one represents a dogma, the other an ideal; the one is a monster of stone, the other a monster of wood. Hugo offers his historical explanation through the grotesque, which makes the guillotine the necessary product of the tower. Constructed of wood, the guillotine is a "sinister tree" that has grown on the land, watered by the sweat, blood, and tears of every tyranny. Hence the guillotine "had the right" to say to the tower: "I am your daughter"—a daughter who is therefore a matricide (376). The present time is "a tempest," a "great wind" that delivers civilization from the "plague" by which it was afflicted. The "horror of the miasma" explains the "fury of the wind" (372). Piling up image upon image, each more overblown than the last, Hugo justifies the Revolution even in its greatest excess. *Quatrevingt-treize,* finally, is politics as cultural performance.

III

La révolution est une action de l'Inconnu.
Hugo, *Quatrevingt-treize*

Revolution is an action of the Unknown.

"I am not a political man." Gauvain's response to Cimourdain's reproaches of failing to heed the dictates of political expediency (229) could very well be Hugo's. His politics too, were cosmic, transcendent, larger than life, certainly larger than the social order. In exile the writer saw himself as he later represented Gauvain, as a martyr: "There must always be someone to say: I am ready. I sacrifice myself."[13] Hugo's revolution is an "idea," "an action of the Unknown" (170), in which individuals participate but whose outcome they do not effect. "What must pass passes" (171). In the Hugolian universe the very notions of guilt and innocence no longer obtain. "No one is innocent, no one is guilty" (231), in Gauvain's words. "Events dictate, men sign." Desmoulins, Danton, Marat, Grégoire, and Robespierre are only scribes. The true author is God (171).

Yet, even though absolved of responsibility for events, the individual must answer to God for his actions. "What does the storm matter," Gauvain observes in a moment of exaltation, "if I have the compass? What do events matter if I have my conscience?" (372). Hugo situates political action on the level of individual conscience. Nevertheless, Gauvain's sacrifice is necessary for the Revolution to move beyond '93 to the future. Will Hugo's sacrifice have a similar effect in 1871?

The defining struggle of *Quatrevingt-treize* is only secondarily the battle between the Blues and the Whites; though it commands the story line and supplies extraordinary scenes, that war is almost epiphenomenal. Metaphor after metaphor, image after image, speech after speech, ensure that the Revolution can only win. Is it not "a form of the immanent that presses upon us from all sides and that we call Necessity?" (171). Even though he goes free at the end, Lantenac cannot win. He is the past, and the past must yield before the winds of change. La Tourgue, the emblem of feudal tyranny, must lie in ruins at the end, and it does.

Yet there is vital political debate in the novel, and it is this debate that makes *Quatrevingt-treize* a novel for the 1870s. The victory of the republic is assured, but the nature and, hence, the course of that republic remain in doubt. The fundamental conflict of the novel is not the opposition between the Blues and the Whites but the contest within the camp of the Revolution, the blue of Gauvain against Cimourdain's red flag of revolution. How would the tricolor of the republic combine the three colors? Would the Revolution rally around Gauvain's republic of mercy or Cimourdain's republic of harsh justice? "The republic was winning . . . but which republic? In the coming triumph two forms of republic faced each other, the republic of terror and the republic of clemency, the one wishing to conquer by rigor and the other by kindness. Which would prevail?" (226)

Such was the question that Hugo posed for the Third Republic: How would it treat the Communards? The savage repression of the Commune translates into the subjugation of the Vendée. But Paris is incomparably more important, precisely because of the connection with the Revolution. For him at any rate, his condemnation of the empire excused crushing civil dissent; the engendering of the republic justified every cost. A tempest sweeps clean. Notwithstanding his support for the Third Republic, Hugo, like Gauvain, chose compassion against strict justice. That he thought the Commune "idiotic" did not keep him from issuing a public notice immediately after the destruction of the Paris Commune that he would open his home in Brussels to Communards fleeing France. (Whereupon the Belgian government obliged him to quit the country.) In 1876, 1879, and 1880 he made formal pleas for amnesty in speeches before the Assemblée Nationale.[14] The novel of 1874 makes the same case. Clearly, Hugo sides with Gauvain's "republic of the ideal" against Cimourdain's "republic of the absolute." "Your republic," Gauvain tells Cimourdain, "measures and regulates man, mine takes him into the sky" (368). Gauvain envisions a society that is "nature sublimated," that places equity above justice, that makes men and women equal, that strengthens a prosperous France. This revelation of the future in 1793 concerns the future in the present, the future that is the present in 1871.

Quatrevingt-treize places the legitimacy of the Third Republic in the rejection of Cimourdain's republic of the sword (371–72). Cimourdain's suicide—he has no arguments to oppose Gauvain and shoots himself at the very moment that the blade of the guillotine falls on Gauvain—acts out the failure of his conception of relentless justice. There may be no immediate effect. The novel simply ends with the double execution-suicide of Gauvain and Cimourdain: "These two souls, tragic sisters, flew off together, the shadow of the one mingled with the light of the other" (380). Nevertheless the choice must be made, and made anew at each juncture. The performance of *Quatrevingt-treize* forces this question upon the reader. With which republic will the vote be cast? The tour de force of the novel consists in its insistence on the starkest, Manichaean terms. Hugo offers a choice not among diverse political positions but between good and evil, between light and darkness, between the future and the past. The ultimate contraries will be resolved in heaven.

Put another way, the future is on the side of Paris. The city forces the choice that Hugo presses. Hugo does not simply associate Paris with the Revolution, he defines the city by the Revolution. In its turn the city defines the Revolution. And that city exists beyond topography, the city of ideas, the city of an idea—the Revolution. If the Revolution is an ideal in search of a "visible envelope" (151), *Quatrevingt-treize* is that envelope. The novel stabilizes the Revolution by containing its movement, and it dramatizes the Revolution by giving it form. Like *Notre-Dame de Paris* forty years earlier, *Quatrevingt-treize* views Paris from afar. The first novel is dominated by views from above the city, from the top of the cathedral or from various undetermined points in the sky; the second is viewed from Brittany, where most of the novel takes place, but more importantly, from the point of view of the end of '93, the end of the Terror, the end of the war in the Vendée. Hugo observes that when they voted the execution of Louis XVI in January 1793, Robespierre had eighteen months to live, Danton fifteen months, Marat five months and three weeks. Thus the end of the Terror is contained in its beginning just as the end contains the beginning. The guillotine that has been sent to Brittany will return to Paris, where, in carrying out the murderous decrees of the Committee of Public Safety, it will also end the Terror. The future is in the present. Gauvain's vision of the future republic is already written in the terrible events of the present, the republic of compassion originates in the republic of terrible justice, that is, where it first becomes a necessity. Paris will swing back, for it is "the enormous pendulum of civilization; it touches in turn one pole and the other, Thermopylae and Gomorrah" (115).

IV

> La Révolution littéraire et la Révolution politique ont fait en moi leur jonction.
>
> Victor Hugo, *Océan*

> The literary Revolution and the political Revolution have joined in me.

The power of Hugo's portrait of Paris in *Quatrevingt-treize* lies in its idealization and in the way that the city, like the Revolution, is placed beyond dispute. Personification is no longer adequate to render the idea of Paris that sustains this novel. Hugo forswears the traditional images of Paris. The most grandiose personification cannot convey the immensity of the city. By 1874 Hugo's Paris is an idea, the idea of the Revolution that Hugo dramatizes in *Quatrevingt-treize*. (Literally as well, since *'93*, the dramatic adaptation of 1881, had over 100 performances.)

A further comparison with *Notre-Dame de Paris* illuminates the striking transformation in Hugo's conception of the city. Forty years, two failed revolutions, and an extraordinary metamorphosis in the city as place separate the two novels. *Notre-Dame de Paris* is a novel of urban places, a novel that hears and sees and feels the city. *Notre-Dame de Paris* bespeaks the optimism of 1830 that produced the myth of Paris, the sense of discovery of the city, its present and its history. It is this myth that sustains Balzac's artist-flâneur as he takes hold of the city, explores its furthest reaches and lays bare its secrets. *Notre-Dame de Paris* too stages the city. Despite the 348 years that separate Hugo's Paris of 1830 from the Paris of Claude Frollo and Quasimodo, *Notre-Dame de Paris* is firmly anchored to place. Strongly delineated particular places structure the novel: the cathedral in the center of the city that centers the novel; the Latin Quarter, where the students throng; the Place de Grève, where Quasimodo is pilloried and Esmeralda is hung; the Court of Miracles, the city-state within the city governed by the band of gypsies; and, finally, brooding over all, the prison-fortress of the Bastille. *Notre-Dame de Paris* gives life to the stones of the city. Hugo even claims the origins of the novel in the mysterious inscription that he saw carved in a stone within the cathedral. *Notre-Dame de Paris* not only reads the old Paris beneath the new, it resurrects the old text in the new. The new Paris that we see is the city of this text as well as the topography before our eyes. "For those who know that Quasimodo existed," Hugo maintains, "Notre-Dame is today deserted, inanimate, dead."

The Paris of *Quatrevingt-treize* utterly lacks this sense of place. Its primary space, as the title indicates, is not topographical but chronological. The Revolution that *Notre-Dame de Paris* foreshadows, *Quatrevingt-treize* enacts, but the revolution is peculiarly detached from the city in which it is nevertheless incarnated and in which it originates. Where the Revolution foreshadowed in *Notre-Dame de Paris* is fixed in the city by the Bastille, the Revolution in *Quatrevingt-treize* is embodied by a distinct and movable object, the guillotine. The mobility of this instrument of revolution figures perfectly the mobility of the Revolution itself, an idea that can take hold anywhere. Modernity and the Revolution are rendered by movement and thought. The Convention as Hugo presents it in *Quatrevingt-treize* is an endless flux of words; "intemperance of language reigned" (169), speeches multiplied. Continual movement submerged the contributions of the individual members, "even the greatest" among them. "To impute the revolution to men is to impute the tide to the waves" (171). The chapter entitled "The Streets of Paris in Those Days" begins with a paragraph lasting almost five pages in which Hugo endeavors to encompass the sense of public life in revolutionary Paris through a succession of sentences and phrases beginning with the impersonal "on" and rendered in the imperfect. The reader comes away with a sense of perpetual motion, of effervescence, a sense of movement, not of site.

> People used to live in public, they ate on tables set up in front of door-ways, the women seated on the church steps made bandages while sing-ing "The Marseillaise," the Parc Monceau and the Luxembourg gar-dens were drill fields . . . ; No one seemed to have time. Everyone was in a hurry . . . Everywhere newspapers. . . . On all the walls, posters, big, small, white, yellow, green, red, printed, handwritten, where one read this cry: *Long live the Republic*! (111–14)

Hugo had long associated the Revolution with movement. The whole of *Notre-Dame de Paris* is structured by the opposition of the medieval civilization imprinted on the cathedral and the modern civ-ilization that will come from the printing press (see bk. 5, chap. 1, "Ceci tuera cela"). Any number of images and metaphors contrasts the stasis of the cathedral, where knowledge is bottled up in the secret researches of Claude Frollo, with the volatility of the printed word. The word will eventually bring down the Bastille just as the guillotine will vanquish La Tourgue. The marquis de Lantenac does not have Hugo's sympathy, but he voices Hugo's belief in the power of the word. "When I think," the marquis laments, "that none of this would have happened if Voltaire had been hung and Rousseau sentenced to hard labor" (352). "No scribblers! as long as there are Voltaires, there will be Marats" (353).

The triumph of print is assured and the connection to revolution is confirmed because movement is life. Thus Hugo ties his properly sociological and political analysis of the connection between the printed word and revolution to his belief in nature and the eternal forces of the divine. The word is, for Hugo, the ultimate manifestation of the divine: "Words are the Word, and the Word is God" ("Suite" à la "Réponse à un acte d'accusation"). Hugo's identification with the movement of the word, his belief in the efficacy of the printed word, inevitably detach him from that which is fixed. The writer in-habits words not places. Moreover, the words that he inhabits—better still, the word by which he accedes to a higher realm—necessarily detach him from place. Paris is powerful less as a place that individuals inhabit than as an idea that produces the words of revolution. Whence its power. "Paris, being an idea as much as a city, is ubiquitous."[15]

The staggering self-confidence of Hugo in these matters may keep us from appreciating an important truth. The story of Paris and its place in his thought is peculiarly enabling both as device and re-source. All of his assurance flows from his recognition that Paris is both place and idea, both context and word. Only by accepting Hugo's utter faith in this power of the word can we understand the extraordinary claim that "the literary Revolution and the political Revolution have joined in me."[16] *Quatrevingt-treize* stages this juncture. Whereas the introduction to *Paris-Guide* historicizes the Revolution as idea, *Quatrevingt-treize* dramatizes the movement that propels the idea. For both texts, Hugo writes from the distance of the far removed Hauteville House, and in both instances he has chosen exile. Thus the imperatives of performance drive a mythology that is at once personal and historical and a rhetoric that requires for its effect the excessive, the monumental, even the monstrous. The Terrible Years of 1793 and 1871 were all of these. *Quatrevingt-treize* contains the Terror, and it does so by proposing a cosmology in which evil is a temporary but vital, even positive, element in the good that necessarily follows. The city of progress, this novel reassures us, will itself progress and will carry that progress to the world beyond. In this way Hugo not only fuses literature and revolution, as he claims, but also subsumes both into the encompassing myth of Paris.

V

AUX MORTS DE 1871.
À tous ceux qui, victimes de l'injustice sociale, prirent les armes contre un monde mal fait et formèrent, sous le drapeau de la Commune, la grande fédération des douleurs,
je dédie ce livre.
JULES VALLÈS.

TO THE DEAD OF 1871.
To all those who, victims of social injustice, took up arms against a poorly made world and formed, under the flag of the Commune, the great federation of suffering,
I dedicate this book.
JULES VALLÈS.

If for Victor Hugo 1871 was an intellectual challenge, for Jules Vallès the Terrible Year, and most particularly, the extraordinary two months of the Commune, was the high point of his life, the year when, as he tells it in the autobiographical novel *L'Insurgé* (1886), he "had his day."[17] Born in 1832 and therefore still in school in the provinces during the Revolution of 1848, Vallès was prevented from manifesting his opposition to Louis-Napoléon's coup d'état of December 1851 by his father, who had him forcibly interned in an insane asylum. During the Second Empire, Vallès lived a more or less precarious existence as an opposition journalist. In 1870, after the fall of the empire, the socialist Vallès actively opposed the newly proclaimed Government of National Defense and, in the newspaper that he founded in February 1871, stridently refused the armistice that the government had concluded with the Prussians. Elected to the Paris Commune in March, Vallès was from then on, arguably, the most vocal of its leaders, particularly for the immensely popular journal that spoke for the Commune, *Le Cri du peuple*. Barely escaping the appalling repression of the Commune in May 1871, he spent months hiding in Paris and in the provinces and then fled first to Belgium and then to London, where he spent most of the next nine years. Condemned to death in absentia by a military tribunal in July 1872 for his participation in the Commune, Vallès could not return to France until July 1880 when, after many years, several tries, and much debate, the Assemblèe Nationale finally voted full amnesty for all of the Communards. The day after he received a telegram announcing the news, Vallès left for Paris, so that he arrived in Paris in time for the first official celebration of 14 July as the national holiday.

Like Hugo, though in a very different mode, Vallès was what he himself called, in one of the neologisms that make his work a linguistic delight, a "parisianizing Parisian" ("Parisien parisiennant", 2:1394). There are other parallels with Hugo. Both men died the same year, 1885, Hugo at a great age (he was born in 1802), Vallès a full generation younger. More than the accident of their contemporaneous deaths connects Hugo and Vallès. Most important, for both writers, revolution was a guiding principle of their lives and their work; and, again for both, revolution meant the Paris that Vallès called "this classic land of rebellion" (2:1394). Finally, both engaged the Terrible Year in texts that are all the more significant for the very different conceptions of literature, of politics, and of Paris that they dramatize. There is a temptation to take the two as polar opposites: Hugo the living republican legend, glorified during his lifetime; Vallès, the down-and-out and invariably fractious journalist who managed to get himself in trouble with every kind of authority, a rebel by

Plate 16. Portrait of Jules Vallès by Gustave Courbet (1860). Eleven years after his portrait of the young but already well-known Vallès, Courbet joined the opposition journalist in the Commune. Vallès spent a decade in exile after the bloody repression of the Commune in May 1871, and Courbet spent six months in prison for his complicity in the destruction of the Vendôme Column during the last days of the Commune. (Photograph courtesy of Giraudon / Art Resource, N.Y., from the original held by the Musée Carnavalet, Paris.)

nature even more than by ideological conviction. As he proudly insisted of himself, "I am a rebel. And a rebel I remain" (2:911).

The funerals of Vallès and Hugo reinforce the contrast. Hugo's state funeral in June 1885 was a majestic ceremony that is inevitably invoked, then as now, as the tribute paid to the powers of great literature. Hugo himself would have appreciated the dramatic contrasts of the event. Following a lying-in-state for a night under the Arc de Triomphe, where the poet-patriarch was attended by an honor guard of young poets, Hugo was borne to his final resting place in the hearse reserved for the poor as he himself had directed for the final performance of a life structured by drama. The government respected the letter if not the spirit of his wishes. The hearse of the poor was attended by the National Guard and paraded down the Champs-Elysées before crowds of two million or more. The poet was buried in the Panthéon, the Church of Sainte-Geneviève that the First Republic had transformed into a secular burial ground to honor great men of the republican age and that the Third Republic reinstituted for Victor Hugo. With a vast diffusion in the popular press, Hugo's funeral was one of those rites of passage by which French literary culture celebrates itself and proclaims its existence to French society at large.[18] Indeed, for the drama and exaltation of the moment, there is no better account than that given by Maurice Barrès in his novel of 1897, *Les Déracinés,* in a chapter aptly entitled "The Social Virtue of a Corpse."

Vallès' death in February of the same year was a very different affair, although it too gave rise to a demonstration. It was manifestly sectarian as Hugo's was not, a demonstration of the solidarity of those who had fought with Vallès in what he called in the dedication to *L'Insurgé* "the great federation of sorrows" (2:875). According to *Le Cri du peuple,* the journal that Vallès had founded two years before, some sixty thousand Parisians followed this hearse of the poor, with perhaps two hundred thousand to three hundred thousand spectators lining the streets along the way. Vallès was buried, not in the Panthéon, but in Père-Lachaise, the cemetery located in the northeastern working-class section of Paris and closely associated with the memory of the Commune. On the edge of this cemetery, in front of the Mur des Fédérés (Wall of the Communards), an infamous massacre of Communards had taken place. Père-Lachaise was a fitting resting place for Vallès. It was the cemetery of his idol Balzac as well as the site of the executions, and it would eventually be the cemetery for a number of notable Communards and socialists (including Karl Marx's daughter Laura Lafargue and her husband, Paul, founder of the French Workers Party).

Politics directed Vallès' life, although, curiously enough, he was not much more of a politician than Hugo. He embraced his notoriety as a political journalist and scorned the very notion of the man of letters who placed himself beyond the everyday and the political. He did not undertake his great *Jacques Vingtras* trilogy until his exile in London, and *L'Insurgé,* the final volume, did not appear in full until after his death in 1885. Still, his politics, and the literary works that went with them, did not fit in with the practice of the Revolution that the Third Republic worked so diligently to establish. The figurative as well as literal "pantheonization" of Hugo bespoke the insecurity of the regime and the political necessity of fixing on a symbol of unity within a republican tradition above suspicion. At the same time, the Third Republic sought to distance itself from the First and Second Republics while still declaring itself the nominal successor. Republicans of the 1870s were haunted by the tumultuous politics and the ultimate failures of the First and the Second Republics, each of which ended in a coup d'état by a Bonaparte. The nascent and still shaky Third Republic had to claim and to disclaim the Revolution simultaneously. It had to convince France (and the world) that, while fulfilling the promise of the Revolution, it was not itself a revolutionary regime.[19]

In its search for unimpeachable heroes, the Third Republic looked for figures connected to but not directly involved in the Revolution. Like the First Republic it turned to Voltaire. As the First Republic staged a great ceremony for the transfer of Voltaire's body to the Panthéon in 1794, so the Third Republic almost immediately turned the boulevard Prince-Eugène (named after the son of Napoléon III) into the boulevard Voltaire, placed Voltaire's portrait in every town hall in the country, and in 1878 staged a vast centenary celebration of his and Rousseau's deaths. Similarly, Victor Hugo offered a precious asset to the Third Republic by virtue of his simultaneous association with the Revolution and independence from any identifiably revolutionary activity. Like Voltaire, Hugo embodied the Revolution without revolutionaries, an almost legendary event in the past that legitimated the present without constricting it.

With Jules Vallès the contrast could scarcely have been greater. For Vallès, revolution means practice in the present and through the present into the future. Revolution is not an event, it is a state, a phenomenon that can never be assimilated into a society that remained, as the dedication to the novel *L'Insurgé* proclaimed, "ill-made." All of Vallès' work and this novel in particular declare the Revolution unfinished business. It is hardly surprising that a republic in search of stability should studiously dismiss Vallès' politics of presence or that it should reject the texts sustained by such an understanding. What is perhaps less obvious is why it has taken so long for Vallès to get much of a hearing in our own time, when Hugo no longer offers a viable literary model. Even at the time of his death Hugo was a survivor of an earlier age, his work relegated for the most part to the musty nineteenth century. (Reference is almost invariably made to the flip answer of the young André Gide when asked to name the best poet of the nineteenth century: "Victor Hugo, hélas!") Modern poetry descends from Baudelaire not Hugo; twentieth-century prose looks to many models but not often to the grandiloquence of Hugo. The cultural figure is less easily displaced. Sartre's recollections in *Les Mots* of his grandfather's cult of Victor Hugo testify to the tenacity of that figure. Today as well, Victor Hugo lives on in textbooks and anthologies as a cultural reference and a nineteenth-century icon.[20]

More than age is in question. Hugo was not simply thirty years older than Vallès. He was a literary giant, the most celebrated of the heroic line of romantics who had decisively shaped the literary field that Vallès entered in the 1850s. After Hugo, after Lamartine and Vigny, after Balzac, no writer would, or could, dominate the literary world as they had. In the 1850s, of the pioneers of the 1820s only Hugo continued to be a vital force. His stature continued to increase at a time when the others of his generation were either dead (Balzac) or in semiretirement (Vigny, Lamartine, Sand).

Despite governments that kept a vigilant eye on every publication, the continuing expansion of journalism made it an ever more powerful determinant of place in the literary field as well as a significant source of income for aspiring writers. The introduction of advertising made it possible to lower subscription rates and paved the way for the serialization of novels to attract readers for the advertisements. The same Émile de Girardin who came up with the idea of coupling advertising and the serial novel in the 1830s turns up in *L'Insurgé* in the

1860s as a quite extraordinary, immensely powerful (and not entirely antipathetic) figure in the world of letters: a cat, in Vallès' extended metaphor, that always lands on his feet and is always on the lookout for prey, "a man all nerves and all claws who has pushed his paws and his muzzle everywhere for the past thirty years" (2:902). Vallès' Girardin comes straight out of Balzac's great novels of journalism. This sense of a society and a literary world of constant struggle does much to explain why Vallès the journalist looks to the royalist Balzac for a model rather than to the revolutionary Hugo.

This journalistic world was largely peripheral to Hugo and his career. Hugo was not a journalist but a man of letters who wrote for reviews and journals only occasionally. Although he founded a journal with his brothers in 1819 (*Le Conservateur littéraire*) and another with his son in 1849 (*L'Événement*), Hugo placed himself in the nobler species of man of letters. Vallès kept himself firmly in the world of journalism; Hugo burst onto the literary scene at the age of seventeen, when his poetry was awarded a prize by the oldest extant literary academy in France, the Académie des Jeux Floraux. If Hugo offered Vallès and his generation a model of the successful writer—and he assuredly did—it was a model that the younger generation knew it could not possibly emulate.

Nor, in Vallès' very strong view, should it do so. "Just as there is an out-of-date politics, there is a sterile and dangerous art, living off crumbs, sleeping on debris, that has to be relegated to the catacombs" (1:883). The writer, the artist, must write in the present, not the past. They have to have "felt and seen what they want us to feel and see" (1:891). For the true artists who are of their time, and who have been actors in the debate, Vallès coins the term "news-er" ("actualiste"). Perhaps, he says, the word has no future, but at least it has no past; "and I am not for the past" (1:891). Writing in 1857, Vallès contends that the second half of the nineteenth century needs a new politics, and it needs a new poetics, a poetics of prose. Romanticism "tolled the death knell" of poetry (1:9). "A new society, with other emotions, other sentiments, other weapons, . . . has opened the second half of the 19th century; what was beautiful yesterday will be ridiculous tomorrow. You have to move with the times." It was time, Vallès announced with his usual truculence, to give up poetry and to "live in prose" (1:10). If Hugo would not have appreciated being targeted as the "pall bearer" at the funeral of poetry (1:9) and might not have found Vallès' acerbic style especially congenial, he should have recognized in the combative Vallès of the 1860s the equally contentious Hugo of the 1820s and 1830s, who called for a new literature to fit a new society and boasted of having put a revolutionary's red cap on the fusty dictionary of the Académie française.

That the erstwhile revolutionary romantics had grown fat upon the land needed no more evidence than the performance of *Hernani,* Hugo's reputedly "revolutionary" play of 1830, when it was specially authorized for the World's Fair in 1867 (performances had been forbidden since Hugo had gone into exile). Vallès was not so faintly disgusted at the spectacle presented by the aging, corpulent romantics and the disciples they had produced: "Either romanticism has aged or, stuffed with fat, it has produced children with rickets" (1:949). Still and all, Vallès had to admit, these skinny second-generation romantics had a spot in the literary world, and he did not. It was incumbent upon Vallès—a "realist," as he identifies himself in the same article—to define success differently. That definition, in the literary world of the Second Empire, would come through journalism, which meant that it would come through politics. And those politics, for Vallès, were ultimately a politics of and for Paris.

VI

C'est donc Paris, Paris misérable et glorieux, Paris dans sa grandeur et son horreur . . . ce grand corps fiévreux.
                                        "La Rue," *La Rue*

It is then Paris, miserable and glorious, Paris in its grandeur and its horror . . . this great fevered body.

In the assimilation with Paris, Hugo is a model, but again one that Vallès could not but oppose. When Vallès began writing in the 1850s, so forceful was Hugo's identification with Paris, on the one hand, and with political opposition, on the other, that Vallès could not escape the connection. The affective and ideological distance that Hugo maintained during the empire was denied to those on the scene, who had to deal not only with the instability of the quotidian but also with the particular circumstances of censorship and the other tribulations of literary life during the empire. Well before he joined the Commune, Vallès had a long history of run-ins with the authorities. An impassioned lecture on Balzac brought him an interdiction from the Ministry of Public Instruction preventing him from speaking in public. He served two months in prison and paid a substantial fine for one article that the government judged incendiary, and for another was fired by the all-powerful newspaper magnate Émile de Girardin under pressure from the minister of the interior. Vallès' journals led a very precarious existence as they steered, with varying success, between the shoals of the censors.

In view of the obstacles encountered in actual literary life under the empire, Hugo had a relatively easy time of it. He maintained his credentials as a revolutionary by never having to put them into practice. The *Hernani* that caused so much ink to flow in 1830 appears to Vallès in 1867 no more than a pathetic substitute for a truly revolutionary work. The vast antitheses for which Hugo claimed divine example seem a pernicious rhetoric. "Let's not confuse a maker of antitheses with a leader of people. . . . M. Victor Hugo is only a superb monster . . . a hollow statue," so that to call Hugo a revolutionary "would be a lie and a danger!" (1:951). (A few years later, when he himself would be forced into exile, Vallès would express greater sympathy for Hugo.)

If Vallès' fixation with Paris was surely the equal of Hugo's, his Paris was a very different city. It was assuredly not the Paris of monuments. Indeed, Vallès criticizes the vast, multiauthored *Paris-Guide* for its excessive attention to monuments and institutions and, hence, the past. "All stones look alike," declares the narrator of *L'Enfant,* dismissing monumental Paris without a second thought (2:338). The aversion to monuments and statues is, in turn, part of a larger antipathy to anything or to anyone who claims to be larger than life—or to anyone for whom the claim is made.

The deflationary perspective that Vallès brings to such apparently diverse subjects as the past, nationalism, literary style, and governmental authority is distinctly modern and even modernist. "I don't believe in the Panthéon, I don't dream about the title of a great man, I don't care about being immortal after my death—I care about living while I'm alive!" (2:891). In the presentation of his journal *La Rue* in 1867, Vallès warns his readers that the journal "will attack all aristocracies, even those of age and genius" (1:939). Replying in the next issue to cries of outrage protesting just this comment, he makes the point with even greater force: "I want *La Rue* to show you flycatchers of glory ("gobe-mouches de la gloire") that there is no more need for providential men in literature than in politics" (1:941).

Although these barbs may not be aimed directly at Victor Hugo, Vallès makes it abundantly clear in a number of other articles that Hugo certainly fits the description of the "monumental" writer, the writer who preaches and "makes phrases for the pleasure of making phrases" (1:941). Even the largely favorable review of *Quatrevingt-treize* Vallès writes in the *Revue anglo-française* reproaches Hugo for "bible-ized sentences" ("biblisme de phrases") that "drown the idea in shadow or dampen it in fog." The "solemn and vague manner" of the narrative fails to serve the "terrible precision" of the drama being played out. Finally, Vallès cannot help closing with an injunction to the "great poet" to stop talking to the clouds (2:79).

Vallès assuredly does not talk to the clouds. Against Hugo's aesthetic of the monumental, the transcendental, and the symbolic, Vallès proposes a very different aesthetic that is part and parcel of very different politics. Against Hugo's politics of performance, Vallès sets his own very personal performance of politics. For Vallès, the emblem of the city, the part that best expresses the whole of Paris, is the street, and it is the street that renders best the originality of Vallès' conception of Paris. The significance of the street for his work is patent. Vallès gave the name to not one but three journals that he edited (1867, 1870, and 1879), to a number of articles, as well as to two books (*La Rue* in 1866 and *La Rue à Londres* in 1884). He used "Jean La Rue" as a pseudonym. In fact, the most devastating criticism that Vallès can think of for the collection of poetry that Hugo published in 1865, *Les Chansons des rues et des bois,* is that the book "has nothing of the street: the title is a lie" (1:568). As movement, the city cannot possibly be represented by a monument. Jacques Vingtras knows very well why he dislikes monuments: "I like only things that move and shine" (2:338). In a later issue of *Le Cri du peuple* Vallès notes laconically that "we aren't in favor of statues." Why? The "petrification of a reputation conflicts with our ideas about the progress of the human spirit" (2:1094). "Fewer statues, more men!" (1:896) is the battle cry of this critic. Vallès nevertheless, if unsuccessfully, opposed the destruction of the column in the Place Vendôme with its statue of Napoléon.

The street has just the kind of movement that, for Vallès, marks true art. It is the repository of the human spirit, filled with just the sparkle of life that Vingtras loves. It is not a place fixed and defined by externals but rather a space of circulation. "Originaux" and "ex-centriques," rich and poor, mix in a space that itself has no hierarchy. "Heaven forbid that I should establish hierarchies—I detest them!" (1:324). Vallès thinks of literature as he thinks of society and refuses hierarchy in the one as in the other. The movement by which the street is defined and the egalitarian principle by which the street is governed make this open space the paradigmatic expression of Vallès' literary practice and political commitment.

In contrast to the visionary mode of Hugo's characteristic bird's-eye view from the towers of Notre-Dame or from even further in *Quatrevingt-treize,* Vallès places himself, and his text, squarely in the street. Distance disables. Climbing to the top of the Panthéon, he gets dizzy (1:957). And when he goes up in a balloon, Vallès sees only the map of the city, not what he recognizes as the city itself (1:960). To write about the city, Vallès needs its streets. Escaping from France, having just crossed the border into Belgium, Vingtras turns back to look at the sky in the direction "where he senses Paris" (2:1087). Whereas Hugo deliberately distanced himself from contemporary Paris to write about the Paris of 1793, Vallès had to return to Paris to write his saga of Paris in the Terrible Year. The first two novels in the *Jacques Vingtras* trilogy, *L'Enfant* (1881) and *Le Bachelier* (1884), could be written in exile, but *L'Insurgé,* the epic tale of the battles on and of the streets of Paris, required that the space be lived in the moment. The same need to experience directly the distinctive nature of urban space meant that to write *La Rue à Londres* Vallès returned to London.

An aesthetic of the street produces a politics of the street. The collective politics of the Commune as Vallès presents it in *L'Insurgé* are at the opposite pole from Hugo's politics of transcendence. Similarly, Vallès' participatory poetics stands against the prophetic stance that Hugo assigns to the great writer. In Vallès' version of the nineteenth century, every one of us can write a masterpiece if we will only write "frankly and simply." Then the "immense book of human emotions" written by all will replace the "monstrous work" made by those "who are claimed to have genius." No more "literaturizing litera-ture" ("littérature littératurante") that only talks about itself. No more mysteries, no more great men, no more fixation on the Pan-théon or the Académie française. Thus *La Rue,* as Vallès envisaged the journal, would not be "the paper of a few, but the work of everyone." True to his conception of participatory poetics and to the logic of journalism, Vallès invited his readers to be as well "our collaborators and our friends!" (1:941, 942).

Vallès aims at being a very different kind of writer. Accordingly, he takes the side of a very different kind of literature. There have been too many "Victims of the Book," too many who believe what they read, too many who believe only through what they have read. "Not one of our emotions is direct." In contrast to Hugo's vision of the democratic utopia that would be initiated by the printing press, Vallès depicts a society where the book has taken over, where "everything is copied," and it is copied from a book. "The *Book* is there. Ink floats on top of this sea of blood and tears" (1:230).

The danger that threatens any book, the danger that Vallès strives to counter, is petrification. Vallès seeks a society, and a literature, without models, that will not be copies, that will not look to monuments, or books, in the past but will look around in the present. As a student with revolutionary aspirations he would look upon the Convention that executed Louis XVI and legislated much of modern France as the "culminating point of history," this "Iliad," and its actors "our fathers these giants" (2:481). The older Vallès, as convinced as ever of the necessity of working for the revolution, realizes that there is no point in copying the theatrical gestures of one's ancestors (2:907). The political problem facing the Commune is not to repeat '93 (2:926) (or, for that matter, 1789) but to invent the revolution, to produce a new society, and with that new society, a new literature. Above all, he assumed that the best literature in the best society required the city, a real Paris.

VII

> Il fallait une phrase, rien qu'une, mais il en fallait une où palpitât l'âme de Paris; il fallait un mot à Paris pour prendre position dans l'avenir.
>
>   Vallès, *L'Insurgé*

> A phrase was needed, just one, but one in which the soul of Paris beat; Paris needed a word to take its position in the future.

Published in full only a year after his death, *L'Insurgé* is Vallès' political as well as literary legacy, both a statement of his political convictions and a handbook of his literary practices. Like his first book, whose conception and delivery are recounted in *L'Insurgé*, this novel is "the son of [his] suffering" (2:889). Its readers gave him the sense of family that he never had, "a family that loves you more than your own ever did" (2:908). It records the liberation of the very autobiographical Jacques Vingtras from the traumas of *L'Enfant* and the misery of student days detailed in *Le Bachelier*. In the extraordinary fraternity of the Commune, in the "grand federation of sorrows," Vingtras finds vindication for his loneliness and his suffering. "Many other children have been beaten like me, many other students have gone hungry, and have arrived at the cemetery without having their youth vindicated" (2:1087). His rancor is dead—he "has had [his] day" (2:1087). *L'Insurgé* is not the reporter's chronicle of the Commune; it is not even a participant's testimony; it is instead Vallès-Vingtras' wrenchingly personal record of "his day."

In literature too, Vallès moved from revolt to revolution. The narrative itself is as self-consciously revolutionary as the political program elaborated by Vallès and his fellow Communards. *L'Insurgé* also recounts the passage from literary rebel (*révolté*) to revolutionary, from an awareness that the nineteenth century needed a new aesthetic to the realization of that aesthetic, first in his journalism, and then in the *Jacques Vingtras* trilogy. It testifies to the success of the literary insurgence even as it recounts the ultimate failure of the political insurrection.

Early on in *L'Insurgé*, when Vingtras-Vallès is a minor clerk in the town hall of the fifteenth arrondissement in Paris, he is invited to lecture on Balzac to an audience that largely opposes the imperial government of Napoléon III. But if these bourgeois contest the current political regime, they firmly support the reigning literary mode. Like Robespierre and his imitators, they are austere fanatics of classical form (2:897). Vingtras gets carried away, he forgets Balzac, and finally "breathes freely." But why, he wonders, does the audience not protest? Why are they still in their seats? And he realizes that he has dressed up his language as he himself has dressed up, in overcoat, hat, and gloves, in bourgeois black formal attire. "These imbeciles let me insult their religions and their beliefs because I do it in a language that respects their rhetoric" (2:898).[21] Even so, the subversive content of the lecture gets him sacked.

Vingtras learns his lesson. Language does not simply carry revolutionary content. It must itself be revolutionary. Henceforth his insurgency would be as much linguistic as political. Aesthetic insurgency creates as many dilemmas as political revolt. When Vingtras endeavors to obtain a position as a regular contributor to a paper, he finds that "no place is there any place for my brutalities." The mighty Émile de Girardin sends him away and refuses his collaboration on the grounds that, even if he steers clear of overtly political subjects, Vingtras' very distinctive language will be too strong. The sound of his trumpet will drown out the "clarinets" of the other collaborators (2:903–4). True enough, Vingtras admits, he always manages to wave a bit of the red flag in the most innocuous articles and to slip in among the roses and the violets of his "Saturday bouquets" for *Le Figaro* "a bloody geranium, a red aster" (2:905). Vallès protests vehemently against the segregation of language, of "style," of "good writing." He is "almost ashamed" at the praise heaped on the style of his first book, so great is his outrage that the critics do not see "the arm hidden under the black lace of my sentences like Achilles' sword at Scyros" (2:907), that, in sum, they close literature off in a world apart.

In *L'Insurgé* Vallès confronts the predicament faced in the novel by Jacques Vingtras and three other men of letters charged with drawing up a proclamation of resistance to the Prussian army then encircling Paris. Men of letters, bourgeois, they had to devise a language that would do justice to the situation and, more importantly still, to the people in whose name this proclamation was to be made. This proclamation in the name of the people had to avoid both bourgeois platitudes about the lower classes and the equally deadly and equally false high-blown rhetoric: "We had to have the people speak a language that was both simple and ample. Before history they were taking the floor, in the most awful of storms. . . . We had to think of Country and Revolution at the same time" (2:1017). The Prussian bombardments of Paris that began the very morning that the proclamation was to be made public made this task more urgent than ever: "A phrase was needed, just one, but one in which the soul of Paris beat; Paris needed a word to take its position in the future" (2:1017–18). The word "commune," the phrase "Place au Peuple! Place à la Commune!" And it was this final phrase that would declare the Commune two months later. "Commune" was the word they were seeking, the fateful word that expressed the conjunction of the people and the city, the word that soon thereafter would turn into a reality. Here was proof that the right word had been found, a word that contained the soul of the city.

This new city—the "country of honor, the city of salvation, the bivouac of the Revolution" (2:1031), the "city of combat" (2:1395)—is also a creation of words. The need to find the right word haunts Vingtras throughout the novel. Bourgeois especially by virtue of his studies, he fears falling into the trap of rhetoric. He himself is necessarily another victim of the book, which explains his admiration for the comrades in the Commune who care not a fig for the niceties of grammar or the elegance of the well-turned phrase. One character in particular, Vingtras' deputy at the town hall of La Villette, "signs orders paved with barbarisms but paved as well with revolutionary intentions." Not the least of the revolts his deputy has organized is "a formidable insurrection against grammar" (2:1033). Vingtras rejoices when the minister of public instruction of the Commune, a cobbler in his cups, boasts of having introduced "leather" into the Conservatory of the French Language—"leather" being the slang term for solecism—and having given tradition a kick in the backside (2:1037). Yet this same man apologizes to Vingtras the journalist for the grammatical errors that "gum up" his plan for public education. But the plan for public education that this untutored, aggressively ungrammatical shoemaker comes up with leaves Vingtras almost speechless. In these "dirty crumpled sheets" of paper scribbled by a funny looking quasi illiterate, Vingtras finds more good sense and more wisdom than in all the schemes put forward by the "bilious looking scholars" who spend all their lives on the subject (2:1038).

At every turn Vingtras confronts the dilemma of the bourgeois revolutionary: he chooses the people, but do they choose him? *L'Insurgé* records the ceaseless effort of the writer to bridge the gulf that society erects between Vingtras and his chosen people. The virulence of the condemnation of the Commune by most writers of the time flows from the fear of what abolition of hierarchy would do to the very conception of literature and the literary. That Vallès himself was a member of the Commission de l'Enseignement of the Commune was, for writers like Edmond de Goncourt, almost the worst that could be said about the insurrection. Classical France, Goncourt declared, would never accept such theories and still less the practice they implied.[22]

VIII

On est en révolution, on y reste . . . il s'agit seulement d'avoir
le temps de montrer ce qu'on voulait, si on ne peut pas faire
ce qu'on veut!

Vallès, *L'Insurgé*

We are in revolution, and we're staying there . . . we only need
the time to show what we wanted to do if we cannot do what
we want!

Vallès' conception of a lived revolution and a communal literature could not differ more from the prophetic sense of self and grandiose conception of literature that guided Victor Hugo for over half a century. By the time he gets to *Quatrevingt-treize*, Hugo has transformed Paris into a heavenly city, not of God but of revolution. Vallès, on the contrary, from the beginning to the end of his career, writes against such sublimation. His Paris is the city of combat, not a cosmic struggle between good and evil but the struggles of everyday life to build a better future. Vallès is at once more ambitious and less universal. His literary ambitions are tied to his political actions; he would undoubtedly be content to claim for his writing what he insisted upon for his political actions: "My name will remain posted in the workshop of social wars as that of a worker who was not idle" (2:1087). To the aesthetic of inflation that governs Hugo's apocalyptic imagination Vallès responds with an aesthetic of deflation, of compression and contraction to the quotidian of the worker.

No single example better displays the distinctive nature of the two aesthetics than the way each represents the guillotine. From the executions of Louis XVI and Marie-Antoinette through those of the Terror, the guillotine came to symbolize the dark side of the French Revolution. A life-long opponent of capital punishment, Hugo wrote his first denunciation of the guillotine in *Le Dernier Jour d'un condamné* in 1829. Continued recourse to the guillotine offered telling evidence of the lack of progress in a supposedly progressive age. The final chapter of *Quatrevingt-treize*, with its confrontation of the guillotine sent from Paris and the medieval Breton tower, sets up the guillotine as the ultimate symbol of the Revolution and of '93. Hugo turns the guillotine itself into a figure of rhetoric, a giant oxymoron: the agent of modernity that is at the same time the product of feudalism, a terrifying machine that originates in nature. Hugo projects a guillotine that dwarfs the Revolution itself.

Vallès, instead, sees the guillotine in very prosaic terms. The machine terrifies precisely because it is so commonplace. There is no need for rhetorical flourishes. Vallès' account of an execution (1:930–36) insists upon the ordinary quality of the event, upon the absence of drama and the want of spectacle. He deliberately deflates the rhetoric of the guillotine to cut the machine itself down to size. Vallès paints himself as a victim of books, for here again the grotesque, inflated narratives have left him totally unprepared. He expected a sinister executioner; he envisioned the guillotine itself "like a supplicating angel holding its red arms toward the sky" and terrifying all those who looked upon it. If the spectators shiver at this execution, Vallès makes it clear that the shivers have nothing to do with the dramatic horror of the situation: the prison yard was freezing. The "puny scaffold" that arrives in pieces and has to be put up by carpenters wrapped up in scarves so as not to catch cold reminds Vallès of provincials setting up a float for the annual Corpus Christi parade. There is not much to see at all, and whatever drama there is comes from Vallès' imagination fired up by all the books he has read. Monsieur de Paris, the executioner, resembles nothing so much as the bourgeois that he so obviously is, with his long overcoat, his cigar, his sleepy and vaguely bored look, and his innocuous conversations about gardening. He has a job to do, and he does it with a minimum of fuss and a maximum of attention to detail. A final blow to an overwrought imagination, the Provençal accent reveals that Monsieur de Paris is not even from Paris![23]

Behind and sustaining this deflationary rhetoric is the aesthetic of the street. Once people and places and language are brought down to the level of the street, then the street takes over to put forward its people and places and language. The revolution is permanent in *L'Insurgé* because there is always deflationary work to be done: the monuments of the bourgeoisie to be torn down, the pretentious language of the bourgeoisie to be punctured, the Paris of the bourgeoisie to be redefined. Jacques Vingtras traces the first stirrings of this book to the funeral of Henry Murger, the author of *Scènes de la vie de Bohème* (on which Puccini based his even more maudlin opera, *La Bohème*).

Seeing the hearse pass by, Vingtras swears that he will set the record right. In the place of Murger's happy-go-lucky "bohemia of cowards," who turned into dull and proper bourgeois once they sowed their wild oats, he will show the true bohemia of "desperate and threatening individuals." His book will speak to and for "those who have kept their anger," who have not sold out, and who have not been beaten down by poverty (2:889).

Vallès' Paris will be the city of workers and the poor, the city of combatants for a better world. This Paris is the city of revolution not because it embodies the idea of revolution but because the struggle continues there, in the street and on the page. If for Hugo, Paris is the place where the revolution took place, for Vallès the city is the space that remains open to revolution. In the very last lines of *L'Insurgé*, just as he crosses the border to freedom, Jacques Vingtras looks in the direction where he "senses" Paris. The deep blue sky and the red clouds over the city remind him of "an immense worker's shirt drenched in blood" (2:1087). In this, the final line of the novel, Vallès proposes the bloodied worker's shirt (*la blouse*) as a badge of his participation in "the great federation of sorrows," the community that frames the novel, from the dedication to its reappearance on the final page. Vingtras finds the justification for his existence in the larger community forged in suffering and in combat. *L'Insurgé* displaces the christological implications from the martyrdom of the exceptional individual to the collectivity, from Gauvain-Hugo to the community of the faithful. Vingtras designates "our crucifix" as the stake on an execution ground near Versailles where so many Communards had been lined up to be shot after the most summary of military judgments. The reprise of the familiar images only highlights the distance from the usual referents of those signs. Like Hugo, who envisions the city as a totality from contrary perspectives—the bird's-eye view of *Notre-Dame de Paris* and the sewer in *Les Misérables*—Vallès views the city through the oxymoronic duo of revolution and revelation.

The bloodied worker's shirt that betokens the federation of sorrows also serves Vallès as an emblem of the city. It is not the inexorable guillotine that represents Paris nor again the ship that figures on the seal of the city. The flag for Vallès' Paris is the red flag of revolution, which is hallowed by its metonymic connection to the article of clothing associated not with a martyred individual but with an oppressed social class. The Commune and, by extension, this text of the Commune have produced a new city.

And yet, however much Vingtras aims to submerge his individuality in the voice of the community, and despite his stated ambition on the last page of the novel that he be remembered simply as "a worker who was not idle" (2:1087), it is as an individual that we remember the man and read the writer. There is no mistaking the distinctive voice, which moves with astonishing rapidity from bitter satire to self-mockery. There is no possible confusion in picking out a writer whose journalistic fervor for the fragmentary of the here and now is not afraid to indulge in a commanding rhetoric of the whole. Vallès' visual imagination fixes on the most ordinary of scenes and almost at the same time paints in sweeping strokes. He actually hears the great variety of tones that swirl about in a great, modern city. The movement of revolution that is the end of *L'Insurgé* is also its means. The power of *L'Insurgé* to move readers today derives in no small measure from the absolute fit between language and ideology. *L'Insurgé* is a modernist text *avant la lettre,* and it is as a modernist text, a text of fragmentation, of rupture, of dissolution, that this novel claims our attention.

The confrontation of Hugo and Vallès across their texts of the Terrible Year constitutes rather more than a fascinating exercise in comparative textual analysis. To be sure, it is that, but more is at stake than unquestionably arresting differences between two writers who took on the same challenge of representation. This encounter over the representation of revolution brings to the surface a still larger crisis of definition, one faced by the city itself. Once again, representative texts construe a major issue of urban meaning. As the Revolution of 1789 required reconceptualization of the city and a rewriting of its traditions no less than its topography, so too 1870–71 brought into serious question texts of the city and their claims to define the urban experience and, especially, the experience of Paris. The Terrible Year challenged the conception of the city on both literary and political grounds. What is Paris in the late nineteenth century? What models, what metaphors, what paradigms, make sense of this "re-revolutionized" city? Is it the revolutionary Paris of the First Republic?

The aggressively modernized and modernizing city of the Second Empire? To whom will the city belong in the Third Republic? What texts will turn out to bear the privileged interpretations? Which ones will be the carriers of meaning to the end of the century and beyond?

Answering fundamental queries of this sort invariably tests modes of representation. Hugo and Vallès responded to this challenge from antithetic conceptions of politics, of literature, and, hence, of the city. Vallès contested Hugo on all fronts. His performance of politics countered as it undermined the politics of performance. The "worker who was not idle" defied the prophetic stance of the older writer. And finally, the "city of combat" that took the bloodied worker's shirt as its emblem repudiated the visionary city of the Revolution.

Vallès' Paris cannot be represented by the vision of a single individual because it was not, or was no longer at the end of the nineteenth century, a city to be read from on high. Distance lends itself to myth, and the myth of Paris is precisely what Vallès writes against. The Paris that Vallès writes is written from within. His city is not a place situated in time by a particular event, no matter how riveting. This Paris is not one site but any number of places, each defined and continually redefined by certainly diverse and possibly contradictory practices.

This perception of diversity and of fragmentation effectively explodes the myth of Paris. The ability to conceive the city as a whole, the plausibility of the grandiose, often excessive metaphors and images so often used to construe and explain the city, depended upon a sense of the whole. The Terrible Year destroyed that sense. It is no accident that to recapture the principles that had guided his entire career, Victor Hugo situated his vision of 1870–71 in the past. Vallès, in struggling to capture the sense of the community, acknowledges the need for a work, a phrase, to sum up the situation. ("A phrase was needed, just one, but one in which the soul of Paris beat"). The word chosen, "Commune," is a social institution, not a metaphor, not an image, but a product of a collective understanding beyond an individual rhetoric.

In the search for perspective, Hugo's narrative faced the past, his own past as a writer and an actor in French society for a half century and more. His driving impulse in this process is one of recovery and integration, and often enough he is himself the heroic model for holding things together, the capacious figure unifying everything through language in the controlling symbol of the Revolutionary city. Vallès' gaze, in contrast, is always on the present and the future in the process of revolution. He sees instead that a changing and changeable city will always demand other kinds of texts—texts that capture the diversity of urban life and that renounce the all-seeing prophet in favor of the worker who needs to see and understand an immediate context, literally the street of the moment.

French literary culture has never made up its mind across this great divide. Although the prophetic figure is not the model of the great writer in the twentieth century, France nonetheless dwells upon and continues to celebrate the emblematic figures in a literary tradition. Hugo to this day is seen more clearly than Vallès, and, to that extent, the lessons of Vallès are yet to be learned, the more disjointed but concrete modernistic city of his conception yet to be fully fathomed. *L'Insurgé* remains, in consequence, a revolutionary work as well as a work of revolution, a strange anti-book within a tradition of books. And the city that both men portray divides between them.

6

Judgments of Paris

Monument vengeur! Trophée indélébile!
...... ô Colonne française
"À la Colonne de la Place Vendôme," Victor Hugo

Monument of revenge! Indelible Trophy!
...... oh French Column

On 16 May 1871, allegedly under the watchful eye of Gustave Courbet, the Commune pulled down the great commemorative column
in the Place Vendôme. Modeled on Trajan's column in Rome and
topped by a statue of Napoléon as a Roman emperor, the 144-foot
monument had marked the very center of Paris since 1810. Its
seventy-six bronze bas-reliefs, cast from enemy cannons captured in
battle, depicted the heroic actions of Napoléon's stupendous victory
at Austerlitz in 1805. Marx predicted in *The Eighteenth Brumaire* that
the statue of Napoléon would crash to the ground when Louis-
Napoléon Bonaparte became emperor, but it took the fall of the empire to realize the prophecy. In the most obvious sense, the demolition of the column reenacted the fall of the Second Empire. Less
obviously perhaps, the ruins of the column restaged the depredations
of haussmannization, which had made rubble such a familiar sight in
Paris. The fallen column reached at once to the new, modern city
and to old Paris. Like the brutal urban renovations of the Second
Empire that wiped out much of old Paris, the column strewn about
the Place Vendôme figured the collapse of the city that writers like
Hugo and Balzac and others had interrogated for a half a century
and more. It spelled the end, as well, of Benjamin's capital of the
nineteenth century. What Paris would replace it?

In Paris, as Victor Hugo observed in *Paris-Guide*, the old text invariably shows up under the new. And so it was for the Place Vendôme.
The column erected in the middle of the square originally stood on
a thirty-three-foot pedestal built in 1699 for an equestrian statue of

Louis XIV, once again in the obligatory Roman dress. That statue was torn down in 1792 and sent to a foundry, most likely to make cannons for the war against the Allied armies then besieging republican France. The statue of Napoléon I that stood atop the column in 1871 was just eight years old at the moment of its destruction. Inaugurated by Napoléon III, it was the third such statue of the emperor to top the column, the previous ones coming and going in accordance with the iconographic priorities of a succession of regimes.

Once again, politics reconfigured topography. And, once again, the changes are significant. The fate of the Vendôme Column, along with the controversies that it provoked, compressed into a single dramatic event the ideological strife that set France against Paris. In pitting republic against revolution in 1871, the government of the Third Republic set the stage for the end of revolutionary Paris. It was not simply that the Commune set itself against the republic and was repressed. The leveling of the Vendôme Column and the annihilation of the Commune that followed called into question the place, the identity, and the symbol system on and through which revolutionary Paris had been constructed. The mythic city of revolution so carefully elaborated over the century suddenly tumbled off its foundation.

The column exalted a long tradition of military prowess that linked the France of Louis XIV to that of Napoléon and identified both with Rome. From the ancien régime to the nineteenth century, military conquest forged important links between the various monarchies, republics, and empires that marched across nineteenth-century France. The name initially envisaged for the square—the Place des Conquêtes—would have been appropriate for every one of these regimes. Consequently, the statue of Napoléon that fell in the Place Vendôme in May 1871 was more than yet another monument destroyed. It stood, and fell, like the Terrible Year as a whole, a powerful expression of the pervasive despair in the wake of the onerous armistice imposed by the Prussians and the ongoing civil war in Paris. For some, clearing the square promised new beginnings, for art and for society; for others, quite to the contrary, it dealt one more blow to the legacy of French military honor and glory that spanned the most divergent of political regimes. For Courbet, in particular, it led to a punishment absolutely without precedent. The painter had proposed dismantling the column several months before its actual destruction and, in ad-

dition to spending six months in prison, would actually be sentenced
to bear the entire cost of restoration![1]

To explain this extraordinarily vindictive action compels us to consider the exceptional significance of this urban icon. With the scenes
of military triumph that spiraled up the monument, the column narrated the history that it represented, yet another chronotope of
nineteenth-century Paris that, like the master chronotope of revolution, merged time and space. As with the changes of street names
during the Revolution and thereafter, the very volatility of this urban
icon makes it an especially valuable evidence for the urban ethnographer. Like the rebaptisms of streets or the alterations of the city
seal from one regime to the next, the shifting fortunes of the Vendôme Column show history at work in the construction of urban narrative.

If revolution supplied the master metaphor of nineteenth-century
Paris, Napoléon provided the figure of legend. A potent force
whether absent or present, the emperor's power was alternatively
used and feared by his successors, from Louis-Philippe, who brought
Napoléon's ashes back to France for burial in the Invalides in 1840,
to Louis-Napoléon Bonaparte, who based his bid for the presidency
in 1848 on imperial filiation and who legitimated the Second Empire
by cultivating connections with the First. But the Terrible Year did
more than put an end to the Second Empire. Even though the statue
and the column were back in place within two years, the heroic Paris
that they exemplified had been vanquished. Like Napoléon I at St
Helena, Napoléon III never returned from exile, and neither Napoléon II—the Eaglet—nor the son of Napoléon III ever reigned. The
final defeat of the empire came not in 1815 on the battlefield of
Waterloo but in 1871 with Paris in flames. The Communards who
toppled the column and its statue were not attacking a single regime.
In the column they aimed at all the old régimes of France in this
memorial officially declared by the Commune as "a monument of
barbarism, a symbol of brute force and false glory, a militaristic affirmation, . . . a perpetual outrage to one of the three great principles
of the French Republic—fraternity."[2]

An integral part of Napoleonic glories, the city necessarily participated in the imperial defeat. Once again, Victor Hugo makes the
connection. His ode "À la Colonne de la Place Vendôme," written
in 1827 during the Bourbon Restoration, celebrates the "avenging

Le XI Aout 1792, les parisiens reprennent une mesure qu'ils avoient eu tort de ne pas ?
mettre a execution le 20 Juin 1791. Ils abbatirent les Statues de Louis XIV, Place des ?
victoires et place vendôme.

Plate 17.   Destruction of the statue of Louis XIV, Place Vendôme, August
1792. This act, pulling down the original statue of Louis XIV that had stood
in place for nearly 100 years, was one of many during the Revolution that set
in place the idea of destroying the monuments of a displaced politics. The
Parisian palimpsest would emerge through a dynamic interaction of tearing
down and building up. (*Révolutions de Paris*, no. 161. Photograph courtesy of
Maclure Collection, Special Collections, the Van Pelt-Dietrich Library, the
University of Pennsylvania.)

Monument," "the indelible Trophy . . ." of this uniquely "French
Column." In Hugo's vision, the scenes of military triumph that draw
the spectator's eyes upward to the statue of Napoléon at the top keep
victory vivid in French memory and remind foreigners of the power
that France once was and might be again. Napoléon's victories, in
Hugo's eyes, belong to all of France and to every regime. The Napoleonic eagle would not return—the Emperor had died in exile in
1821—but the "sun of Austerlitz" might well rise again; and the
Bourbon lily would join forces with the republican Chanticleer, the
Vendée with Waterloo.[3] The destruction of the column in 1871 finally

Plate 18.   Demolition of the Colonne Vendôme, 16 May 1871. In 1810 the Colonne Vendôme was raised on the pedestal that remained from the destruction of 1792 with a statue of Napoléon in Roman dress at the top. Demolition of the 144-foot column, here in the very act of tumbling, was an event much commented upon by both sides during the Commune of 1871. Even though the Parisian icon that Victor Hugo had called the "Monument of revenge! Indelible Trophy! . . . Oh French Column!" was soon rebuilt, its demolition gave a final blow to at least one of the myths of nineteenth-century Paris. (Photograph courtesy of Roger-Viollet.)

brought the eagle down. It brought down as well the city in which Hugo could make the column a manifestation of country and characterize his own generation as so many "eaglets" bereft of a father.

The end of the romantic Paris of Hugo and Balzac also announced the end of the romantic writer. Although Paris remained the site of revolutions past, the city was no longer conceived or dreamed or, more importantly, practiced as the space of vast revolutions yet to come, hoped for or feared. The representative writer no longer took an identity through the Revolution. As observers at the time were not slow to recognize, the defeat of the Commune deposed Paris. The Third Republic did its utmost to dissociate the present from revolution even as it harked to the originary moment of 1789. Thereafter, the Revolution and the city would make separate representations of country. The column was restored to the Place Vendôme, but the city in which that monument made sense could not be reenacted or restaged. At best, it was remembered. Like the city that arose from the Revolution and needed imaginative reconstruction at the beginning of the century, so too Paris at the end of the century, the defeated city, had to be rethought and reimagined. What could be the touchstone of Paris in the wake of the failure of revolution? What could be the master metaphor that would take Paris into the twentieth century?

I

lui, vaincu à Sedan, dans une catastrophe qu'il devinait immense, finissant un monde . . .

Émile Zola, *La Débâcle*

and he, defeated at Sedan, in an immense catastrophe, ending a world . . .

In the many forms taken by the reconfiguration of fin-de-siècle Paris, no writer better than Émile Zola illuminates the complex process of representational change.[4] Immensely prolific and most probably the best-known writer of the period, Zola undertook to rewrite the city as the century drew to a close. From *La Débâcle* in 1892 to *Paris* six years later, the novelist traced a route from the old Paris to the new, from the haussmannized Paris of the Second Empire to the metropolis of the Third Republic and beyond, to a vision of the twentieth century. In works that radically reconstrued the relationship of place and idea, Zola reformulated the connection between writer and space. He re-viewed the tie between the writers of Paris and the space that was their setting, their inspiration, and even their raison d'être. From Hugo, Balzac, and Vallès, who spoke from and to Paris as the place of revolution par excellence, the writer qua intellectual that Zola epitomized spoke from no place and addressed every place. Site no longer anchored the exemplary intellectual in anything like the way that the city of revolution fixed and directed the urban novelist early in the century. From *La Curée* and *La Débâcle* to *Paris* and the

Quatre Évangiles, Zola moved steadily to separate revolution from Paris.

La Débâcle is Zola's narrative of the Terrible Year. Where *La Curée,* written at the very moment of transition from the Second Empire to the Third Republic, straddles regimes, *La Débâcle* is unambiguously retrospective, coming as it does twenty years after the cataclysmic events that brought an end to the regime the writer had taken as his subject—the social and natural history of a family under the Second Empire. A year later Zola completed the family narrative with *Le Docteur Pascal,* but *La Débâcle* effectively terminated the social narrative. In this, his last judgment, Zola takes the final measure and ultimate representation of the regime around which the saga of the Rougon-Macquart family coheres. For *La Débâcle* fulfills the premises of the earlier works. The collapse of the Second Empire, Zola had already affirmed in 1871, is necessary to the very conception of the cycle. *La Curée* leads to *La Débâcle* as inexorably as the coup d'état of December 1851 brings the defeat of France in September 1870 and the massacre of Paris the following spring. The catastrophe and ruin that *La Curée* visits upon Renée Saccard are extended in *La Débâcle* to the city as a whole when Paris is thrown to the hounds of the German and Versaillais troops.

Debacle signifies more than the rout of French troops at Sedan on the eastern front. Within Zola's imaginative construction of the Rougon-Macquart cycle, the military defeat of France ends the regime without ending the narrative. The new regime dictates the fall of Paris, the fall of the revolutionary Paris incarnated in the Commune. Napoléon III is only the titular head of a recent regime of doubtful legitimacy. His abdication and exile finish the empire, but they cannot found the republic. As the true king of nineteenth-century France, Paris must be deposed to institute the republic. Another execution is in order.

Yet, obviously, France is inconceivable without Paris. Too many metaphors, too many images, and too many texts over several centuries insist upon the inextricability of city and country. Revolution sets Paris apart, but the end of the century rejects rather than embraces revolution. In 1870–71, the act of political and social formation takes place against, rather than for, the Revolution. The Commune realizes the hopes but also the fears of 1848, and its fate is the same. Once again, in a savagely ironic twist, a republic takes it upon itself to crush revolution. Where *Notre-Dame de Paris* and *Quatrevingt-treize* imprint the Revolution on the city-text, *La Débâcle* effaces the Revolution from that same text. For Hugo's politics of transcendence in *Quatrevingt-treize,* which merge revolution into a vast progression of history, Zola substitutes a politics of "naturalization" by subsuming the political into the eternal cycles of birth, growth, and death.[5] However different their modes of presentation and their understanding of literature, Hugo and Zola alike write political novels that set politics apart from the social and moral responsibilities of everyday life.

La Curée and *La Débâcle* are linked by more than the particulars of plot or setting or family interactions that tie all the novels in the Rougon-Macquart cycle. The exceptionally dense network of metaphors and images woven around Paris creates a specific intertextuality for these two novels. Zola's concern with disease and health, and his preoccupation with the reciprocal influence of heredity and milieu on individual and societal behavior, structure the entire novel cycle. But these novels of Paris give especial prominence to the tropes of disease, fever, debauchery, and madness to characterize not only the society and the individual but also, very pointedly, the rebellious city and its inhabitants. Whether at the top of Second Empire society in *La Curée* or with the drifting population of malcontents in *La Débâcle,* Paris suffers from a malady that contaminates all of France. Renée Saccard is the sacrificial victim in *La Curée,* but the city continues the hunt, oblivious to the portents of the day of judgment that must surely come.

That day of judgment comes in *La Débâcle.* Thus the early descriptions of the emperor in *La Curée* and in the companion study of the Second Empire government, *Son Excellence Eugène Rougon,* reveal a man who walks with difficulty, his mouth opening weakly, a man with a half-extinguished eye and a dissolved, vague face. *La Débâcle* darkens the already somber picture of human dissolution. In the emperor who suffers from kidney stones and dysentery and flees into exile after surrendering to the Prussians, the reader recognizes the hesitant walk, the "dead eye," the "heavy eyelids," the "ravaged face" (84, 197, 312) of this man who has become no more than "a shadow of an emperor" (68). Similarly, *La Débâcle* realizes the destiny of Paris that is implied in *La Curée* as the city succumbs to the fever and folly adumbrated in the earlier work.[6]

La Débâcle chronicles the improbable friendship across class lines of the stolid peasant Jean Macquart, corporal in the French army, and Maurice Levasseur, one of his men, a bourgeois who, after the defeat at Sedan, returns to the besieged capital and sides with the Communards. As luck and the novelist would have it, Jean, who rejoins the regular French army that attacks the insurgent Communards, kills Maurice. For the peasant to rebuild the country, the Parisian must die, and the city must die with him. In the logic of the peasant close to the land that justifies the novel, "the rotten limb" (576) has to be lopped off in order for the organism to live. The vast enterprise of reconstitution of the country, in the literal as well as symbolic sense, cannot occur in Paris. To start that rebuilding, Jean Macquart quits the still smoldering city to return to the south that his family had left at the beginning of the Second Empire, "walking toward the future, toward the great and arduous task of rebuilding a whole France" (582).

The familiar associations of Paris—with a woman, with weakness, with intelligence—come together in *La Débâcle* to doom both Maurice and the city that he embodies and represents. Maurice "has his letters," having taken his law degree in Paris, and is, in contrast to the uneducated Jean, a "monsieur." Weak physically and temperamentally (25), Maurice is further endowed with a "woman's nervousness" (191).[7] France will be rebuilt by unambiguously masculine men, who, like Jean, come from and return to the country. So strongly is Maurice presented as an outgrowth, an emanation, of the city's own madness and fevers that the distinction between the man and the city all but disappears.[8] From the interpretive register of disease, *La Débâcle* moves to another, even stronger one in Christian allegory. In an image familiar from *La Curée*, the Paris of the Second Empire appears as Sodom and Gomorrah (562), the conflagration of Paris constitutes a holocaust (541, 576), the nation is "crucified" (576), and the "city of hell" (575) expiates its faults. To be sure, the biblical language is closely associated with the characters in the novel. But Zola's frequent recourse to free indirect discourse blurs the distinction between character and narrator. He assigns the images of disease, destruction, and punishment to individuals and also incorporates them into the narrative descriptions. We can never be sure just who is responsible for the images and metaphors or where they are to be applied as the point of view slides between narrator, character, and description.

The Commune thus deals the final blow to the Second Empire of Napoléon III and to the whole century that sprang from the first Napoléon. Maurice is the last, corrupt offspring of the empire. To the grandfather, the resounding victories of the Grand Army; to the grandson, the devastating defeat at Sedan and the depravity of the Commune. As Napoléon III perverts the legacy of Napoléon I, so too Maurice dishonors his inheritance. "This degeneration of his race . . . explained how the victorious France of the grandfathers could become the defeated country of the grandsons" (365). The military glories of the empire are evoked with ever greater poignancy as the defeats multiply (25, 71–73, 365). Notably, all of these defeats cohere for Zola in the destruction of the Vendôme Column. In the moment Maurice pauses to remember the litany of imperial victories from his grandfather's tales (541). The reader at the time most likely paused as well, to ponder the psychological investment in topography, an investment deepened by the intertexts that had accumulated over the century, from Hugo's original ode to his final protest against the demolition in "Les deux trophées" in *L'Année terrible*. With the sunset that ends the novel, a "bloody sun," the "sun of Austerlitz," sets for good, never to rise again. Nor will Victor Hugo write an ode to the restored Vendôme Column, to predict the rebirth of the Napoléonic eagle, or to enjoin the "eaglets" left behind, as Hugo called his generation, to keep the faith. As in *Quatrevingt-treize,* Hugo calls upon the French to resolve their quarrels as he resolves his antitheses: "Versailles has the parish, and Paris the commune. / Yet above them both, France is one."[9]

Yet, even as Jean Macquart looks at the sun setting over the city in flames in *La Débâcle,* he sees, or rather intuits, another dawn in preparation: "It was the definite rejuvenation of eternal nature . . . , the renewal promised to everyone who hopes and works, the tree that puts out a strong new limb once the rotten branch . . . has been cut off" (581). The "new limb" cannot grow in the old Paris, in the degenerate Paris of the Second Empire where the revolutionary insurrection "grew naturally" (533). Somehow the ashes of the old city will fertilize the earth for a new city, a city without revolution. *La Débâcle* intimates a narrative of regrowth even as it recounts a drama of destruction and defeat. The Second Empire, in Zola's vision, destroys revolutionary Paris, not with the coup d'état of its beginning but in the apocalypse of its end. Politics recede before this vision of

a future that will come from the earth itself. The eternal cycles or-
dained by nature overcome the social institutions or political arrange-
ments devised by humans.

II

> Paris flambait, ensemencé de lumière par le divin soleil, rou-
> lant dans sa gloire la moisson future de vérité et de justice.
>
> Zola, *Paris*

> Paris was all ablaze, fertilized with light by the divine sun, turn-
> ing over in its glory the future harvest of truth and justice.

The evacuation of the social and the political by the natural becomes still more pronounced in Zola's next cycle of novels, *Les Trois
Villes* (*Lourdes,* 1894; *Rome,* 1896; *Paris,* 1898). Even more than *La
Débâcle, Paris* splits between the city that is the setting and the city that
is dreamed, both by various characters in the novel and by the narrator. With its antagonistic social classes, implacable anarchists, corrupt politicians, and decadent upper classes, Zola's republic of the
1890s resembles nothing so much as the Second Empire of the
Rougon-Macquart. Zola's rare achievement in this novel is to have
transformed this familiar city into something uncommon. *Paris* "de-
urbanizes" Paris by reconceiving the city as country. The return to
the land on which *La Débâcle* places all hope is effected, paradoxically
enough, in the reimagined and rewritten city of *Paris.*

In this naturalized Paris, revolution is a thing of the past, a distant
memory of the failures of 1848 and 1871. Political action of any sort
is a delusion. Instead of a model of democracy at work, the parliamentary debates of the Third Republic expose a morass of corruption, venality, and moral turpitude. At the opposite end of the political spectrum, Zola's anarchists place themselves outside society
altogether. Their rage for destruction, wild dreams, and delusory mys-
ticism tie the anarchists of *Paris* to the Communards of *La Débâcle.* In
Paris too the "wind of violence" passes over the city in a "contagion
of madness" (603), and the crazed dream of annihilation, the long-
ing for a purified society and a "golden age" (566–67), produce a
"chimera" (575). These hallucinations consume Guillaume Froment,
the scientist, and his anarchist associates in *Paris* much as the "black
dream" of destruction and the vision of a new golden age ravage

Maurice Levasseur and the Paris of the Commune in *La Débâcle*. But there is a difference. The fraternal reconciliation of *Paris* balances and overcomes the fratricide of *La Débâcle*. In a highly charged, over-wrought scene in the crypt of Sacré-Coeur, the unfrocked priest, Pierre Froment, persuades his older brother, Guillaume, not to ignite the fuse that would explode the basilica and massacre the ten thousand pilgrims gathered for mass. The scientist must, Pierre insists, turn his scientific knowledge to positive account.

Guillaume Froment converts from the destructive vision of the anarchists to the pacific vision of beneficent science enunciated by the eminent chemist Bertheroy early in the novel. Politics, for Bertheroy, are totally irrelevant. Only science counts, for "only science is revolutionary" (476). The anarchists are "too dumb" if they think that bombs can change the world. Is it possible, reflects Guillaume Froment, that this "singular revolutionary" actually works harder and more effectively than any anarchist, than any politician, to overthrow the "old and abominable society?" (476). The motor powered by Guillaume's explosive that purrs away to everyone's admiration in the final scene—here is the "real revolution" (604). Intellectual creation, not mindless destruction, engenders a new world. "Science alone is revolutionary, . . . beyond miserable political events, beyond the vain agitation of sectarianism and ambition" (605). Revolutionary Paris has moved full circle from the destruction of the Bastille as the primal, emblematic revolutionary act. Against Hugo, against Vallès, Zola removes revolution from the public space of the city and encloses it within the eminently private space of the laboratory, the workshop, and the home.[10]

Although *Paris* draws upon a number of the traditional images of Paris, Zola radically alters their sense. In affirmations that recall Hugo's impassioned statements of *Paris-Guide,* Zola's new city "rule[s] over modern times," "the center of all peoples," "the initiator, the civilizer, the liberator." In and through Paris the one century ends and the new one will begin (606). But Zola's city is not Hugo's. Its sovereignty no longer derives from the revolutionary tradition but from science. "Science . . . makes Paris, which will make the future" (477).

Paris is doubly powerful because it draws on the vitality of nature as well as the intellectuality of science. The city that Bertheroy perceives as a "boiler where the future is bubbling, under which we scientists maintain the eternal flame" (606) appears to Pierre Froment

as a vat or cask (*cuve*) "where the wine of the future [is] fermenting."[11] Despite the obvious differences between the two containers—
the one tended by the scientist, the other tended by nature—the two
domains converge insofar as nature, like science, exists beyond conventional morality. The wine made in this cask is produced from "the
best and the worst" (591), the dissolute no less than the pure. Zola
invokes the image several times at the end of the novel to resolve,
metaphorically at least, the moral dilemma that has beset Pierre ever
since his trip to Lourdes and his subsequent loss of faith. In the long
run and in spite of itself, the profoundly degenerate society that Zola
condemns nevertheless does its part in the great work of nature. Revolution conceived as purposive, directed action disappears in a world
no longer determined by Hugo's march of history but by the discov-
eries of science. Its conversion into a historical event relegates the
Revolution to the past, a moment of preparation for the new century
and its singular revolutionaries.

In redefining revolution, Zola reimagines the city. In place of the
synecdoches by which Balzac and Hugo, even Flaubert and the earlier
Zola, convey a powerful sense of the lived city, of the streets and the
neighborhoods, of the houses and the shops, in *Paris* Zola detaches
the idea, or the ideal, of the city from the urban site. True, the novel
situates the action squarely in Paris, and we follow the characters all
over the city, from the elegant neighborhoods of the rich to the
squalid hovels of the poor. There is an amazing scene of a manhunt
in the Bois de Boulogne that is characterized as a *curée,* and a moving
narration of an execution in the Prison de la Roquette. But, in the
end, the scrupulous location of familiar characters and their actions
in an easily recognizable city counts for little. Zola's Paris lies elsewhere, in the space constructed by the metaphors that take Paris off
location, off site—and beyond revolution.

Very much unlike that of writers who display urban topography as
a means of leading the reader to an understanding of the city, Zola's
metaphorization in *Paris* ends up denying the city as a distinctively
urban space. Balzac and Hugo count heavily on metonymy for their
portrayals of Paris. Notre-Dame de Paris is a synecdoche for Paris,
which Hugo elaborates into a metaphor for the medieval city and the
civilization that it subsumes. Even organic metaphors have an urban
resonance. The notorious associations of Paris with a woman, and
particularly a sexually aggressive woman, owe much to the readily
observable prostitutes in the city streets. Or again, the metaphor of

Paris as the "head" of France appears especially appropriate in view of the concentration of French intellectual life in the capital. So too Zola in *Le Ventre de Paris* (1873), a novel about the central food market, takes the metaphor of the "belly" of the city to such an extent that it acts like a synecdoche. Then too, in *L'Assommoir* (1877) the constitutive metaphor for working-class life in Paris is suggested by the city itself. The bar called L'Assommoir which takes its name from the machine that dispenses the alcohol (*assommer* means "to beat up, to knock out") offers a striking and powerful example of metonymy veering into metaphor.[12] Indeed, the metonymic associations of many of the metaphors of Paris are what give that myth its characteristic intensity. Clearly, as well, the metaphor of "revolution" also draws its vitality on the associations with place.

When the metaphors of Paris begin to lose their metonymical foundation, because either the metaphors themselves change or the altered city fails to offer the places or the practices to generate the metonymy and ground the metaphor. *Paris* confirms this shift away from metonymy. The cask of wine, of which Zola makes so much as a metaphor for the city and the civilization beyond, and, later, the field have nothing to do with Paris. Lacking metonymical associations, they seem foreign, imposed from without, unjustified. They can almost be seen as anti-metonymies. Within an urban context the cask is surely an oddity if not an outright anomaly. Its associations are not with the city but with vineyards, the land, and the countryside. These associations with the land reconfigure both Paris and revolution and convert urban culture into agriculture. To the extent that the strength of the myth of Paris lies in the affinities between Parisian metonymies and metaphors, then the anti-metonymic force of Zola's metaphors undermines that myth. Zola simply discounts the public city and its narratives of corruption, seduction, venality, and misery—all traditional associations with the city, and, moreover, associations of which he had made much in earlier novels. Finally, what counts in *Paris* is not the familiar dramas of the public city but the very private drama of the ideal (and idealized) family that takes place within the home, within the artisanal workshop, that is, within the space of the novel itself.

Paris charts the inner voyage of Pierre Froment from doubt to a new faith, a voyage that takes him from the dark, cold city to the light and warmth of a field ready for harvest. Appropriately enough, given the solar logic of the novel, Pierre embarks upon his spiritual journey on a dark, cold January morning in front of the Sacré-Coeur basilica on Montmartre. Alone, the priest tormented by uncertainty and the failure of human charity looks down at a Paris "drowned under a dreary, shivering thaw" under a sky "the color of lead," enveloped by "the mourning" of a thick mist (1).[13] Paris seems a "field of houses . . . a chaos of stones . . . , veiled with clouds, as if buried under the ash of some disaster . . ." (2). Notwithstanding the banality of the parallels drawn between life and the seasons as a literary strategy, the properly ideological nature of this vision is nevertheless remarkable. And Zola keeps Pierre in tune with the sun throughout the novel. The priest chooses "a bleak twilight falling on Paris" (380) to confess his anguish at his loss of faith. Not surprisingly, his future wife, the exuberantly healthy, tranquilly atheistic Marie, sees Pierre as "crazy" and suffering from "a black madness" (380). Pierre can emerge from uncertainty and darkness only in the brilliant, resplendent sun of a September day, surrounded by his family, with Sacré-Coeur resolutely out of the line of vision. "Paris was all ablaze, fertilized with light by the divine sun, turning over in its glory the future harvest of truth and justice" (608).

To connect the dark beginning and the luminous end Zola elaborates what turns out to be the constitutive metaphor of the book, by which Paris is transformed into a field planted by the scientist, nourished by the sun of truth, and to be harvested by all humanity. *Paris* moves from the almost sinister sterility of the church in the opening scene to the fecundity and productivity of the happy extended family at the end, from visions of the Last Judgment visited on the iniquitous city reminiscent of Maurice's "black dreams" in *La Débâcle* to a divination of the future reign of truth and abundance.

Zola does not entirely abandon more traditional associations of Paris. The panoramic view of the city that he surveys in the opening scene reminds Pierre, conventionally enough, of an "immense ocean," and the image recurs in one form and another a number of times throughout the novel.[14] But the defining image of the novel, which both charts Pierre's regeneration and contains Zola's vision of one century ending and another beginning, remains the field. The comparison is by no means original (although it is far less conventional than the ocean / sea parallel). Yet the weight that it bears in *Paris* makes the metaphor a distinctive interpretation of the city that gives striking expression to Zola's depoliticized politics for the Third Republic.

Four visions of the future, each closing a chapter and the fourth closing the novel, establish the field as the key to the novel and to Zola's revelation of a new Paris. The very first page sets up the movement of darkness to light and the transformation of the city that structure the book as a whole. The chapter opens on a grey, cold Paris day, but it ends with Pierre's dream of "a great sun of health and fecundity, which would make the city an immense field of a fertile harvest, where the better world of tomorrow would grow" (25).

His first visit to his brother's home on Montmartre gives Pierre a sense of what that Paris might be. Instead of the city of working-class poverty and upper-class degeneracy that he knows so well as a committed working priest, he finds his atheist, scientist brother and his three sons hard at work in a vast, open studio-laboratory. In place of the "terrifying" Paris and the "endless sea" to which he is accustomed, the late afternoon sun over the city outside the window discloses an endless field over which the sun seems to be scattering seed. The urban landscape of roofs and monuments covers the field, the streets become the furrows made by a giant plow. Is this, Pierre wonders, the planting that will lead to the future harvest of truth and justice?[15]

Later that spring, when Pierre has become part of the household, the scene recurs with still greater insistence on the connection between Paris and a field, between the sun and a planter sowing wheat. Zola renders spectacularly visual the associations of Paris with birth, germination, and growth that recall Hugo's introduction to *Paris-Guide* and his affirmation that "Paris is a sower" ("Paris est un semeur").[16] The scattering of the grains of wheat by the sun specifically implicates the Froment family (*froment* means "wheat") in the destiny of the city. And it is specifically the earth of Paris that will yield the longed-for harvest: "This good earth . . . , worked over by so many revolutions, fertilized by the blood of so many workers," is the "only earth in the world where the idea can germinate" (384).

The final scene in the novel brings together the three controlling images of Paris: the motor that turns Paris itself into a vibrating engine, alive and strong like the sun; the gigantic cask where the next century will be born; and finally, the field covered with wheat that now stands ready to be reaped. The time of planting is past. The light of science has engendered the motor ("the father and the son had given birth . . . to this marvel" [584]) as the warmth of love has produced Pierre and Marie Froment's child. So moved is Marie by the splendid sight of Paris in the sun that she "offers" her infant son to the city below "as a majestic gift." He, his mother prophesies, will harvest these Parisian fields and put that harvest in the granary. The novel ends in this apotheosis of the city transformed by nature and science.[17]

The concluding paragraph of the novel transforms Paris yet again, this time into a heavenly body, a lesser sun revolving in the universe, in tune with the divine laws of nature. The warmth of the sun that brings all life revolutionizes the City of Light by eliminating revolution. The City of the Sun succeeds the City of Light, Zola's Parisian fields replace the City of Revolution. The dreams of a new golden age that haunt the Communards of *La Débâcle* and the anarchists of *Paris* are impossible because they depend on an act of destruction. The new world is, for Zola, profoundly an act of creation.

In this manner, *Paris* affirms for society as a whole what *Le Docteur Pascal* (1893), the final novel of the Rougon-Macquart cycle, only suggests for the individual. The science defended as knowledge by the earlier novel is legitimated in the later work by the promise of a better society that it holds out for all humanity. The children born at the end of these novels speak to fundamentally different hopes. The fatherless infant alone with his mother in the last scene of *Le Docteur Pascal* becomes, in *Paris*, Jean Froment surrounded not only by an impressive extended family of parents, uncle, cousins, surrogate great-grandmother, and friends but also by three generations of scientists: his cousin Thomas (the inventor of the motor), his uncle, Guillaume (the discoverer of the explosive that powers the motor), and Bertheroy (the "master"). Surely, Jean Froment will make good on the combined pledge of his name, his family, his milieu—and Zola's very extended metaphor! The scientist will sow, and the next generation will reap. Indeed, the three novels of the *Quatre Évangiles* that follow *Paris* trace the reaping of that harvest, with the three younger sons of Pierre and Marie: Matthieu in *Fécondité*, Luc in *Travail*, and Marc in *Vérité*. (Jean was to be the protagonist of the unfinished *Justice*.)

And where is Paris after *Paris*? The force of the metaphor is such that the city all but disappears in the "luminous dust" (164), the "golden rain of sun" (383), and the "gold dust" (607) that suffuse the novel. The city of *Paris* would seem to be the antithesis of the misty, passably dreary city of *L'Éducation sentimentale*, its contours clouded by the omnipresent rain, fog, drizzle, and haze. Yet, the glittering motes and specks of Zola's golden Paris achieve much the same effect of unreality, paradoxically dissolving the cityscape in an abundance of light. In these crucial scenes, the actual city of streets and monuments all but evaporates, whether under the moon's "calm dreamy light" that renders the city "vaporous and trembling," or in the morning sun that fashions a "city of dream" (467). The city of revolution, the city of historical events and monuments and politics, melds into the infinite field of grain, everything subsumed in a blaze of light.

The utopian impulse so evident in the determinedly apolitical yet highly ideological stance of *Paris* becomes even more pronounced in the novels that follow, which make even less place for Paris and a visionary conception of revolution. In the *Quatre Évangiles* Paris either serves as the traditional source of immoral ideas and depraved practices (contraception in *Fécondité,* the exploitation of the working class in *Travail*) or is altogether irrelevant. The new society demands new sites: Chantebled ("Singing land"), the joyous, fruitful farm of Matthieu Froment's extended family in *Fécondité;* Luc Froment's cooperative industrial venture of *Travail;* and Marc Froment's public schoolrooms in *Vérité.*

In their exaltation of fertility, work, and education, Zola's modern gospels offer so many utopics—that is, texts that themselves constitute the ideal society, in a time and space that exist outside history and beyond topography. These novels are utopic chronotopes. But they are not, strictly speaking, "no place," as the term utopia implies. For all that they exist outside of contemporary society and ostensibly outside contemporary political debates, these works conceive and represent the future as a direct extension of the present.

III

Les hommes de littérature, de philosophie et de science, se
lèvent de toute part, au nom de l'intelligence et de la raison.
                    Émile Zola, Declaration to the Jury

Men of literature, of philosophy and of science are rising from
all over in the name of intelligence and reason.

This reconceived urban space at the end of the century, de-urbanized and de-revolutionized, produced a distinctive personage. As the

city early in the century produced its characteristic figure in the flâneur, so the very different Paris at the end of the century begat the
intellectual. Although it by no means invented the intellectual, Zola's
spectacular intercession in the Dreyfus affair unquestionably fixed the
figure in the cultural repertory of modern France and the West. The
debates began immediately, over who should be counted an intellectual, over whether the identification was a matter of individual choice
or collective affiliation, and over whether, in the end, intellectuals,
however defined, were a good or bad thing. At a moment of deep
crisis in French society, Émile Zola thrust the intellectual to stage-
center, fueling on-going debates over the nature of contemporary
society and the roles particular groups play within that society.

Much is made, and rightly so, of how unusual, and how unexpected, it was for this established writer—president of the Société des
Gens de Lettres, Officer of the Legion of Honor—to take up the
cause of the disgraced army officer and to embark upon a campaign
that he knew would cost him dear (in the event, two trials, fines, close
to a year's exile in England, suspension from the Legion of Honor,
threats on his life, and public vilification that did not end even with
his death). Neither the sympathy for the downtrodden and the oppressed evident in the Rougon-Macquart novels, nor the battles in
defense of naturalism, nor again the spirited vindication of Manet
would lead anyone to predict that this writer would set himself so
intractably against the combined powers of the government and the
army.

Even though Zola's action was unprecedented, he was not unprepared for the part that he undertook with such zeal. A close reading
of *Paris* reveals, on the contrary, that the writer was in fact preparing
himself for the role that he invested with such conviction and performed with such consummate skill. Although it would be excessive
to see *Paris* as Zola's dress rehearsal for his engagement in the Dreyfus
affair, the novel nevertheless provides strong evidence that the writer
already possessed a firm sense of the special role that should devolve
upon the intellectual in contemporary society.

A simple juxtaposition of dates speaks volumes: having completed
Paris in August 1897, Zola entered the *dreyfusard* lists only three months
later on 25 November, with an article in *Le Figaro*. The explosive "J'accuse" hit the newsstands the following 13 January. The novel was se-
rialized during the fall and appeared in volume form in March, that

Plage 19.   Émile Zola at the time of the Dreyfus affair. The writer's impassioned defense of the military officer condemned for espionage took the case out of the military courts and put it before the civil courts and the public. If the novelist in *Paris* could look with equanimity to "the future harvest of justice and truth," the intellectual who took up the cause of Alfred Dreyfus was not so patient. His very metaphors, from a future harvest to an imminent explosion, show his urgency, and suggest his complete identification with revolutionary rhetoric. "J'accuse," Zola specified, was "a revolutionary means to hasten the explosion of truth and justice." (Photograph courtesy of Roger-Viollet.)

is, between Zola's first trial in February and his second in July of 1898. Finishing *Paris* indisputably afforded Zola the time and the psychological space necessary for the Dreyfus adventure. Had he been in the middle of a novel, he later admitted, he wasn't sure what he would have done.[18] Still, it has not been appreciated how much this work has to do with Zola's intervention in the course of the Dreyfus affair—far more than juxtaposition of dates alone allows. For *Paris* proposes something of a blueprint for the model intellectual. This novel in which

Zola articulates the rights, the duties, and the mission of the intellectual prepares as it confirms the impassioned defense of Alfred Dreyfus. The dramatization of the intellectual coincides with the end of the revolutionary city, and *Paris* confirms both phenomena.

For Zola as for French society as the century draws to a close, the intellectual is a new figure, indisputably a product of modern society. In Zola's later work, representatives of intellectual milieux make a notable addition to the social classes recognizable from the Rougon-Macquart novels. The Dreyfus affair would reveal how modern the intellectual was. In contrast to earlier champions of justice, who typically spoke from a moral high ground, the intellectual also bases claims to a public hearing on knowledge. To take the most striking of Zola's predecessors in France (examples he had in mind), neither Voltaire nor Hugo claimed to know more than the authorities about the condemnation of Jean Calas, on the one hand, or the coup d'état that established the Second Empire, on the other. They knew more or less what everyone else knew but saw things differently. Accordingly, they make their case almost entirely on moral grounds. Of course, Zola passes a moral judgment. His strident rhetoric is overwhelmingly a rhetoric of morality. But he grounds that moral judgment in facts, in knowledge, or, to use the term to which he returns again and again, in "truth." In "J'accuse" (officially a letter addressed to Félix Faure, president of the republic), Zola assumes that Faure does not know the truth ("For your honor, I am convinced that you are ignorant of it") and needs only to be enlightened. The explosive list of accusations that gave "J'accuse" its name and provoked Zola's trials occupies fewer than two of the twelve pages of the letter. The rest retell the narrative of Dreyfus' condemnation, citing "facts" and making a "demonstration." Again and again Zola invokes "truth" as the necessary constituent of the justice that he demands for Dreyfus.[19]

The precise nature of the connection between the intellectual's moral stance and knowledge has been a vexed question ever since, usually revolving around the question of who is, or can claim to be, a bona fide intellectual. Why should membership in the inelegantly termed "knowledge professions" qualify one to speak on issues outside the realm of professional expertise? Contemporaries like the conservative critic Ferdinand Brunetière rebuked Zola for meddling in things that he had no reason to know anything about. In both cases, judgment turned on the question of knowledge much as it would in innumerable instances in the twentieth century—the "truth" about the Soviet Union for the intellectuals of the 1930s, a different "truth" about the Soviet Union for the intellectuals of the 1970s.

Intellectuals dominate *Paris.* For in this novel haunted by the idea of the future, these representatives of modernity—the scientists, the scholars, and the professors—bear the burden of bringing the new century into existence. Guillaume Froment is an experimental scientist who works on his own, but the chemist Bertheroy (who most directly articulates Zola's faith in the beneficence of science) is a member of the Institut de France and lectures at the École Normale Supérieure, where Guillaume's son François is a student. The three sons cover several of the possibilities of this newly prominent social configuration: Thomas, the applied scientist (the motor is his invention), François, preparing to be a teacher-scholar, and Antoine, the artist.

Even the master solar metaphor focuses on the intellectual classes. The sun, explicitly equated with truth ("truth finally exploding like the sun" [590, *cf.* 599]), singles out the Left Bank with all its schools, which "occupies a vast field in immense Paris" (200). In one of the structuring scenes of Paris as field, the rays of the sun fall alternately on the Latin Quarter with its great schools and on the neighborhoods of factories and workshops, thereby highlighting the alliance of knowledge and commerce necessary to bring the new era into existence (383). Further, Pierre Froment's conversion from the priesthood to the ethos of science clearly signals the shift in spiritual direction that society will and must take.

No matter what alliance is made, within the moral and social hierarchy established in the novel, it is nonetheless the intellectual who leads. Disinterested, unmoved by material considerations, the intellectual devotes himself to the common good. Guillaume will give his new explosive powder "to everyone." More than banter is at issue in François' self-conscious observation, as he watches the setting sun, that the École Normale and the Panthéon remain in the light long after night has plunged the commercial districts into obscurity (553). Politics fade before this unbeatable combination of science and commerce as Paris vanishes in the luminous apotheosis of the sun. The fin-de-siècle intellectual works from and with a very particular conception of space, one that embraces the whole that is somehow disconnected from the parts. The juxtapositions of synecdoche give way to the displacements and transference of metaphor.

The intellectual whose engagement in the body politic so marks the late nineteenth century differs from earlier types of "public writers" on a number of dimensions.[20] Zola in the 1890s confronted an array of literary institutions more numerous and more complexly stratified than those with which Hugo had contended only twenty or thirty years previously. Political institutions too altered. The most vocal and most dramatic opposition to the Second Empire had come from dissidents outside the political sphere, and, for Hugo and others in exile, from outside of France altogether. By contrast, once the serious crises of the 1870s settled, opposition in the Third Republic played out almost entirely within the established rules of the game. Zola was denied the distance that allowed Hugo the implied mastery and omniscience of a bird's-eye view of politics.

What is notable about Zola's writing during the Dreyfus affair is the dissociation of his eminently political act from a particular time and from a particular space. In *Paris* those with the greatest attachment to the actual city are, paradoxically, the anarchists who seek with their bombs to obliterate specific signs of history and symbols of contemporary society. Guillaume finally chooses to dynamite Sacré-Coeur because it symbolizes the old society, the unenlightened world, the obscurantism of the church, and also the repression of revolution.[21] Against Guillaume's obsession with this church and the anarchists' fixation on topography, Zola sets out the ahistorical visions of Paris that punctuate the novel. Only when he has renounced the project to blow up the basilica is Guillaume able to see the ecstatic vision of the future harvest. Here is the real explosion of truth. The potential destruction of Guillaume's invention turns to construction of a new world.

When Zola invokes the Revolution in his articles on the Dreyfus affair, it is as a set of eternal principles. With the exception of the anarchists, revolution has lost its connection to Paris, to the city whose stones bear witness to this seismic event. Revolution becomes a function of overriding principles and metaphors of illumination. "J'accuse," Zola specifies, "is only a revolutionary means to hasten the explosion of truth and justice. . . . I have only one passion, that of light, in the name of humanity which has suffered so much and which has a right to happiness" (124). Precisely these terms abound in *Paris,* which similarly divests "revolutionary" of any specific political content. Rather, Zola associates the legacy of the Revolution with an idea of France. His declaration to the jury during his first trial in February 1898 speaks to and for the nation: "We have to know if France is still the France of the rights of man, the France that gave liberty to the world and should give it justice. Are we still the noblest, the most fraternal, the most generous of peoples?" (132). "I have on my side solely the idea, an ideal of truth and justice" (134), he declares, echoing the many declarations of *Paris*. In the "Impressions d'audience," written during his first trial, he exhorts France to fulfill its promise. "To stay at the front of nations, to be the nation that will hasten the future, we must henceforth be the soldiers of the idea, the combatants of truth and right. Our people must be the most free and the most reasonable. It must fulfill at the earliest possible moment the model society, the one that is being born in the decomposition of the old society that is crumbling" (246).

The Dreyfus affair "is small indeed, . . . far from the terrifying questions that it has raised" (132). It is no longer a question of a man's fate but of "the salvation of the nation" (132). "The innocent man who suffered on Devil's Island was only the accident, a whole people suffered with him. . . . In saving him, we were saving all the oppressed" (204). France itself fades into the background before the vision of a transfigured society of supranational proportions that, once again, recalls the final scene of *Paris*. Accordingly, although Guillaume Froment originally plans to give his invention to his country to enable France to win the inevitable war with Germany, he eventually puts it at the disposal of humanity (reasoning that if every country possesses ultimate destructive potential, none will dare to use it). He will derive no personal gain from his invention, which he leaves for others to market. In an article written from his exile in England, Zola too insists that he has no desire to take personal profit from his action (152). In the disinterested intellectual, Zola reiterates again and again, lies all hope for the future. "Intellectuals [*savants*] tomorrow, the hope for more truth and more justice; . . . Who does not feel that we are heading toward this truth, and to this justice, and who would dare to not side with this hope of work, of peace, of intelligence that is finally mistress of universal happiness?" (246).

In the Dreyfus affair Zola had only to follow the logic of his own metaphorical constructions, a "sower" of light and truth, who, like

his fictional characters, cultivates the future harvest of truth and justice. To the ideal that he propounds Zola adds a very distinctive in-
gredient, an element that is often lost in the campaigns of intellectuals in the twentieth century. Intelligence and reason do not suffice.
Love is also essential. And it is not a universal love for all mankind,
but the love generated in the family and focused on the individual,
and especially the individual child. This is the sense of Pierre's marriage and the final scene in *Paris* that unites the family of scientists
around the infant as well as the motor—both creations, infant and
engine, equally necessary for the new society and the new century.
The love embodied in the one is the necessary counterpart to the
intelligence that materializes in the other.

Such is also the signification of Zola's claim at the very end of
"J'accuse" to speak "in the name of humanity which has suffered so
much and which has a right to happiness" (124). He speaks of humanity but through and for an individual. Zola's unequivocal condemnation of the Communards in *La Débâcle* and the anarchists in
Paris originates in just this indifference to the human element. His
ideal intellectual is moved by compassion as well as reason. Otherwise,
woe to humanity. In the single usage of "intellectual" as a substantive
in *Paris,* Zola denounces the "cold intellectual" who fails to temper
intellect with understanding and sets a bomb that kills three people.
This young man, an erstwhile student, does not resemble any of the
other anarchists in the novel. Within the economy of the novel, his
execution is not only inevitable but appropriate. For there is

> no excuse for his abominable act, no political passion, no humanitarian
> lunacy, not even the exasperated suffering of the poor. He was the pure
> destroyer, the theoretician of destruction, the energetic and cold in-
> tellectual who put all the effort of his intelligence in justifying murder
> . . . And a poet as well, a visionary, but the most horrifying, . . . (581)

Only by renouncing his delusion of absolute justice can Guillaume
Froment become the complete intellectual, just as Pierre must resolve
his spiritual crisis by abjuring his passionate desire for absolute belief.
"Did not his torment come from the absolute . . . ?" (378). The absolute, whatever the domain, is deeply asocial, whereas the intellectual, for Zola, is profoundly social, deeply committed to humanity
and to individuals even as Zola himself serves the idea of justice and
the case of Alfred Dreyfus. The Parisian field and its abundant harvest

join the opposites in a vision of what human effort can accomplish. This vision of a new golden age is Zola's legacy of Paris to the twentieth century.

IV

> Bergère ô tour Eiffel le troupeau des ponts bêle ce matin
> Apollinaire, "Zone"

> Shepherdess oh Eiffel Tower the flock of bridges is bleating
> this morning

If the representative figure of this new Paris and the new age foretold is the intellectual, assuredly the exemplary monument is the Eiffel Tower. As the fall of the Vendôme Column sealed the end of romantic Paris, so the Eiffel Tower proclaimed the modern Paris that faced the twentieth century. So familiar has the tower become, so inconceivable is Paris without it, that we forget not only how singular a structure it was in 1889 but also, over a hundred years later, how unique it still is. It has the simplicity of the triangle, a spire reminiscent of a cathedral, and intricate iron tracing that makes ascent an experience of a moving collage. There exists no other structure like it. Because the tower is *sui generis,* it is instantly recognizable as the emblem of modern Paris. Like the ideal of the intellectual in fin-de-siècle France, the Eiffel Tower claims our attention without reference to its particular site, a detachment that makes the association with the city as a whole all the easier, all the more "natural." There is no necessary connection between the tower and the Champ-de-Mars. Its singular form would set the tower apart whatever the site. And, unlike the Vendôme Column, unlike monuments generally, the Eiffel Tower neither commemorates an event nor honors an individual. It appeals to no cultural memory other than those that it has itself created. Nor, whatever uses are made of it (telegraph, radio, and now television station, restaurants, historical exhibits) does it serve a purpose other than representational. Even the shops in the tower sell the tower itself, in what seems to be an infinite number of forms.* The Eiffel Tower

---

*The variety of forms in which the tower is presented is truly astonishing: statuettes, paper weights, tee shirts, ashtrays, and such, but also bottles of perfume and brightly colored bath sponges shaped like the tower. And any visitor who just might possibly have forgotten to pick up an appropriate souvenir on the spot can repair the omission in the gas stations on the main autoroute leaving the city.

Plate 20. The Eiffel Tower at the World's Fair of 1889. As the fall of the Vendôme Column sealed the end of romantic Paris, so the Eiffel Tower proclaimed a new and aggressively modern Paris. Built for the World's Fair of 1889 and for the celebration of the centennial of the French Revolution, the Eiffel Tower resolutely faced the twentieth century. The allegorical statues of Progress in the left foreground, all curves, wings, and drapery, throw the stark, geometric lines of the tower into even sharper relief. The classical allegory dwindles before the very different grace and power of the modern representation as the clouds of change hover on the horizon. (Photograph from the Bibliothèque Nationale, courtesy of Giraudon / Art Resource, N.Y.)

is, as Roland Barthes observes in a marvelous essay, a "pure sign," open to interpretation by every user.[22] Viewing in this context is, of course, using.

Representing only itself, the Eiffel Tower is the indisputable synecdoche for modern Paris, ostensibly above the history that ties Paris to its past and, for that very reason, resolutely open to the future. So too Zola's *Paris,* with its metaphorization of the cityscape into a landscape, turns the city away from its site, its past, and its history toward a vision of future grandeur that will, by implication, eclipse the present as well as the past. Apollinaire's celebrated shepherdess tending her bleating flock of automobiles on the bridges of Paris magnifies by modernizing Zola's version of urban pastoral.

Although the Third Republic put the Vendôme Column back in place, it looked elsewhere to fix the imagination of the city and the country. The column was henceforth only one of the many monuments to dot the Parisian landscape—the landscape that the Eiffel Tower defined. The Vendôme Column, like all the other monuments and buildings that harked back to one or another ancien régime, proclaimed its connections to a past, even to several pasts. It made sense only in relation to the past, however dimly perceived or, for that matter, misperceived. To the contrary, the Eiffel Tower visibly had no ties to any past. It fit within no tradition. It was truly one of a kind. The deliberate absence of manifest historical reference opened the tower to every future, and does so still today. In a city where history so obviously marked virtually every corner, the Eiffel Tower was indeed, as it was accused of being, "foreign," indisputably not Parisian, not French. Its manifest ahistoricity challenged history itself and provoked very vocal protests like the manifest signed in 1887 by writers, artists, and other "passionate amateurs of the beauty of Paris" who spoke "in the name of French art and history" against "the useless and monstrous Eiffel Tower" then in the process of construction "right in the heart of our capital."[23] Its size alone—at 984 feet it is almost seven times the height of the Vendôme Column—meant that it could be neither ignored nor avoided.

Yet, as Haussmann's Paris had become nineteenth-century Paris, so the Eiffel Tower created its own space and its own history to become synonymous with the twentieth-century city. Now all comers could master the city from above. No longer was the bird's-eye view restricted to the powerful or the imaginative. The tower became quintessentially Parisian. By the time of its fortieth anniversary, in 1929, a poll on whether or not it should be torn down found few advocates of demolition. The painter Robert Delaunay, for whom the tower was a favorite subject, even went so far as to call the tower "one of the marvels of the world."[24]

That the Eiffel Tower presents itself as resolutely modern and aggressively ahistorical does not, of course, place it outside history. The very ahistoricity of this extraordinary structure fits rather neatly within the larger political project of the Third Republic. To forge a national consensus and to stabilize the country, the republican governments after 1871 slowly but surely de-revolutionized the Revolution. It took over a decade of often bitter political debate punctuated by constitutional crises for the regime to settle into the patterns that would make it the longest French government after the Revolution (1870–1940, a record that will hold for many years to come).

Not the least of these battles concerned the emblems through which the republic exemplified itself to France and to the world. A symbol system had to be reconstructed. The Third Republic worked diligently to build a republic that would accommodate the past with the future, a republic whose glory would draw upon Louis XIV and Versailles as well as Napoléon and the Civil Code and even the fall of the Bastille. A series of key dates charts this delicate process of ideological negotiation as the republic went about selecting its ancestors and overhauling its symbolic arsenal: 1878, the centennial celebrations of the deaths of Rousseau and Voltaire, the twin deities converted to republican duty; 1879, the vote for "La Marseillaise" as the national anthem; 1880, declaration of 14 July as the national holiday; 1885, the gigantic state funeral of Victor Hugo, the ecumenical republican par excellence; and finally, 1889, the joint celebration of the centenary of the Revolution and the World's Fair. Inaugurated in 1889 the Eiffel Tower thus participated in both the revolutionary celebration and the celebration of scientific and technological progress. Even though the organizers of the centennial most certainly bore in mind the revolutionary festivals held there, it was with the intention of rewriting revolutionary history. The Champ-de-Mars was to be the site of a festival for a new revolution. On the erstwhile military parade ground, the revolution of science and commerce made its claims. The Eiffel Tower signaled the determination of the republic to face resolutely forward. It would take from the past only that which could be turned to account for the France of tomorrow.[25]

Because the violence of revolution had no place in the new France, the Paris explained by the Revolution had to be redefined, reconstructed, and reimagined. Bastille Day became the national holiday, but the animation was confined to commemorating not reenergizing the Revolution. No single image of Paris at the end of the century carries the powerful charge of revolutionary Paris. The myth had lost its force.[26] The Eiffel Tower could remain the emblematic urban icon because, figuring none of them, it could signify them all. It was in a sense the "degree zero" of the city.

The hold of the Revolution of 1789 on the collective imagination of France and Europe throughout the nineteenth century lay in its proleptic powers. The Bastille and the guillotine, the Declaration of the Rights of Man and the execution of the king, cast a long shadow forward, inviting, even requiring that the present be understood through a certain past. The future, as well, was a function of that past, one in which order and turmoil cohered. The French Revolution of 1789 substituted prophecy for teleology, a vision that gained strength from the ensuing revolutions that occurred with distressing (or exhilarating) regularity in the decades that followed the siege of the Bastille.

Paris as Revolution has claimed that nineteenth-century re-visions of Paris, and especially the myth of Paris that structured so much writing about the city, depended upon a concerted need to create and, thereby, fix and place through the language and symbols at hand. Like any other interpretation that proposes an order, these reconfigurations of Paris arrested change, the better to determine its course. Haussmann's willful transformation of Paris illustrates to perfection how "rewriting" the cityscape redirected and then determined new imaginative practices of the city.

The texts that produced the mythic city of Paris depended on a distinct nineteenth-century sense of the whole. Paris stood for something complete and, above all, knowable. Accordingly, when writers no longer felt the desire, the will, or the imaginative capacity to grasp the city as a whole, the myth of revolutionary Paris lost both imaginative force and literary significance. The traditional metaphors, the conventional metonymies, and the standard synecdoches no longer conveyed the complexity of the modern city; their power to define space and to determine place diminished rapidly. By the end of the century, the holistic metaphor of revolution that had guided so much thinking about the city had run its course. It was, after all, a profoundly disquieting metaphor. It channeled change, to be sure, but it did so with the promise, or the warning, of still more change to come, more movement, more mobility, more confusion, and, of course, more bloodshed. Revolution proposed change as the norm, as the fundamental category of social existence. In the end, revolution as metaphor necessarily came into conflict with the Revolution as the primal, founding event of modern French society. This historical revolution was still a catalyst, but it came increasingly out of a fixed and determined past.

There was never a scarcity of competing definitions in the nineteenth century. The conception of revolution proved extraordinarily capacious. That one talks about an "Industrial Revolution" in spite of egregious dissimilarities from the political events of the same period points both to the versatility of revolution as an abstraction and also to the need to make sense of change in terms of a comprehensive sign or emblem. Belief in revolution meant acceptance of change as a way of life and mode of perception. It would be no wonder, then, that the fin-de-siècle, quite apart from the cultural colorations that it took on in particular settings, turned toward an interrogation of time in its own search for meaning.

The myth of Paris that unfolded over the nineteenth century developed out of this perception of temporal and spatial mobility and from a concomitant urgency to check that movement. Moreover, the historical novel at its most serious and most modern—from Scott and Balzac to Flaubert and Zola—exemplifies exactly this conflation, one in which chronology and topography combine. The two, a myth of urban history and the historical novel, join in the chronotope of revolutionary Paris, the topos that infuses urban space with recognizable movements in history. The same conjunction is fundamental to making sense of the modern city, and in particular to an informed understanding of Paris as the paradigmatic city of modernity. The chronotope proves an apposite figure to the degree that it translates into textual terms the double vision that imposes time upon place and the corresponding triple vision that brings past, present, and future together in a meaningful whole. The passion for being modern inheres in this perception of living in a place and a time that make sense only when interpreted as a function of change, disruption, and transformation. It is, then, not by chance that the central novels in the nineteenth-century tradition produced a powerfully urban model of history. Nor is it an accident that so much of the debate over the novel as a genre should take place among French critics and about French novels, in which that model carries such intensity.

Much is made of the disruptive force of modernity and of the instability that, at least since Baudelaire, is taken as its essential feature. Analyzing and dramatizing both the social forces that produce the condition and the condition itself preoccupied writers and intellectuals of every persuasion throughout the century—from the "mal du siècle" diagnosed by Chateaubriand to the "bovaryisme" dramatized by Flaubert to the deracinement attacked by Barrès and the anomie diagnosed by Durkheim. Each interpretation, even as it accepted the universe of perpetual motion, offered meaning and stability of a sort, however illusory stasis inevitably turned out to be.

As one would expect, the exhaustion of revolution as an organizing scheme for conceptions of the city coincided with the advent of other models of interpretation. By the end of the century, urban narratives began to work through other elective affinities as literature engaged the city on other terms. Paris splintered into many cities, and revolutionary Paris dissolved into any number of images. The literature of the twentieth century moved elsewhere, and decisively inward. Writers took their inspiration from the many new cities and their myths—the idealized urban landscape of the Impressionists, the Gay Paree of cabarets, the intellectual's city of university and academies, the Paris of art studios and galleries and cafés that drew writers and artists from all over the world, and the greatest of the literary cities of the Belle Époque, the Paris of Proust filtered through the lens of memory. The Paris of the Eiffel Tower and the World's Fair of 1889 did not celebrate revolution but rather the centennial of 1789. The republican present sought to assimilate the turbulent insurrectionary tradition by removing it safely to an increasingly remote past.

Each of these new cities at the end of the century forged its own myths and lived off its own legends. But none of them depended, as before, on the totality of conception inherent in revolution. No modern author claimed the city as Balzac, Hugo and Flaubert, and Vallès and Zola once claimed it. The reconceptualization of the city brought new practices of urban space and new visions of revolution. The revolutionary tradition that Zola invoked so dramatically during the Dreyfus affair has no privileged space in the twentieth century. It is, rather, a sensibility, a consciousness, a set of abstract principles. The modern intellectual that Zola put into circulation does not write from or identify with a special place. No urban icon, no urban narrative can contain the principles of right and justice that guide the intellectual. Henceforth the intellectual who claims to speak for humanity does so disengaged from the particulars of time and place as a relatively disembodied figure.

For the century before, the interpretation of meaning meant Paris, and Paris arranged itself around revolution—revolution in its streets and revolution in its narratives. Making sense of the one always entailed making sense of the other. Indeed, the great works of this city and this time centered on that interaction and invariably reached for some larger form of integration. Over and over again, writers turned to place within a narrative of revolution to fix but also to convey the meaning of change in that movement. Paris was the subject; revolution, the inevitable theme.

By the end of the century, the virtuoso metaphor that served the urban imagination so long and so well served no longer. The cityscape disaggregated, and the bird's-eye view revealed not overall design but fragmentary scenes of almost unimaginable diversity. Zola's *Paris* made one final attempt to comprehend the city as a whole, but the knowledge came at a great price. This final Paris dissolved into a utopian vision of the future with little connection to the dynamic, revolutionary, and eminently visible cities of Hugo, Flaubert, Vallès, and even the young Zola. Like Zola in the articles on the Dreyfus affair, the intellectual of the twentieth century sees largely within the mind's eye.

Of course, Paris does not disappear from literature. On the contrary, in some senses the city is never more present. But, somewhere, early on, the twentieth century loses both the certainty that Paris can be known and the conviction that revolution holds the key to that knowledge. Writing the twentieth-century city implies different urban practices, entails very different strategies, and works with different symbols. Louis Aragon's marvelous *Le Paysan de Paris* (*The Peasant of*

Paris) (1921), by way of example, takes on the city but in a decidedly surrealistic mode. Aragon works off the fragments of a public discourse (the signs and the advertisements in the Passage de l'Opéra, which he reproduces in loving detail), but he does not suppose any global coherence, much less one with revolutionary connotations.

The real coda to the myth of Paris comes with Raymond Queneau's *Zazie dans le métro* (1959). During the whirlwind Paris visit of Zazie, an inordinately precocious girl of eleven or twelve, even the most inveterate of her Parisian guides—a taxi driver—is never altogether sure whether he is looking at the Sacré-Coeur or the Invalides or the Panthéon (they all have domes), and there is always a sneaking suspicion that the building in question just might be the Gare de Lyon. Queneau's spoof of the modern guided tour to Paris also parodies the whole literary tradition of urban exploration. This *Paris-Guide,* or antiguide, for the twentieth century systematically effaces the historical and topographical differences crucial to the sense of history that informs the great urban narratives of the nineteenth century. At the same time, as parody, *Zazie* presupposes that history, that topography, and that tradition. The humor depends on the reader knowing that the monuments are from very different historical eras and are located in quite different parts of Paris. It also depends on catching the connections to Hugo's epic *Les Misérables* when Zazie is rescued from the police by her uncle's transvestite lover, who carries her through a sewer into the métro to the train station. For Hugo's christological Jean Valjean, who carries the wounded Marius through the sewers to his home in the city, Queneau gives us a complicated figure of uncertain meaning who takes Zazie out of, not into, the city.

Even the view from the top of the Eiffel Tower fails to make anything clearer since the only construction identifiable with certainty is the part of the subway that goes above ground. But that, as Zazie has already observed, is not the real métro. And the point is, obviously, that, because the métro is on strike, Zazie never gets to see the only thing that interests her in all Paris. In the one short trip that she actually takes on the métro, she faints and sees nothing.

Only the surfaces attract in *Zazie.* The depths of place have no meaning, no lessons to impart. The métro like the metropolis itself remains forever out of reach. Queneau explicitly refuses the mastery of the bird's-eye view and rejects the knowledge of the encompassing metaphor. We who live in the city are condemned and, like Zazie, live without knowledge. What has she done, her mother asks on the train home, if she hasn't seen the métro? "I've aged," replies Zazie in the emblematic last line of the book, one that utterly resists the implicit notion of renewal in a revolutionary construct.

The coherence of the new, modern city derives from singular, private experience, from Queneau's fantasy that plays on even as it disavows the sense of the city as a whole. The faith that gave such assurance to the writers of the revolutionary tradition becomes just one more urban practice. Queneau celebrates not Paris but the absence of Paris. Finally, it makes no difference whether we are looking at Sacré-Coeur or the Invalides or the Panthéon. Gone are the time-space and especially the dream-time that made it possible to write the nineteenth-century city. Dreams, though, have a way of recurring, and they also have a life of their own.

Notes

PROLOGUE

1. It is useful, and enlightening, to follow the varying fortunes of the term *revolution*. See Alain Rey, «*Révolution*»—*Histoire d'un mot* (Paris: Gallimard, 1989). The strength of this work lies in its insistence on chronological development of usages and at the same time the intermingling of different usages, even within the same sentence, moving between the Revolution as a unique historical event and revolution as a sociopolitical concept with cyclical overtones.

2. "La littérature est l'expression de la société comme la parole est l'expression de l'homme." Louis de Bonald, *Législation primitive* (Paris: Le-Clere, An XI [1802]), 2:207. The phrase originally appeared in an article in the *Mercure de France*, no. 41 (An X [1802]), and was appended as a footnote to the later work.

3. Compare the contrast drawn by Claude Lévi-Strauss between cities of the Old World, which are objects of contemplation and reflection, with those of the Americas, which never accede to this status. *Tristes Tropiques* (Paris: Plon, 1958), 106–8. The Revolution is certainly a primal factor in the constitution of Paris as an object of philosophical and cultural as well as economic and political speculation.

4. The chronotope renders Time "artistically visible" and, conversely, invests Space with "the movements of time, plot and history." M. M. Bakhtin, "Forms of Time and of the Chronotope in the Novel—Notes toward a Historical Poetics," in *The Dialogic Imagination*, trans. C. Emerson and M. Holquist (Austin: University of Texas Press, 1981), 84. The extension of "chronotope" to as polysemic a phenomenon as revolution is consistent with Bakhtin's own wide-ranging use of the concept. See Henri Mitterand's analysis of the varying levels of specificity of the chronotope in "Chronotopies: La Route et la mine," in *Zola—L'Histoire et la fiction* (Paris: Presses Universitaires de France, 1990), esp. 179–95.

5. "Le XIXe siècle, un espace de temps <*Zeitraum*> (un rêve de temps, <*Zeit-traum*>), dans lequel la conscience individuelle se maintient de plus en plus dans la réflexion, tandis que la conscience collective s'enfonce dans un sommeil toujours plus profond." Walter Benjamin, *Paris, Capitale du XIXe siècle*, trans. Jean Lacoste (Paris: Éditions du Cerf, 1993), 406 (K 1, 4).

6. This is Bernard Marchand's characterization of the serial novel of the 1840s. *Paris: Histoire d'une ville XIXe–XXe siècle* (Paris: Seuil, 1993), 62. This

work is indispensable for anyone concerned with modern Paris and its usually chaotic, often conflictual relationship to the country and especially to the state.

7. Michel de Certeau elaborates the parallel in *L'Invention du quotidien* (Paris: UGE-10/18, 1974). Translated by Steven Rendell, under the title *The Practice of Everyday Life* (Berkeley: University of California Press, 1984). See, in particular, chapter 8, "Marches dans la ville." The readings of urban and literary texts in the chapters draw on de Certeau's conception of the city as the locus of divergent and even conflictual urban and textual practices.

8. "Les croyances sociales ... ont un double caractère. Ce sont des traditions ou des souvenirs collectifs, mais ce sont aussi des idées ou des conventions qui résultent de la connaissance du présent. ... D'où il résulte que la pensée sociale est essentiellement une mémoire, et que tout son contenu n'est fait que de souvenirs collectifs, mais que ceux-là seuls parmi eux et cela seul de chacun d'eux subsiste qu'à toute époque la société, travaillant sur ses cadres actuels, peut reconstruire." Maurice Halbwachs, *Les Cadres sociaux de la mémoire* (Paris: Presses Universitaires de France, 1952), 295–96. See also Halbwachs, *On Collective Memory*, trans. Lewis A. Coser (Chicago: University of Chicago Press, 1992), 188–89. The urban narratives of nineteenth-century Paris made possible just the sort of reconstruction that Halbwachs had in mind, although he does not discuss literature.

9. In the insistence on the knowability of the city, I part company with the rich analyses of Christopher Prendergast in *Paris and the Nineteenth Century* (Oxford and Cambridge, Mass.: Blackwell, 1992). Writing from a perspective informed by the work of Raymond Williams, Prendergast focuses on the resistance to as well as the construction of dominant ideological representations of Paris and is greatly concerned with the discrepancy between these representations and actual life in the city. See, in particular, chapter 1, "Parisian Identities." For Prendergast the very possibility of knowledge of the city is problematic.

10. One of the most interesting of recent works is Sandy Petrey, *Realism and Revolution: Balzac, Stendhal, Zola, and the Performances of History* (Ithaca: Cornell University Press, 1988). Working from the speech-act framework of J. L. Austin, Petrey argues that realist fiction "performs" the Revolution rather than "reflecting" the world produced by a neatly identifiable series of events. This performative quality, which Petrey analyzes to great effect in close readings of individual texts, turns realist fiction into an active participant in history, not the passive recorder constructed by several generations of critics.

11. When asked by the king to justify the choice of Rouen over Paris as the first city of France, the emperor allegedly maintained that Paris was a great country unto itself and later, in Paris, made the celebrated proclamation "non urbs, sed orbis." The frequency of the image made it a cliché before the end of the sixteenth century. See Jean-Pierre Babelon, *Paris au XVIᵉ siècle* (Paris: Hachette, 1986), 15–35 (quotation on p. 28).

CHAPTER 1

1. Walter Benjamin argues that the naming of things completed the work of God and constituted, therefore, the very sign of human existence. "On Language as Such and on the Language of Man," in *Reflections,* ed. Peter Demetz, trans. Edmond Jephcott (New York: Harcourt Brace Jovanovich, 1978), 314–32.

2. "Die Stadt hat—was sonst nur den wenigsten Worten zugänglich war; einer privilegierten Klasse von Worten—, oder doch einer grossen Menge möglich gemacht: in den Adelsstand des Namens erhoben zu werden. Diese Revolution der Sprache wurde vom Allergemeinsten, der Strasse, vollzogen.— Die Stadt ist durch die Strassennamen ein sprachlicher Kosmos." (Die Strassen von Paris) (P 3,5) in Walter Benjamin, *Das Passagen-Werk,* ed. Rolf Tiedemann, in *Gesammelte Schriften,* ed. Rolf Tiedemann and Hermann Scheppenhauser (Frankfurt am Main: Suhrkamp, 1972–89), 5:650; Benjamin, *Paris, Capitale du XIXᵉ siècle,* trans. Jean Lacoste (Paris: Éditions du Cerf, 1993), 539.

3. "Guillot, qui a fait maint bias dis / Dit qu'il n'y a que trois cent et dix / Rues a Paris vraiement." There were more, but Guillot did not bother with cul-de-sacs: "Les autres rues ai mis hors / De sa rime, puisqu'ils n'ont chief." Guillot, *Le Dit des rues de Paris,* reproduced in Émile de Labédollière, *Le Nouveau Paris* (Paris: Barba, 1860), 437–40. See also Jean-Pierre Leguay, *La Rue au Moyen Age* (Rennes: Éditions Ouest-France, 1984).

4. Guillebert de Metz (1407–34) offers the explanation that "a la croix du Triouer se trioient les bestes; et pour ce, a proprement parler, est elle appellée la Croix du Triouer pour les bestes que len y tiroit. Au carrefour Guillori estoit le pillori ou len coppoit les oreilles; et pour ce, a proprement parler, il est appellé le carrefour Guigne oreille. . . ." Les Planches de Mibray is, "a proprement parler, les Planches de Mibras; car cestoit la moitié du bras de Sainne." Guillebert de Metz, *Description de la Ville de Paris,* cited in Antoine Leroux de Lincy and L. M. Tisserand, *Paris et ses historiens aux XIVᵉ et XVᵉ siècles* (Paris: Imprimerie Impériale, 1867), 138–39. I am indebted to Jody Enders for this reference.

5. The concept of "sacred geography" was developed by Robert Redfield, "The Culture of Cities," in *Human Nature and the Study of Society* (Chicago: The University of Chicago Press, 1962), 1:326–50. For "landscape of power," see the discussion of Sharon Zukin, *Landscapes of Power* (Berkeley: University of California Press, 1991), chap. 1.

6. "Très Chers et bien amez, pour ce que nostre intention est de doresnavant faire la plus part de nostre demeure et séjour en nostre bonne ville et cité de Paris et alentour plus qu'en aultre lieu du royaulme; cognoissant nostre chastel du Louvre estre ce lieu plus commode et à propos pour nous loger; à ceste cause, avons délibéré faire réparer et mettre en ordre ledict chastel. . . ." François I, letter to the municipality, 15 March 1528, quoted by Jean-Pierre Babelon, *Paris au XVIᵉ siècle* (Paris: Hachette, 1986), 45. See also the discussion on pp. 45–55.

7. "On verra à la place de la nouvelle salle de la comédie françoise les rues de *Corneille,* de *Racine,* de *Molière,* de *Voltaire,* de *Crébillon,* de *Regnard;* ce qui scandalisera d'abord les échevins (il faut s'y attendre) comme en possession de donner seuls leurs illustres noms à des rues. Mais peu à peu, ils s'accoutumeront à cette innovation, & à regarder Corneille, Molière & Voltaire, comme les compagnons de leur gloire. Enfin, la rue *Racine* figurera à côte de la rue *Babille,* sans trop étonner les quarteniers, les dizeniers et autres officiers de l'hôtel-de-ville." Louis-Sébastien Mercier, "Les Ecriteaux des rues," in *Tableau de Paris,* 12 vols (Amsterdam, 1782–88), 2:202–3.

8. See Paul Lacroix, "La Porte et Place de France sous le règne de Henri IV," *Gazette des Beaux-Arts* (1870), 12ᵉ année, 2ᵉ période, Vol. 3, 561–66. Lacroix does little more than string together a series of (incorrectly cited) quotations from Auguste Poirson, *Histoire du règne de Henri IV* (Paris: Didier, 1866), 3:720–23 and 4:518–19; and Henri Sauval, *Histoire et recherche des antiquités de la ville de Paris* (Paris: C. Moette, 1724), 1:632. The quotations are from Poirson, *Histoire* 3:720–21. See also Hilary Ballon, *The Paris of Henri IV: Architecture and Urbanism* (Cambridge, Mass.: MIT Press, 1991), 202–3. Ballon gives an illuminating analysis of the maps of Paris published in this same period as a parallel symbolization of the royal landscape of power in chapter 6, "The Image of Paris: Maps, City Views, and the New Historical Focus."

9. "Bon Dieu! quel genre d'esprit préside donc à la dénomination de toutes ces rues? Ne diroit-on pas que c'est toujours le même qui fut parrain des rues du *Pet du Diable,* des *Rats,* du *Foin,* des *Marmouzets,* de celles de *Pierre-au-lard* ou *Jean-pain-mollet?...* Les noms obscènes, quoique défigurés, de la plupart de nos anciennes rues, attestent la turpitude de nos ancêtres." Mercier, "Marivaux," *Tableau de Paris* 11:243–44.

10. J. B. Pujoulx, *Paris à la fin du XVIIIᵉ siècle ou esquisse historique et morale des monumens et des ruines de cette capitale; de l'état des sciences, des arts et de l'industrie à cette époque, ainsi que des moeurs et des ridicules de ses habitans* (Paris: Mathé, 1801). My discussion here and below quotes from chap. 19, "Noms des rues," pp. 73–76, and chap. 20, "Projet sur les dénominations à donner aux rues de Paris," pp. 77–83.

11. Paris was not alone in cleaning up its streets. In 1797 the residents of Cow Lane in Boston petitioned for the name of their street to be changed to High Street (just as the Dominicans had replaced their cows with Saint Dominique); in the early nineteenth century Maidenhead, New Jersey, changed its name to Lawrenceville, Staten Island eliminated its Cuckold Town section, and Copenhagen replaced Skidenstraede (Filthy Street) with Krystalgade. See George R. Stewart, *Names on the Land,* 3d ed. (Boston: Houghton Mifflin, 1967), 242–43; and Bent Jørgensen, *Dansk Gadenavneskik* (København: Akademisk Forlag, 1970), chap. 12 (English summary, pp. 213–15).

12. "Ainsi ces anciennes cités ... sont ordinairement si mal compassées au prix de ces places régulières qu'un ingénieur trace à sa fantaisie dans une plaine ...; toutefois, à voir comme [les édifices] sont arrangés, ici un grand, là un petit, et comme ils rendent les rues courbées et inégales, on dirait que

c'est plutôt la fortune, que la volonté de quelques hommes usant de raison, qui les a ainsi disposés." Descartes, *Discours de la méthode* (1637), in *Oeuvres philosophiques,* ed. F. Alquié (Paris: Garnier, 1963), 1:579–80.

13. "A peine dans toute cette multitude de rues . . . en voyez-vous une qui rappelle un nom cher à la nation? Vous chercheriez en vain ceux de Duguesclin, de Turenne, d'Amboise, de Sully? Croit-on que les noms de La Fontaine, de Massillon, de Fénélon [sic] & de tant d'autres ne rappelleroient pas des idées bien plus gracieuses & se fixeroient pas bien autrement dans la mémoire que celui de *Croulebarbe?*" Mercier, "Marivaux," *Tableau de Paris* 11:244. On cultural changes, see Serge Bianchi, *La Révolution culturelle de l'an II: Élites et peuple, 1789–1799* (Paris: Aubier, 1982), 214–36.

14. Villette's letter of April 1791 to the Jacobin Club is cited in full by Paul Lacombe, *Les Noms des rues de Paris sous la Révolution* (Nantes: Imprimerie Vincent Forest & Emile Grimaud, 1886), 9. See also Jules Cousin, "De la nomenclature des rues de Paris," in *Mémoires de la Société de l'histoire de Paris* (1899), 26:8; and Daniel Milo, "Le Nom des rues," in *Les Lieux de mémoire: La Nation,* ed. Pierre Nora (Paris: Gallimard, 1986), 3:292–301. Milo situates the great wave of debaptisms between 1792 and 1794, followed, after the fall of Robespierre in July 1794, by general apathy and the collapse of the national system, especially in the provinces.

15. Abbé Grégoire, *Système de dénominations topographiques pour les places, rues, quais, etc. de toutes les communes de la République* (1794), 3.

16. Citoyen Avril, *Rapport au conseil général de la commune de Paris, sur quelques mesures à prendre en changeant les noms des rues* (Paris: Printed for the Comité de l'Instruction publique, 1793), 1–4. The speech of E. Chamouleau is reported by Lacombe in *Les Noms des rues de Paris sous la Révolution,* p. 16. The abbé Grégoire, *Système de dénominations topographiques,* p. 26, n. 24, refers to the brochure, *Plan pour la régénération des moeurs en France,* by Citoyen Chamoulaud. (Prior to the nineteenth century spelling was highly variable.)

17. Preceding citations taken from Grégoire, *Système de dénominations topographiques,* 10, 14, 4, 10, 14.

18. "Et si on considère qu'il y a eu néanmoins de tout temps quelques officiers, qui ont eu charge de prendre garde aux bâtiments des particuliers, pour les faire servir à l'ornement du public, on connaîtra bien qu'il est malaisé, en ne travaillant que sur les ouvrages d'autrui, de faire des choses fort accomplies." Descartes, *Discours de la méthode,* in *Oeuvres,* 580.

19. Until recently, American cities seldom accorded first names even for "people" streets, and those American cities that have begun to employ full names rarely include titles. See my article, "Reading the City," *The French Review* 61 (February 1988): 386–97.

20. Thomas Jefferson to Benjamin Rush, 23 September 1800, *The Writings of Thomas Jefferson,* ed. Andrew Lipscomb and Albert E. Bergh (Washington D.C.: The Thomas Jefferson Memorial Association, 1905), 10:173–74.

21. "Description of the City of Washington," *A Spectator, The Maryland Journal,* 30 September 1791, and *Gazette of the United States,* 8 October 1791,

quoted in "Editorial Note," in *The Papers of Thomas Jefferson*, ed. Julian P. Boyd (Princeton: Princeton University Press, 1982), 20:53.

22. *Essai sur la Ville de Washington par un Citoyen des États-Unis* (New York: J. Delafond, 1795); and William Howard Taft, "Washington: Its Beginning, Its Growth, and Its Future," *National Geographic Magazine* 27 (March 1915): 221–92. See also Edwin Melvin Williams, "The L'Enfant Plan of 1791," in *Washington Past and Present: A History*, ed. John Clagett Proctor (New York: Lewis Historical Publishing Co., 1930), 46. The quote from L'Enfant below is taken from Williams, *Washington Past and Present*, 46.

CHAPTER 2

1. Abbé Edgeworth Firmin (the king's confessor), *Histoire de la captivité de Louis XVI et de la famille royale* (Paris: I.G. Michaud, 1817), 222; and Jean-Louis Soulavie, *Mémoires historiques et politiques du règne de Louis XVI* (Paris: Treuttel et Würtz, 1801), 6:517–18. For an exceptionally interesting reading of the primordial role of patriarchy in the Revolution, see Lynn Hunt, *The Family Romance of the French Revolution* (Berkeley: University of California Press, 1992).

2. The following discussion cites from Gilles Corrozet, *La Fleur des antiquitez de Paris* [the second edition of 1533] (Paris: Aux Editions de l'Ibis, 1945) and Gilles Corrozet, *Les Antiquitez, histoires, croniques et singularitez de la grande & excellente cité de Paris, ville capitalle & chef du Royaume de France: Avec les fondations & bastimens des lieux: Les Sepulchres & Epitaphes des princes, princesses & autres personnes illustres* (Paris: Nicolas Bonfons, 1577) (Bonfons added considerable material to the original edition of 1550). See also the meticulous research of M. Dumolin, "Notes sur les vieux guides de Paris," in *Mémoires de la Société de l'histoire de Paris et de l'Ile de France* 47 (1924): 209–85; and Paul Lacombe, *Bibliographie parisienne—Tableaux de moeurs, 1600–1880* (Paris: P. Roquette, 1887).

3. Germain Brice, *Description de la Ville de Paris, et de tout ce qu'elle contient de plus remarquable* (9th ed., 1752; reprint, Geneva-Paris: Droz-Minard, 1971), 20.

4. Jèze, *Tableau de Paris* (Paris: Chez C. Herissant, 1759). The interminable subtitle conveys the author's pretensions, which both work from and aim beyond extant models: *Formé d'après les antiquités, l'histoire, la description de cette ville, & c. contenant un calendrier civil; le précis de l'histoire de cette ville, un état abrégé du ministère: les noms, les demeures & les districts de tous les premiers commis des quatre secrétaires d'état, du lieutenant général de Police, du prévôt des marchands, du controlleur général et des intendans des finances. Le gouvernement, les divers établissemens pour les sciences & arts libéraux: la demeure des maîtres dans les langues, sciences, & ce. Les spectacles, les cabinets de tableaux, d'histoire naturelle, & autres curiosités: les manufactures, la compagnie des Indes, la bourse & la définition des principaux effets qui s'y négocient, & c.* The 1760 *État ou Tableau de la Ville de Paris considérée relativement au nécessaire, à l'utile, à l'agréable & à l'administration* (Paris: Chex Prault, 1760) has much of the same material, but the material

is subjected to far greater systematization. See also Michel Delon, "Piétons de Paris," in *Paris le jour, Paris la nuit* (Paris: Laffont, 1990), i–xxiv.

5. P.-J.-B. Nougaret, *Paris, ou le rideau levé. Anecdotes singulières, bizarres et sentimentales. Pour servir à l'histoire de nos moeurs anciennes et nouvelles; avec des faits qui n'avaient point encore été publiés* (Paris: 1799); J. B. Pujoulx, *Paris à la fin du XVIIIe siècle ou esquisse historique et morale des monumens et des ruines de cette capitale; de l'état des sciences, des arts et de l'industrie à cette époque, ainsi que des moeurs et des ridicules de ses habitans* (Paris: Mathé, 1801); Louis Prudhomme, *Voyage descriptif et philosophique de l'ancien et du nouveau Paris. Miroir fidèle qui indique aux étrangers et même aux Parisiens ce qu'ils doivent connoître et éviter dans cette capitale; contenant des faits historiques et anecdotes curieuses sur les monumens et sur la variation des moeurs de ses habitans depuis vingt-cinq ans . . .* (Paris: Chez l'auteur, 1814).

6. References to Mercier in the text can be found in the selections in Delon, *Paris le jour, Paris la nuit.* The volume numbers and chapter titles in the text refer to the complete edition of Mercier, *Tableau de Paris,* 12 vols. (Amsterdam, 1782–1788).

After the Revolution, Mercier returned to the genre that he had himself defined. *Le Nouveau Paris* in 1798 has less to do with customs than with politics and is a decided disappointment after the *Tableau.* Such is also the assessment of a rival, J. B. Pujoulx (*Paris à la fin du XVIIIe siècle*), 2, who contrasts his own independence with Mercier's political role during the Revolution. In Pujoulx's view, Mercier's political role makes *Le Nouveau Paris* the work of a political historian rather than that of a man of letters.

7. The scope of his enterprise set Mercier apart from Restif de la Bretonne, whose *Les Nuits de Paris* appeared the same year as Mercier's final edition of his *Tableau.* Mercier greatly admired Restif (to whose novel *Le Paysan perverti* the *Tableau* devotes its chapter 3). As Alexandre Dumas put it in one of his novels, "les deux amis s'étaient partagé le cadran: l'un avait pris le jour, et c'était Mercier; l'autre avait pris la nuit, et c'était Restif de La Bretonne." Dumas, *Ingénue,* cited as epigraph to Delon, *Paris le jour, Paris la nuit.*

8. "Ce qui n'est pas clair n'est pas français . . . Ce qui n'est pas clair est encore anglais, italien, grec ou latin." Antoine Rivarol, *De l'universalité de la langue française* (Paris: Cocheris, 1791), 40. On Mercier's *Tableau,* "un ouvrage pensé dans la rue et écrit sur la borne; l'auteur a peint la cave et le grenier en sautant le salon." Rivarol quoted by Jeffry Kaplow, "Introduction," *Le Tableau de Paris* (Paris: Maspero, 1979), 10.

9. Victor-Joseph Étienne, known as Étienne de Jouy, 1764–1846, is best known to posterity as the author of the libretti for Rossini's *Guillaume Tell* and *Moïse.* These represented a tiny bit of the literary and journalistic output of a writer, and member of the Académie française, whose *Oeuvres complètes,* published in 1828, ran to twenty-seven volumes. *L'Hermite de la Chaussée d'Antin* appeared in the *Gazette de France* from August 1811 to April 1814 and was published in five volumes between 1812 and 1814. *Guillaume le Franc-Parleur* took up where the *Hermite de la Chaussée d'Antin* left off (Jouy kills off the first

Hermit)—again in the *Gazette de France,* from May 1814 to July 1815—and was published in two volumes in 1815 (and immediately translated as *Paris chit-chat*). So successful was the formula that other Hermits followed: the Hermite de la Guiane arrives in France from Guyana in July 1815, just after the battle of Waterloo, to find France topsy-turvy. *L'Hermite de la Guiane* (3 vols., 1816–17) was followed by *L'Hermite en province* (14 vols., 1818–27), *Les Hermites en prison* (2 vols., 1823, which may not be by Jouy), and *Les Hermites en liberté* (2 vols., 1824). The success can be judged by the number of imitations, including *L'Ermite du faubourg St-Honoré* (1814), a violent diatribe against Jouy; *L'Hermite de la Chaussée du Maine* (1819); *L'Hermite du Marais, ou le rentier observateur* (1819); *L'Hermite rodeur* (1824); and *L'Hermite du faubourg St-Germain* (1825).

Quotations below for l'Hermite de la Chaussée d'Antin are from *L'Hermite de la Chaussée d'Antin* (Paris: Pillet, 1815), 2:111, and for Guillaume le Franc-Parleur, from *Guillaume le Franc-Parleur ou observations sur les moeurs et les usages parisiens au commencement du XIXe siècle,* 3d ed. (Paris: Pillet, 1815), 1:1, 1:86, 1:11.

10. Théophile Gautier, in *Paris et les parisiens au XIXe siècle—Moeurs, arts, et monuments* (Paris: Morizot, [1856]), i. This is also the subtitle of two other works that overlapped considerably, *Le Tiroir du diable* (Paris: [1845]) and *Le Diable à Paris: Paris et les Parisiens* (Paris: Marescq-Havard, 1853). *Paris, ou le livre des cent-et-un,* 15 vols. (Paris: Ladvocat, 1832–34). The most extensive collection remains *Les Français peints par eux-mêmes,* 9 vols. (Paris: L. Curmer, 1840–42).

11. Benjamin, "Paris, Capitale du XIXe siècle" (originally written in French in 1939), in *Gesammelte Schriften,* ed. Rolf Tiedemann and Hermann Scheppenhauser (Frankfurt am Main: Suhrkamp, 1972–89), 5:60. The German version of 1935 is found in *Reflections,* trans. Edmond Jephcott (New York: Harcourt Brace Jovanovich, 1978). On the *physiologies,* see Richard Sieburth, "Une Idéologie du lisible: Le Phénomène des physiologies," *Romantisme* 47 (1985): 39–60; and *Les Français peints par eux-mêmes,* in *Panorama social du XIXe siècle,* ed. Ségonène Le Men and Luce Abélès (Paris: Réunion des Musées nationaux, 1993). For a detailed (but probably not exhaustive) listing of *physiologies,* see Lacombe, *Bibliographie parisienne,* 112–57.

12. "Au Public," *Paris, ou le livre des cent-et-un* (Paris, Ladvocat, 1831), vi.

13. Jules Janin, "Asmodée," *Paris, ou le livre des cent-et-un* (Bruxelles: Louis Hauman, 1831), 1:29 (also for the quotation in the following paragraph).

14. Jules Janin, "Introduction," *Les Français peints par eux-mêmes* (Paris: L. Curmer, 1843), 1:vi; and for the citation in the next paragraph, 1:ix.

15. Philippe Hamon identifies this transformation from *description* (lists) to *tableau* (presupposes an order) as a primary problem in the construction of especially realistic narrative. *Introduction à l'analyse du descriptif* (Paris: Hachette, 1981), 183.

16. Pierre Citron locates the transformation from theme to myth in just this tendency to conceive of Paris as a whole. *La Poésie de Paris de Rousseau à Baudelaire* (Paris: Éditions de Minuit, 1961), 2:249–63.

17. H. Temple Patterson argues for Hugo's mostly unacknowledged use of the *Tableau de Paris. Poetic Genesis: Sébastien Mercier into Victor Hugo,* vol. 11 of *Studies on Voltaire and the Eighteenth Century* (Geneva, 1960). *Cf.* Mercier, *Tableau de Paris* ("Physionomie de la grande ville" [1] and "A vue d'oiseau" [11]); and Mercier, "La ville de Paris en relief," *Le Nouveau Paris* (vol. 4, chap. 120), in Delon, *Paris le jour, Paris la nuit,* 440–49. The striking connections between Mercier and Balzac have not been explored in the depth and detail they warrant.

On the illusion of power fostered by these views from above, see Michel de Certeau's discussion of the view from the World Trade Center in *The Practice of Everyday Life* (Berkeley: University of California Press, 1984), chap. 7.

18. Père-Lachaise opened in 1804 and by the 1820s was a favorite promenade. On Parisian panoramas, see Citron, *La Poésie de Paris* 1:387–95. The top three in his sample are Notre-Dame, Père-Lachaise, and Montmartre, the latter especially after 1848. Walter Benjamin points to "Das panoramatische Prinzip bei Balzac," *Das Passagen-Werk,* in *Gesammelte Schriften* 5:63 (Q4,1). See also Jeannine Guichardet's discussion in *Balzac «Archéologue de Paris»* (Paris: SEDES, 1986), 321–27. Other Balzacian panoramas include *Les Proscrits* (1831); *La Femme de trente ans* (1831), the beginning of pt. 4; and *L'Envers de l'histoire contemporaine* (1842–44), where the topographical panorama gives rise to a historical one.

19. Christopher Prendergast takes Hugo's introduction to *Paris-Guide* as symptomatic of the meshing of republican and imperial images in a glorification of a city that obscures when it does not altogether deny omnipresent political conflict. Looking through the lenses of Raymond Williams and Walter Benjamin, Prendergast writes in order to read that conflict back into the city text. *Paris and the Nineteenth Century* (Oxford and Cambridge, MA: Blackwell, 1992), 7–9. See also the discussion of Hugo's "politics of transcendence" in chapter 5 below.

20. *Paris-Guide par les principaux écrivains et artistes de la France* (Paris: Librairie Internationale, 1867), xxxiv. Further references to this edition will be cited in the text by page number. Contributors to the first, more institutionally oriented volume devoted to *La Science* and *L'Art* include Louis Blanc ("Le Vieux Paris"), Renan ("L'Institut"), Sainte-Beuve ("L'Académie française"), Bertholot ("L'Académie des Sciences"), Littré ("La Médecine à Paris"), Michelet ("Le Collège de France"), A. Firmin-Didot ("L'Imprimerie à Paris"), Gautier ("Le Musée du Louvre"), Edgar Quinet ("Le Panthéon"), Viollet-le-Duc ("Les Églises de Paris"), Dumas *fils* ("Les Premières Représentations"), Dumas *père* ("L'École des Beaux-Arts"), and Taine ("L'Art en France"). The second volume, *La Vie,* is at once more sociological (with sections titled "Physiologie de Paris" and "Les Étrangers à Paris") and more practical, with sections on food supplies, underground Paris (water and gas), the administration, cemeteries, and the morgue. *Paris-Guide* thus combines the sketches of the earlier literary guides, the historical and official descriptions with the information on current institutions, although it does not give practical information about hotels, museums, and such. To return to my ear-

lier distinction, *Paris-Guide* is a *guide,* not a *conductor.* The introduction was also published separately (1867). See Hugo, *Oeuvres complètes,* ed. Jean-Claude Fizaine (Paris: Laffont, 1985), 10:3–43.

21. The list comes from Pierre Citron's "Index-Catalogue des images relevées des origines à 1862," in *La Poésie de Paris* 2:408–44.

22. References in the text will be page numbers for Jules Vallès, *Le Tableau de Paris* (Paris: Messidor, 1989) (a reprint of the edition of 1971 published by Editeurs Français Réunis).

CHAPTER 3

1. Benjamin's fullest discussion is found in "Le Flâneur" (1939), a chapter of his unfinished *Paris du Second Empire chez Baudelaire,* which was to have itself been part of a larger work, *Charles Baudelaire: Ein Lyriker im Zeitalter des Hochkapitalismus,* ed. Rolf Tiedemann (Frankfurt am Main: Suhrkamp, 1974). The Baudelaire dossier is found in *Gesammelte Schriften,* ed. Rolf Tiedemann and Hermann Scheppenhauser (Frankfurt am Main: Suhrkamp, 1972–89), bk. 1, vol. 3. See the edition by Jean Lacoste, *Charles Baudelaire: Un Poète lyrique à l'apogée du capitalisme* (Paris: Payot, 1982), which has Benjamin's own notes, full references to the works of Baudelaire cited or mentioned by Benjamin, and excellent explanatory notes by Lacoste (the last two missing in the English translation). See also "Le Flâneur" (M), in the translation of the *Das Passagen-Werk, Paris, Capitale du XIXe siècle,* trans. Jean Lacoste (Paris: Éditions du Cerf, 1993), 434–72.

2. The first recorded usage dates from 1585 in Touraine. The Norman *flanner* deriving from old Scandinavian *flana* ("courir étourdiment ça et là") appears in 1645. Oscar Bloch and Walther Von Wartburg, *Dictionnaire étymologique de la langue française,* 6th ed. (Paris: Presses Universitaires de France, 1975), 265.

For 1808: "*flaner*—Rôder sans motif de côté et d'autre; fainéantiser; mener une vie errante et vagabonde; *Flaneur: Un grand flaneur*—Pour dire un grand paresseux; fainéant, homme d'une oisiveté insupportable, qui ne sait où promener son importunité et son ennui." D'Hautel, *Dictionnaire du bas-langage ou des manières de parler usitées parmi le peuple,* 2 vols. (Paris, 1808; reprint Geneva: Slatkine Reprints, 1972). Dictionaries (*Le Grand Robert de la langue française, Trésor de la langue française,* 1980) misquote D'Hautel's definitions, giving the later rather than the earlier definition and not noting the absence of the circumflex. No account is taken of the 1806 pamphlet or the 1824–26 guidebooks by Aldéguier that I discuss below.

Flâner, flâneur, and *flânerie* are not accepted by the *Dictionnaire de l'Académie française* until the seventh edition (1878), and then with the warning that these terms are colloquial (*familier*). *Flâneur* as an adjective is attributed to Jules Janin (1829); as a noun to Balzac's *Physiologie du mariage* (1826) (see discussion below).

3. The works discussed in this section of the text are noted below in chronological order.

Le Flâneur au salon ou Mr Bon-Homme: Examen joyeux des tableaux, mêlé de Vaudevilles (Paris: Chez M. Aubry, 1806). The date can be determined by internal evidence (it is also penciled in the copy in the Bibliothèque Nationale). M. Bonhomme witnesses the laying of the foundation at the Étoile of the monument for the heroes of Austerlitz (the battle was in December 1805; work on the Arc de Triomphe began in 1806) and discusses paintings exhibited in the previous and the current Expositions, which are those of 1804 and 1806, respectively.

[J. B. Auguste Aldéguier], *Le Flaneur, ou mon voyage à Paris, mes aventures dans cette capitale, et détails exacts de ce que j'y ai remarqué de curieux, et de nécessaire à connaître,* Recueilli et composé par un Amateur de la grande Ville (Paris, [1825]). This identical work reappears a year later with a new title. *Le Flaneur, galerie pittoresque, philosophique et morale, de tout ce que Paris offre de curieux et de remarquable dans tous les genres, avec des réflexions critiques, philosophiques et historiques sur chaque objet; ouvrage utile aux Provinciaux qui veulent tout de suite connaître Paris, ses usages, ses moeurs, son industrie et ses établissements, publics et particuliers,* Par Un Habitué du boulevard de Gand (Paris, 1826). Reference below will be to chap. 17, ''Boulevards—Flaneurs,'' 186–96.

Honoré de Balzac: *La Physiologie du mariage* (1826); *Une double famille* (1830); ''Le Mendiant'' (1830); *Ferragus* (1833); *La Fille aux yeux d'or* (1834); *Facino cane* (1836); *César Birotteau* (1844); *La Cousine Bette* (1846). References to the *Comédie humaine* (*CH*) will be to the edition by Pierre-Georges Castex, 12 vols. (Paris: Gallimard-Pléiade, 1976–81) and will be indicated by volume and page number in the text.

Un Flâneur, ''Le Flâneur à Paris,'' in *Paris, ou le livre des cent-et-un* (Paris: Ladvocat, 1831), 6:95–110; Louis Huart, *Physiologie du Flaneur* (Paris: Aubert-Lavigne, 1841); and Auguste de Lacroix, ''Le Flâneur,'' in *Les Français peints par eux-mêmes* (Paris: J. Philippart, [1877–78]), 3:25–35 (this is a four-volume edition of articles from the 1840–42 original).

4. Janet Wolff argues that the absence of a *flâneuse*, that is, a female figure in public life, is emblematic of the absence of women from modern social theory, which has focused on the public sphere. ''The Invisible *Flâneuse*: Women and the Literature of Modernity,'' in *Feminine Sentences: Essays on Women and Culture* (Berkeley: University of California Press, 1990), 34–50. In a different light, Cheryl Morgan posits Delphine de Girardin, whose regular newspaper column *Lettres parisiennes* appeared between 1836 and 1838, as a female flâneur. But Girardin is a ''cross-dressed'' flâneur, since her persona in these columns is a titled man-about-town, the vicomte de Launay. Cheryl Morgan, ''Writing Women In(to) the July Monarchy Press: Fashion, Feminism, and the *Feuilleton*'' (Ph.D. diss., Columbia University, 1993).

5. ''Pour moi, Paris est une fille, une amie, une épouse, dont la physionomie me ravit toujours parce qu'elle est pour moi toujours nouvelle.'' Balzac, ''Le Mendiant,'' 5:1422, n. 3. From this sexual urban hermeneutic Michele Hannoosh elaborates a Parisian epistemology that defines the text itself as female, at once the object of desire and the subject of investigation. Balzac's ''ironic realism'' both distances the writer from and immerses him in the city-

text. "La Femme, la ville, le réalisme: Fondements épistémologiques dans le Paris de Balzac," *The Romanic Review* 82 (1991): 127–45.

6. Richard D. E. Burton's provocative study ties figures of ubiquity who see without being seen (from the detective, the capitalist, and the flâneur to the Flaubertian *auctor absconditus*) to the panopticon, the carceral structure identified by Foucault with the emergence of the modern state. "The Unseen Seer, or Proteus in the City: Aspects of a Nineteenth-Century Parisian Myth," *French Studies* 42 (January 1988): 50–68.

7. See in particular "Les Foules" in *Le Spleen de Paris,* which, although it does not explicitly name the flâneur, reviews virtually all the current themes of flânerie. Baudelaire names the flâneur in "Le Peintre de la vie moderne," chap. 3, "L'Artiste, Homme du monde, Homme des foules et Enfant," *Oeuvres complètes,* ed. Claude Pichois (Paris: Gallimard-Pléiade, 1976), 2:687–94. (All works of Baudelaire are cited in this edition.) Benjamin identified Baudelaire's connection to the *physiologies* and what I have called literary guidebooks. See "Le Flâneur," *Charles Baudelaire: Un Poète lyrique à l'apogée du capitalisme,* 55–56. See also Karlheinz Stierle's detailed analysis of the mediating influence of this tradition, "Baudelaire and the Tradition of the *Tableau de Paris,*" *New Literary History* 11 (Winter 1980): 345–61.

8. References to Flaubert's *L'Éducation sentimentale* will be to the excellent edition by C. Gothot-Mersch (Paris: Garnier-Flammarion, 1984) and will be indicated by page in the text and notes. The single occurrence of *flâneur* as a substantive refers to unknown strollers in the crowd (271). For "flâner" or "flânerie" (all in reference to Frédéric) see pp. 129, 136, 140, 159, 267, and 365, to which can be added "au hasard" in reference to walks (116, 210, 262), "vagabonder" (146, 366), "il faisait dans Paris des courses interminables" (73), "s'en allaient par les rues" (104), and "sa promenade" (389). References are translated to this edition from Charles Carlut, Pierre H. Dubé, and J. Raymond Dugan, *A Concordance to Flaubert's "L'Éducation sentimentale,"* 2 vols. (New York: Garland, 1978).

In a perceptive analysis Mark Conroy associates Frédéric with the flâneur, particularly as conceptualized by Walter Benjamin. Mark Conroy, *Modernism and Authority: Strategies of Legitimation in Flaubert and Conrad* (Baltimore: Johns Hopkins University Press, 1985), 51–76. However, Conroy focuses on the rhetorical strategies used to legitimate the modern novel, whereas I consider the flâneur as a literary-historical and sociological type in relationship to (modern) urban culture.

Finally, Christopher Prendergast begins his analysis of *L'Éducation sentimentale* with Frédéric's flânerie, but he reads this flânerie and the novel (which he plays off very effectively against Michelet's *Histoire de la Révolution française*) entirely in political terms. *Paris and the Nineteenth Century* (Oxford and Cambridge, Mass.: Blackwell, 1992), 102–25.

9. As Marie-Claire Bancquart aptly observes in a splendid article, "les monuments se taisent." "L'espace urbain de *L'Éducation sentimentale:* Intérieurs, extérieurs," *Flaubert, la femme, la ville* (Paris: Presses Universitaires de France, 1983), 143–57 (quotation, p. 153). See also P. M. Wetherill, "Paris

dans *L'Éducation sentimentale," Flaubert, la femme, la ville,* 123–37, in which Wetherill also stresses the reciprocal fragmentation of the city and the novel.

10. Émile Durkheim, *Le Suicide—Étude de sociologie* (Paris: Presses Universitaires de France-Quadrige, 1990), 324. The Durkheim quotations in the text are found on pp. 325–26.

11. Citations below are drawn from Benjamin, "Paris, Capitale du XIXe siècle," in *Gesammelte Schriften* 5:60–77; and *Paris, Capitale du XIXe siècle,* 47–59.

12. "Ne t'occupe de rien que de toi. Laissons l'Empire marcher, fermons notre porte, montons au plus haut de notre tour d'ivoire, sur la dernière marche, le plus près du ciel. Il y fait froid quelquefois, n'est-ce pas? Mais qu'importe! On voit les étoiles briller clair et l'on n'entend plus les dindons." Flaubert to Colet 22 November 1852, *Correspondance,* 3d ser. (1852–54) (Paris: Conard, 1927), 53–54.

13. I develop this argument in "The Flâneur on and off the Streets of Paris," in *The Flaneur,* ed. Keith Tester (London: Routledge, 1994).

CHAPTER 4

1. All discussion of the seals of Paris (and the photographs) draws on the wonderful, extraordinarily detailed work by A. de Coëtlogan and L. M. Tisserand, *Les Armoiries de la Ville de Paris,* 2 vols (Paris: Imprimerie Nationale, 1874). See *Les Armoiries* 1:164 for Haussmann's rationale in bringing back the medieval ship that figured on the seal of the Water Carriers Guild (Corporation de la marchandise de l'eau).

2. On the transformations of Paris, see the splendid work of François Loyer, *Paris XIXe siécle: L'Immeuble et la rue* (Paris: Hazan, 1987). Translated by C. L. Clark, under the title *Nineteenth-Century Paris: Architecture and Urbanism* (New York: Abbeville Press, 1988).

3. See Giovanni Macchia, *Il Mito di Parigi* (Turin: Einaudi, 1962), 340. Macchia further proposes Le Nôtre's gardens at Versailles as the model for making over the streets of Paris.

4. As a career civil servant, Haussmann would not have aspired to the prefecture of the Seine, which was a political plum. His napoleonic credentials were strong. Named Eugène for Eugène de Beauharnais (the son of the empress Josephine and Haussmann's godfather), he came to the attention of Louis-Napoléon in the election of 1848 through his diligence in getting out the vote in the department where he was then prefect (the Var, in the south). He was rewarded with an appointment as prefect of the Gironde (Bordeaux) in 1851, before the final appointment as prefect of the Seine in June 1853. After his dismissal in 1870 due to scandalous (even by the loose standards of the Second Empire) fiscal manipulations, Haussmann lived in semiretirement until his election to the Senate where he sat from 1877 to 1881. See his *Mémoires,* 3 vols. (Paris: Victor-Havard, 1890–93); and David Pinkney, *Napoleon III and the Rebuilding of Paris* (Princeton: Princeton University Press, 1958), chap. 2.

5. "Encore quelques jours, et les Piliers des Halles auront disparu, le vieux Paris n'existera plus que dans les ouvrages des romanciers assez courageux pour décrire fidèlement les derniers vestiges de l'architecture de nos pères; car, de ces choses, l'historien grave tient peu de compte. . . . Aujourd'hui, les Piliers des Halles sont un des cloaques de Paris. Ce n'est pas la seule des merveilles du temps passé que l'on voie disparaître. . . ." Balzac, "Ce qui disparaît de Paris," *Oeuvres diverses* (Paris: Conard, 1940), 3:606–7. Citations to the *Comédie humaine* will be to the edition by Pierre-Georges Castex, 12 vols. (Paris: Gallimard-Pléiade, 1976–81) and will be indicated by volume and page number in the text.

6. "Ce ne sera certes pas un hors-d'oeuvre que de décrire ce coin de Paris actuel, plus tard on ne pourrait pas l'imaginer; et nos neveux, qui verront sans doute le Louvre achevé, se refuseraient à croire qu'une pareille barbarie ait subsisté pendant trente-six ans, au coeur de Paris, en face du palais où trois dynasties ont reçu, pendant des dernières trente-six années, l'élite de la France et celle de l'Europe." Balzac, *La Cousine Bette, Comédie humaine* 7:99. Napoléon III did indeed clear the quartier and finish the Louvre. See also Jean-Pierre Babelon, "Le Louvre," in *Les Lieux de mémoire: La Nation,* ed. Pierre Nora (Paris: Gallimard, 1986), 3:169–216.

7. Émile de Labédollière, *Le Nouveau Paris* (Paris: Barba, 1860), 1.

8. The quotations in the text are taken from the following section of "Le Cygne":

> Le vieux Paris n'est plus (la forme d'une ville
> Change plus vite, hélas! que le coeur d'un mortel);
> Je ne vois qu'en esprit tout ce camp de baraques,
> Ces tas de chapiteaux ébauchés et de fûts,
> Les herbes, les gros blocs verdis par l'eau des flaques,
> Et, brillant aux carreaux, le bric-à-brac confus.
> . . . .
> Paris change! mais rien dans ma mélancolie
> N'a bougé! palais neufs, échafaudages, blocs,
> Vieux faubourgs, tout pour moi devient allégorie,
> Et mes chers souvenirs sont plus lourds que des rocs.
>
> Aussi devant ce Louvre une image m'opprime:
> Je pense à mon grand cygne
> . . . .
> A quiconque a perdu ce qui ne se retrouve
> Jamais, jamais! . . .

Baudelaire, "Le Cygne," *Oeuvres complètes,* ed. Claude Pichois (Paris: Gallimard-Pléiade, 1975), 1:85–87.

9. "(1) Portion de la bête que l'on donne aux chiens de chasse après qu'elle est prise. *Donner la curée.* Par ext. Le fait de donner la curée; le moment où on la donne: *sonner la curée* (2) Ruée sur quelque chose, dispute âpre et violente pour quelque chose (places, butin) laissé disponible après un événement. . . . Le fait de s'acharner contre quelqu'un, lorsqu'il est en difficulté." *Le Grand Robert de la langue française,* 2d ed. (1985), s.v. "curée." The metaphorical meaning took over as early as the sixteenth century, largely obscuring

the original hunting reference for the quarry given to the hounds at the kill.

10. "Notes générales sur la marche de l'oeuvre," cited in "Notice," *La Curée*, ed. Henri Mitterand (Paris: Gallimard-Folio, 1981), 358. All further citations to *La Curée* will be to this edition and will appear in the text as parenthetical page numbers. See also my article, "Mobilité et modernité: Le Paris de *La Curée*," *Les Cahiers naturalistes* 63 (1993): 73–81.

11. "Les Rougon-Macquart . . . racontent ainsi le second Empire à l'aide de leurs drames individuels, du guet-apens du coup d'État à la trahison de Sedan.

Depuis trois années, je rassemblais les documents de ce grand ouvrage, . . . lorsque la chute des Bonaparte, dont j'avais besoin comme artiste, et que toujours je trouvais fatalement au bout du drame, sans oser l'espérer si prochaine, est venue me donner le dénouement terrible et nécessaire de mon oeuvre. Celle-ci est, dès aujourd'hui, complète; elle s'agite dans un cercle fini; elle devient le tableau d'un règne mort, d'une étrange époque de folie et de honte." Zola, "Préface" (1 July 1871), *La Fortune des Rougon* (Paris: Gallimard-Folio, 1981), 23–24.

12. 3e "(Rare) Ce qui conserve ou exalte le souvenir d'une personne, d'une chose; ce qui sert de document, d'archives." *Le Petit Robert* (1992), s.v. "monument." Philippe Hamon emphasizes the "monumentality" of the text and the city; see *Expositions—Littérature et architecture au XIXe siècle* (Paris: Corti, 1989). Translated by Katia Sainson-Frank and Lisa Maguire, under the title *Expositions—Literature and Architecture* (Berkeley: University of California Press, 1992). See especially chapter 2, "Le Livre comme exposition."

13. "C'est Haussmann qui a lancé Paris dans le tourbillon des grandes dépenses. Les villes ont imité Paris, les particuliers ont imité Paris. . . . Fantasmagories de calcul. Roman de l'expropriation, de la construction, de la démolition, de la spéculation et au dénouement expiation ou liquidation. . . . " Zola's résumé of an article by Jules Richard in *Le Figaro*, 25 February 1869, cited in *La Curée*, 357.

14. The technical meaning of *liquide*, which dates from the sixteenth century, is "qui est exactement déterminé dans son montant, sa valeur. *Créance, dette liquide:* dont l'existence est certaine et la quotité déterminée." *Liquidité* used to refer to immediately available assets dates from the nineteenth century. *Le Petit Robert* (1992), s.v. "liquide."

15. Balzac's miser Gobseck offers the relevant intertext here for the textuality of money. See also the beginning of *La Fille aux yeux d'or* for Balzac's conception of speculation as the basic structure of contemporary Paris.

16. "La production littéraire se fait de jour en jour, plus énorme, plus menaçante. Le livre monte, déborde, se répand; c'est une inondation. Il s'échappe en torrent des librairies encombrées, croule en cascades jaunes, bleues, vertes, rouges, des étalages vertigineux. On ne se fait pas une idée de tous les noms arrachés des profondeurs de l'inconnu, que cette marée déferlante soulève un instant sur le dos de ses vagues, roule pêle-mêle . . . et rejette ensuite, en un coin perdu de la grève, où nul ne passe, pas même les voleurs

d'épaves." Octave Mirbeau, *Les Écrivains—1ᵉ série, 1884–1894* (Paris: Flammarion, n.d.), 85.

On the transformation of publishing in this period, see the superb study of Jean-Yves Mollier, *L'Argent et les lettres: histoire du capitalisme d'édition, 1880–1920* (Paris: Fayard, 1988).

17. Robert Lethbridge, "Zola et Haussmann: Une Expropriation littéraire," in *«La Curée» de Zola, ou 'la vie à outrance'"* (Paris: SEDES, 1987). Zola was clear about the grandeur of Haussmann's work: "Si les moyens employés sont plus ou moins bons, plus ou moins légaux et prudents, l'oeuvre faite est grande. Personne, je crois, ne songe à le nier." *Le Gaulois,* 8 March 1869, cited in Zola, *Oeuvres complètes,* ed. Henri Mitterand (Paris: Cercle du livre précieux, 1966), 10:801–5.

18. Zola builds the case for madness slowly but inexorably from the beginning of the novel. "[Aristide] la prenait, il la jetait dans cette vie à outrance, où sa pauvre tête se détraquait un peu plus tous les jours" (55); "elle s'éveillerait . . . folle" (55–56). Zola refers to this woman "folle de sa chair" (57) and to "son allure d'écervelée, sa tête folle" (109); "sa tête folle . . ." (131). And of course Renée has migraine headaches (158). Her maid tries to calm her "pauvre tête" (169); "la tête brisée par les affaires" (204); "ses toilettes folles" (217). Madness is not far away: "Elle sentait qu'elle perdait le peu d'équilibre qui lui restait . . ." (232); "Tout se détraqua dans sa tête" (242); "Il craignait réellement qu'elle ne devînt folle, une nuit, entre ses bras" (247); "Tu es un peu fêlée, ma chère, il faut soigner ça" (267); "Des lueurs de folie luisaient dans ses yeux" (270); "Tu perds la tête" (305). Renée is "Une femme . . . folle assurément. . . . [Maxime] cherchait avec désespoir un moyen pour sortir de ce cabinet de toilette, de ce réduit rose où battait le glas de Charenton" (306) and where "la folie montait" (309). Renée displays "l'idée fixe d'une intelligence qui se noie" (310). "Ah! que sa pauvre tête souffrait! . . . sa fièvre de femme malade" (313). "Toute sa face lui disait que le craquement cérébral s'achevait. Maxime . . . avait terminé son oeuvre, épuisé sa chair, détraqué son intelligence" (314).

Nor is Renée alone in her madness in the novel. Lusts "ate away" at Hélène de Mareuil "like an ulcer" and left her in a state of "lucid madness" (161). In Zola's obsession with degeneration, such a woman can only produce a child like Louise, deformed, ugly, consumptive, and consumed with vice from birth—a perfect match for Maxime (162).

Saccard's own "insane" expenditures were "pure dementia" (164), and his continual movement led his associates to predict that he would become "crazy" (166). The move to the Parc Monceau brought on "the insane crisis" (165). Finally, it is the whole society that is led to insanity: at the Saccard *hôtel* "the whole era passed through with its crazy, stupid laugh" (165). Finally, of course, the "fêlure" is that of the Rougon-Macquart family, notably that of the matriarch, Tante Dide.

19. Zola is hardly subtle in his insistence on the animal associations of his heroine. Renée, with her "étranges cheveux fauve pâle" (40), is "pareille à une grande chatte aux yeux phosphorescents" (216); "cette adorable bête

amoureuse'' (216); "tendresse de bêtes farouches" (219); "des sécheresses félines" (220). Maxime is her "proie" (220, 280) "qu'elle rêva de reprendre . . ." (314) in "une colère fauve" (314). In her relationship with Maxime, Renée's masculinity puts her on the side of the hunter; to Maxime her white hand feels like "claws" sinking into his shoulder (247). She has the pose and the smile of the marble sphinx in the greenhouse, the "monstre à tête de femme" (216). The same image is used to describe her as Echo (280).

20. Michael Fried, *Courbet's Realism* (Chicago: University of Chicago Press, 1990), 171–88. The full title of Courbet's painting, now in the Museum of Fine Arts, Boston, is *La Curée, chasse au chevreuil dans les forêts du Grand Jura.* Fried analyzes the painting as Courbet's self-representation, seeing the artist as both the hunter passively smoking his pipe and the huntsman playing a horn. There are, however, traces of blood between the hounds and the deer.

21. The first sentence of the following letter from the period in which Zola was writing *La Curée* is often cited, the rest less so. "Nous voyons la création, dans une oeuvre, à travers un homme, à travers un tempérament, une personnalité. L'image qui se produit sur cet écran de nouvelle espèce est la reproduction des choses et des personnes placées au delà, et cette reproduction qui ne saurait être fidèle, changera autant de fois qu'un nouvel écran viendra s'interposer entre notre oeil et la création. L'écran réaliste est un simple verre à vitre, très mince, très clair, et qui a la prétention d'être si parfaitement transparent que les images le traversent et se produisent ensuite dans toute leur réalité. Toutes mes sympathies, s'il faut le dire, sont pour l'Écran réaliste. . . ." Letter to Valabrègue, 18 August 1864, in *Oeuvres complètes* 14:1309.

22. *Capital*, vol. 1, quoted by Marshall Berman in his very insightful examination of modernism, *All That Is Solid Melts into Air—The Experience of Modernity* (New York: Penguin, 1988), 87. See especially chapter 2, "All That Is Solid Melts into Air: Marx, Modernism, and Modernization."

CHAPTER 5

1. Impossible to specify, estimates of deaths range from ten to thirty-five thousand. The current consensus gives the following estimates: three thousand killed in combat, seventeen thousand killed between 22 May and 15 June (the Communards executed fewer than one hundred hostages), and two thousand deaths in prison or in transport. In addition, more than forty-three thousand prisoners were tried over the next four years, of whom over forty-five hundred were condemned to hard labor in New Caledonia. Jules Vallès was one of almost five thousand lucky enough to escape into exile, principally in Belgium, England, and Switzerland. In contrast, after 1848, fifteen thousand arrests were made in Paris, and judgment after the coup d'état of 1851 concerned some twenty-six thousand people in all of France. See William Serman, *La Commune de Paris* (Paris: Fayard, 1986,) 512, 524, 527, 531, 538. General amnesty was not declared until 1880. The Communes that arose in the provinces (Lyon, Marseille, Le Creusot, Saint-Étienne) were crushed by

the end of March 1871. For two months Paris stood alone against France.

L'Année terrible is the title Hugo gave to the book of poems written from June 1870 to August 1871 and published to resounding success in April 1872.

2. "Par le fait, depuis 89, il y a toujours eu un roi de France, et il n'y en a eu qu'un seul: c'est Paris. La France lui a été dévouée et obéissante, ne lui a refusé ni tributs, ni sang, ni sacrifices, ni caprices. Mais le moment est venu pour Paris de payer de sa personne. S'il veut conserver son empire, qu'il se gouverne en sage, qu'il obéisse en soldat, qu'il combatte et qu'il vainque ou succombe en roi!" Louis Veuillot was a virulently conservative journalist whose articles appeared regularly throughout 1870–71 in *L'Univers* and were published together in November 1871. The citation is taken from "Metz perdue" (1 November 1870), in *Paris pendant les deux sièges, Oeuvres complètes* (Paris: P. Lethielleux, 1928), 13:167.

3. Bernard Marchand presents the Commune as above all an urban and typically Parisian movement, directed again the conservatism of the heavily religious and conservative provinces, which supported the empire and accepted the armistice with the Prussians. *Paris: Histoire d'une ville XIXᵉ–XXᵉ siècle* (Paris: Seuil, 1993), 102–25. To a certain extent, the Commune can also be seen as an attempt by the typically artisanal and working-class Communards to repossess the city of which they had been dispossessed by Second Empire urbanism.

4. "Le genre humain peut-il être décapité?" Hugo, "Paris incendié," "Mai," *L'Année terrible*, in *Oeuvres complètes* (Paris: Laffont, 1985–1990), 6:116.

5. Hugo, "Introduction," *Paris-Guide par les principaux écrivains et artistes de la France,* 2 vols. (Paris: Librairie Internationale, 1867). All references to *Paris-Guide* will be to this edition and will be cited in the text by page number. See also the discussion of *Paris-Guide* in chapter 2 supra and the discussion of the Vendôme Column in chapter 6 infra.

6. *Journal d'Adèle Hugo* (Paris: Minard, 1985), 3:86 (17 January 1854). Clearly Hugo's political position evolved in these years. Hugo traced his own itinerary: "1818, royaliste; 1824, royaliste libéral; 1827, libéral; 1828, libéral socialiste; 1830, libéral socialiste démocrate; 1849, libéral socialiste démocrate républicain." Guy Robert, *Chaos vaincu* (Paris: Les Belles Lettres, 1976), 1:15, cited in Paul Bénichou, *Les Mages romantiques* (Paris: Gallimard, 1988), 330, n. 1. See also Bénichou's superb close readings of Hugo's poetry for the evolution of Hugo's conception of poetry and the mission of the poet.

7. Quotations are from Hugo, *Choses vues: Souvenirs, journaux, cahiers, 1849–1869,* ed. Hubert Juin (Paris: Gallimard-Folio, 1972), 346. The material circumstances of Hugo's exile were never uncomfortable. He was not in any danger from the imperial government, although he had been expelled first from Brussels and then from Jersey by governments anxious not to antagonize France. Hugo traveled freely and prominently in Europe, presiding over the peace congress held at Lausanne, Switzerland, in 1869. He continued to receive his regular stipend as a member of the Académie française, and his editor eagerly published his works (*Les Misérables* in 1862 was an instant international best-seller).

8. "Je vis dans l'exil; là je perds le caractère de l'homme pour prendre celui de l'apôtre et du prêtre." *Journal d'Adèle Hugo* 3:284 (13 July 1854).

9. See Hugo's journals, published as *Choses vues: Souvenirs, journaux, cahiers, 1870–1885,* ed. Hubert Juin (Paris: Gallimard-Folio, 1972). The cannon request comes on 30 October 1870. Hugo, it should be noted, authorized the reading but asked that the cannon be named "Châteaudun." More generally, these volumes, which cover 1830 to 1885, are a mine for Hugo's perceptions of and reactions to public events.

10. "Bref, cette Commune est aussi idiote que l'Assemblée est féroce. Des deux côtés, folie. Mais la France, Paris et la République s'en tireront." Hugo, *Choses vues,* 164 (9 April 1871).

11. Hugo, *Quatrevingt-treize* (Paris: Garnier-Flammarion, 1965), 165. All further quotations will be from this edition and will be cited in the text.

12. Hugo, "Préface de mes oeuvres et post-scriptum de ma vie," *Oeuvres complètes* 12:699. *Cf.* "Avant d'ôter de l'art cette antithèse, commencez par l'ôter de la nature," William Shakespeare, pt. 2, bk. 1, iii, *Oeuvres complètes* 12:346. The discussion below builds on my analysis of *Quatrevingt-treize* in *Literary France: The Making of a Culture* (Berkeley: University of California Press, 1987), 152–56.

13. "Il faut toujours quelqu'un qui dise: Je suis prêt. / Je m'immole. Sans quoi, ma France bien-aimée, / La conscience au coeur de l'homme se rompait; . . ." Hugo, *Les Quatre Vents de l'esprit,* bk. 3, 33, ii (13 September 1854), in *Oeuvres complètes* 6:1334.

14. See Hugo, *Oeuvres complètes* 10:917–25 (22 May 1876); 1007–8 (28 February 1879); and 1017–18 (3 July 1880). As a perusal of Hugo's speeches in these years indicates, amnesty turns up often as well in less formal circumstances.

15. Hugo, "Ce que c'est que l'exil" (1875), *Oeuvres complètes* 10:417. As Suzanne Nash has pointed out to me, this optimistic reading of *Quatrevingt-treize* slights Hugo's evident attraction to the mysterious forests of Brittany and the elemental way of life that they preserve and runs counter to the scene where the three young children imprisoned in La Tourgue tear up a magnificent in-quarto that scatters to the wind ("Le Massacre de Saint-Barthélemy," bk. 3, pt. 3, 258–70). It is not clear what this particular book represents. To the extent that it too has been "imprisoned" in the tower, and imprisoned as well in a form that impedes circulation of ideas, the in-quarto stands for the past of the book ("l'antique livre," 270), not the present and certainly not the future. In this scene, and indeed in the book as a whole, the children represent the future. It is worth noting as well that here Hugo uses the image of the azure ("le massacre se termina par un évanouissement dans l'azur," 270), precisely the terms that he will later invoke to describe the indifference of nature to man's predicament ("l'implacable sérénité de l'azur," 376).

16. Hugo, *Océan: Tas de pierres,* cited in Bénichou, *Les Mages romantiques,* 356.

17. Vallès's work will be cited in the text by volume and page number in *Oeuvres*, 2 vols., ed. Roger Bellet (Paris: Gallimard-Pléiade, 1975, 1990). Volume 1 contains *L'Argent* (1857), *Les Réfractaires* (1865), and *La Rue* (1866); volume 2 contains the *Jacques Vingtras* trilogy: *L'Enfant* (1881), *Le Bachelier* (1884), and, most important for the present discussion, *L'Insurgé* (1885). Both volumes contain an important selection of the journalism. Bellet's introductions and notes provide a superb introduction to a writer whose passionate and detailed involvement with history in the making undoubtedly puts off many readers.

18. On the funeral as a rite of passage in French literary culture see my discussion in *Literary France*, 156–57 (Hugo) and 192–96 (Sartre). On Vallès' funeral, discussed below, see Max Gallo, *Jules Vallès, ou la révolte d'une vie* (Paris: Fayard, 1988), 20–22.

19. The careful deployment of republican emblems offered great opportunities for the constitution of an appropriate symbol system. But even these had to be modified on occasion. "La Marseillaise" was the only clear candidate for national anthem, but lyrics calling for the extermination of royal traitors and their foreign allies were not calculated to convince the crowned heads of Europe of French stability. Not until 1879 did the Third Republic proclaim "La Marseillaise" the national anthem, and then only with significant modification. The rousing marching song came to be intoned with almost liturgical solemnity. It is appropriate that the two socialist heads of state in the twentieth century, Léon Blum and François Mitterrand, speeded up "La Marseillaise." See Michel Vovelle, "*La Marseillaise:* La guerre ou la paix," in *Les Lieux de mémoire: La République,* ed. Pierre Nora (Paris: Gallimard, 1984), 1:85–136.

20. The Fifth Republic financed an extravaganza celebration of 1885 for Victor Hugo and relatively little for Jules Vallès. See *La Gloire de Victor Hugo,* Catalogue de l'Exposition des Galeries nationales du Grand Palais, 1985, Ministère de la culture et Éditions de la Réunion des musées nationaux, Paris; and Jean-Claude Fizaine, "Aspects d'un centenaire," in *Romantisme* 60 (1988): 5–36. As the author of a recent, judicious history of the Commune observes, ideological debates and impassioned arguments weigh heavily on the historiography of the Commune. (Serman, *La Commune de Paris,* 10). In many respects the Commune has never been assimilated into French history.

In contrast to Hugo, Vallès long remained on the margins of literary history. Jean-Pierre Richard, writing in 1947, can speak in terms of "a vast conspiracy of silence" organized around Vallès by French literary historians (Richard, "Un témoin de 48: Jules Vallès," *Annales* 4 [1947]: 430). In 1965 the future editor of Vallès in the prestigious Pléiade edition notes that people "are beginning to know Vallès well." ("Littérature et société selon Jules Vallès 1865–1885," *Europe* [March-April 1965]: 238). *Cf.* Max Gallo, *Jules Vallès,* 471, in which he discusses the "rejection" of Vallès by the literary establishment (beginning with the Goncourts), during his lifetime and after his death, until recently.

One small indicator of the respective ranks on the prestige hierarchy of literary studies is the number of references in the annual Bibliography of the Modern Language Association. From January 1981 through March 1992 (therefore including the period of the centennial celebrations), there are 595 entries for Victor Hugo and 52 for Jules Vallès.

I will also add that Hugo remains, in some quarters at least, a symbol of the republic. In his speech for Bastille Day 1993 M. Aimé Montal, the mayor of Villeneuve-lez-Avignon (Gard), invoked *Quatrevingt-treize* in his eulogy to 1793.

21. "C'est que j'ai gardé tout mon sang-froid, et que, pour faire trou dans ces cervelles, j'ai emmanché mon arme comme un poignard de tragédie grecque, je les ai éclaboussés de latin, j'ai grandsièclisé ma parole—ces imbéciles me laissent insulter leurs religions et leurs doctrines parce que je le fais dans un langage qui respecte leur rhétorique et que prônent les maîtres du barreau et les professeurs d'humanités. C'est entre deux périodes à la Villemain que je glisse un mot de réfractaire, cru et cruel, et je ne leur laisse pas le temps de crier." Vallès, *Oeuvres* 1:898.

22. "Jules Vallès est ministre de l'Instruction Publique. Le bohème des brasseries occupe le fauteuil de Villemain. . . . Et, il faut le dire, cependant . . . c'est l'homme qui a le plus de talent et le moins de méchanceté. Mais la France est classique, de telle sorte que les théories littéraires de cet homme de lettres font déjà plus de mal au nouveau pouvoir que les théories sociales de ses confrères. Un gouvernement dont un membre a osé écrire qu' Homère était à mettre au rancart et que *Le Misanthrope* de Molière manquait de gaieté, apparaît au bourgeois plus épouvantant (*sic*), plus subversif, plus antisocial, que si ce même gouvernement décrétait le même jour l'abolition de l'hérédité et le remplacement du mariage par l'*union libre*." Edmond et Jules de Goncourt, *Journal—Mémoires de la vie littéraire* (Monoco: Éditions de l'Imprimerie Nationale / Fasquelle & Flammarion, 1956), 9:192 (31 March 1871). With characteristic exaggeration, Goncourt promotes Vallès to minister of public instruction. See Paul Lidsky, *Les Écrivains contre la Commune* (Paris: Maspero, 1970) for some truly astonishing denunciations of the Communards.

23. Similarly, Meursault in Camus's *L'Étranger* is astounded at how small and how unimpressive the guillotine is. He too credits all the dramatic stories of the French Revolution for the false impression. Meursault too is a victim of the book, and Camus, like Vallès, insists upon the ordinariness of the guillotine.

In English literature of course Dickens's *Tale of Two Cities* fixed the image of the scaffold forever after for generations of readers.

CHAPTER 6

1. Courbet's involvement with the Colonne Vendôme is a long and complicated tale. In September 1870, as president of the Société des Artistes, he called upon Parisians to "dismantle" or "unbolt" the column (the much

discussed neologism *deboulonner* was crucial to fixing the extent of Courbet's responsibility for the eventual destruction). At the time that the Commune officially decreed the "demolition" of the column, on 12 April 1871, Courbet was not a member of the Commune (he was elected 16 April). But the connection between Courbet and the column was strong, as the caricatures in the press at the time confirm.

Barely ten days after the column had been torn down, on 25 May, the Assemblée Nationale in Versailles voted reconstruction. On 20 June, according to Victor Hugo (*Choses vues*), Courbet was rumored to have offered to replace the column at his expense on the condition that he be released from prison. Courbet himself later acknowledged having written in July to a prominent politician, Jules Simon, that if he could be convicted of such destruction, he would pay for the restoration. After a trial (attended by Zola) in August 1871, Courbet was fined five hundred francs and condemned to six months in prison for "usurpation de fonctions et complicité de destruction de monument publique." In April 1874 the newly elected Bonapartist majority made good on the earlier conviction and charged Courbet with the total expense of the reconstruction—over 350,000 francs! Courbet died in 1877 a ruined and disheartened man, always protesting his innocence. See Rodolphe Walter, "Un Dossier délicat: Courbet et la Colonne Vendôme," *Gazette des Beaux-Arts*, ser. 6, 81 (March 1973): 173–84. My thanks to Gonzolo J. Sanchez for sharing his research with me. " 'The Development of Art and the Universal Republic': The Paris Commune's *Fédération des artistes* and French Republicanism, 1871–1889" (Ph.D. diss., Columbia University, 1994). For details on the construction of the column, as well as drawings of the bas-reliefs on the bronze plaques, see Fernand de Saint-Simon, "Histoire de la Colonne Vendôme," in *La Place Vendôme* (Paris: Éditions Vendôme, 1982), 119–85.

2. *Journal Officiel*, (13 April 1871), cited by Walter, *Gazette des Beaux-Arts*, 177.

3. Almost a half century before *Quatrevingt-treize*, this promiscuous association of symbols from across the political spectrum already resorts to one of Hugo's favorite rhetorical strategies, that is, the creation of a vast synthesis from ideological contraries. Hugo wrote "A la Colonne de la Place Vendôme" in response to a diplomatic incident when four members of the imperial aristocracy were announced at an Austrian reception without the titles that had been conferred by Napoléon. Hugo, whose own title of count derived from his father's imperial title, rushed to defend national honor.

> O Monument vengeur! Trophée indélébile!
> Bronze qui, tournoyant sur ta base immobile,
> Sembles porter au ciel ta gloire et ton néant;
> Et, de tout ce qu'a fait une main colossale,
> Seul es resté debout;—ruine triomphale
>   De l'édifice du géant.
> Debris du Grand Empire et de la Grande Armée,
> Colonne d'où si haut parle la renommée!
> Je t'aime: l'étranger t'admire avec effroi.
> J'aime tes vieux héros, sculptés par la Victoire;

Et tous ces fantômes de gloire
Qui se pressent autour de toi.
. . . .
Que de fois j'ai cru voir, ô Colonne française
Ton Airain ennemi rugir dans la fournaise!
. . . .
Prenez garde!—La France, où grandit un autre âge,
N'est pas si morte encor qu'elle souffre un outrage!
Les partis pour un temps voileront leur tableau.
Contre une injure ici tout s'unit, tout se lève,
Tout s'arme, et la Vendée aiguisera son glaive
    Sur la pierre de Waterlo.
. . . .
Allez!—Vous n'avez plus l'Aigle qui de son aire
Sur tous les fronts trop hauts portait votre tonnerre;
Mais il vous reste encor l'oriflamme et les lis.
Mais c'est le Coq gaulois qui réveille le monde;
Et son cri peut promettre à votre nuit profonde
    L'aube du soleil d'Austerlitz.
. . . .
Non, Frères! non, Français de cet âge d'attente!
Nous avons tous grandi sur le seuil de la tente.
Condamnés à la paix, aiglons bannis des cieux,
Sachons du moins, veillant aux gloires paternelles,
Garder de tout affront, jalouses sentinelles,
    L'armure de nos aïeux!

Hugo, *Odes et Ballades,* 4th ed. (1828), in *Oeuvres complètes* (Paris: Laffont, 1985), (bk. 3) 4:189–94. Hugo came back to the column in 1830, in a hymn more to Napoléon than to France: "Ce bronze devant qui tout n'est que poudre et sable, / Sublime monument, deux fois impérissable, / Fait de gloire et d'airain"; "A la Colonne," *Les Chants du crépuscule* (1835), in *Oeuvres complètes* 4:691–98.

    4. Marie-Claire Bancquart, *Images littéraires du Paris fin-de-siècle* (Paris: Aux Éditions de la Différence, 1979). This work is indispensable for any consideration of the larger context of the literature of fin-de-siècle Paris.

    Citations to Zola's work will be to the following editions: *La Débâcle,* ed. Henri Mitterand (Paris: Gallimard-Folio, 1984); *Le Docteur Pascal* (Paris: Garnier-Flammarion, 1975); *Son Excellence Eugène Rougon* (Paris: Garnier-Flammarion, 1973); *Paris* (Paris: Charpentier-Fasquelle, 1898); *La Vérité en marche* (Paris: Garnier-Flammarion, 1969). For *Paris* in particular, I shall give lengthy citations in the notes, the only means of confirming the extraordinary metaphorical structure of the novel.

    5. See Sandy Petrey, "La République de *La Débâcle,*" *Cahiers naturalistes* 54 (1980):87–95.

    6. The connections between *La Curée* (1872) and *Son Excellence Eugène Rougon* (1876) go beyond the two brothers who are the protagonists, beyond the society whose corruption both novels denounce at such length. The later novel exemplifies to perfection the *curée,* understood as the rush for political spoils. In addition, an actual hunt (chap. 7) ends with the hounds voraciously devouring the entrails of the deer in a striking actualization of the constitutive

metaphor of *La Curée*. "Et, en bas, les chiens achevaient leurs os. Ils se cou-
laient furieusement les un sous les autres, pour arriver au milieu du tas. C'était
une nappe d'échines mouvantes. . . . Les mâchoires se hâtaient, mangeaient
vite, avec la fièvre de tout manger. De courtes querelles se terminaient par
un hurlement. Un gros braque, une bête superbe, fâché d'être trop au bord,
recula et s'élança d'un bond au milieu de la bande. Il fit son trou, il but un
lambeau des entrailles du cerf" (226–27). The scene is analogous to the
tableau vivant near the end of *La Curée* (see chap. 4 supra), since it is a *curée
froide;* that is, the final scene of the hunt is postponed until the evening, when
all the guests can watch the hounds massed in the courtyard of the château
throw themselves at the entrails on command. As in *La Curée*, imperial society
sees itself on display. A final variation on *la curée* is the manhunt in *Paris* in
the Bois de Boulogne, which ends with the capture and execution of the
anarchist Salviat.

7. From *La Curée* to *La Débâcle* Zola remains faithful to his representation
of the city as a diseased individual who must die. Thus the following from *La
Débâcle* for Maurice: "des yeux . . . un peu fous parfois" (26), "tête affaiblie"
(525), "nervosité ombrageuse" (531), "fièvre grandissante" (532), "tête
perdue" (535), "exaltation" (536), "coup de démence" (537), "rêve fou"
(542), "repris de folie" (561), son "grand rêve noir" (541, 580). Compare
note 18, chap. 4 supra, the characterizations of Renée Saccard. Zola's preoccupation with disease is a constant in virtually all his work.

8. *Cf.* "toute une crise de nervosité maladive . . . se déclarait, une épidé-
mique fièvre" (523); "sa fièvre de désespoir" (527); "cette foule hallucinée"
(528); "Paris, alcoolisé . . . tombait à une ivrognerie continue" (532); "les
germes de folie . . . montaient de la foule," "cette population, détraquée"
(533); le "coup de démence . . . emportait Paris entier, ce mal venu de loin"
(537); "la crise aiguë du mal" (540); "le coup d'ivresse générale," "l'épi-
démie envahissante, la soûlerie chronique" (543); "Paris détruit, frappé de
folie furieuse, s'incendiant lui-même" (554).

It is worth noting that *Le Docteur Pascal*, which provides details on what has
happened to all of the members of the Rougon-Macquart family, sets Jean up
as a model of health, for the country and for the individual, as he works the
land and raises a fast-multiplying family (156–57, 161). The earth is "le fond
d'éternel rajeunissement" (157). Pascal places his hopes in Jean's oldest boy,
who "semblait apporter le renouveau, la sève jeune des races qui vont se
retremper dans la terre" (161).

9. From Guernsey, Hugo followed closely the discussions over the possible
demolition of the Vendôme Column. Hearing of the vote of the Commune,
he quickly writes "Les deux trophées," which, in Hugo's view, gave the column a few extra days (8 May 1871).

Versailles a la paroisse et Paris la commune;
Mais, sur eux, au-dessus de tous, la France est une

. . .

Tous ces grands combattants, tournant sur ces spirales,
Peuplant les champs, les tours, les barques amirales,

Franchissant murs et ponts, fossés, fleuves, marais,
C'est la France montant à l'assaut du progrès.
"Les deux trophées," "Mai," *L'Année terrible*, in *Oeuvres complètes* 6:107–11.

10. Zola's promotion of the scientist as savior is part of a general shift in late nineteenth-century France. See Christophe Charle, *Naissance des «intellectuels», 1880–1900* (Paris: Minuit, 1990), 28–38.

11. "L'immense Paris . . . travaillait à l'avenir inconnu, dans le grondement de sa formidable cuve" (468); "Paris, . . . la cuve énorme où fermentait le vin de l'avenir" (473); "l'idée de la cuve géante . . . de la cuve ouverte là" (551); "Paris, c'était la cuve énorme, où toute une humanité bouillait, la meilleure et la pire, . . . Et, dans cette cuve . . . " (591); "Et tout cela bouillait dans la cuve colossale de Paris, les désirs, les violences, les volontés déchaînées, le mélange innomable des ferments les plus âcres, d'où sortirait à grands flots purs le vin de l'avenir" (592); "La lie humaine tombait au fond de la cuve" (593). For the romantics' use of this image and the move of the term from the alchemist's beaker to the vintner's vat, see Citron, *La Poésie de Paris* 2:99.

12. Christopher Prendergast mentions in passing but does not elaborate the metonymical motivation of the metaphorical extension of the "underground" Paris motif. *Paris and the Nineteenth Century* (Oxford and Cambridge, Mass.: Blackwell, 1992), 82.

13. "C'était, après deux mois de froid terrible, de neige et de glace, un Paris noyé sous un dégel morne et frissonnant. Du vaste ciel, couleur de plomb, tombait le deuil d'une brume épaisse" (1).

14. "Il regarda Paris, dont la mer immense se déroulait à ses pieds" (1); "le brouillard qui changeait la grande ville en un océan de brume" (4); "l'océan de Paris, la mer sans bornes des toitures" (153); "la mer sans bornes" (164); "les monuments semblaient des navires à l'ancre, une escadre arrêtée en sa marche, dont la haute mâture luisait à l'adieu du soleil . . . cet océan humain . . . " (209); "Paris, c'est l'océan" (223); "les grandes vagues obscures, qui montaient de l'océan indistinct de la ville" (554); "on dirait des navires, toute une escadre innombrable . . . des milliers de vaisseaux d'or qui partent de l'océan de Paris, pour aller instruire et pacifier la terre" (407). The last example comes just after Pierre has put off his cassock and put on ordinary pants and a jacket. Clearly, Paris can fulfill its civilizing mission only when the Church has been repudiated.

15. "Paris était ensemencé d'une poussière lumineuse, comme si quelque semeur invisible . . . eût jeté à main pleine ces volées de grains, dont le flot d'or s'abattait de toutes parts. L'immense champ défriché en était couvert, le chaos sans fin des toitures et des monuments n'était plus qu'une terre de labour, dont quelque charrue géante avait creusé les sillons. Et Pierre . . . se demanda si ce n'étaient pas là les bonnes semailles, Paris ensemencé de lumière par le divin soleil, pour la grande moisson future, cette moisson de vérité et de justice dont il désespérait" (164).

16. In the final two pages of Chapter 1, book 4, of *Paris,* the metaphor is at the same time a marvelous description of the cityscape, very impressionistic

in its effect. "C'était le même effet qu'il avait vu déjà, lors de sa première visite. Le soleil oblique, qui descendait derrière de minces nuages de pourpre, criblait la ville d'une grêle de rayons. . . . Et l'on aurait dit quelque semeur géant . . . , qui . . . lançait ces grains d'or, d'un bout de l'horizon à l'autre" (383).

Images of sowing, planting, and harvesting are all over late nineteenth-century France, from the emblem and motto of the Larousse dictionary, "Je sème à tous vents," to the immensely popular paintings by Millet. Visually, Zola's use of light to locate the sower is reminiscent of Hugo's poem "Saison des semailles, le soir."

17. ". . . le soleil oblique noyant l'immensité de Paris d'une poussière d'or. Mais, cette fois, ce n'étaient plus les semailles, . . . ce n'était non plus la ville avec ses quartiers distincts. . . . Il semblait qu'une même poussée de vie, qu'une même floraison avait recouvert la ville entière, l'harmonisant, n'en faisant qu'un même champ sans bornes, couvert de la même fécondité. Du blé, du blé partout, un infini de blé dont la houle d'or roulait d'un bout de l'horizon à l'autre . . . et c'était bien la moisson, après les semailles. . . . Paris flambait, ensemencé de lumière par le divin soleil, roulant dans sa gloire la moisson future de vérité et de justice" (607–8). The tight metaphoric construction of this novel that can too easily be seen as merely repetitious shows in the way the dominant metaphor of the golden field plays off the traditional image of Paris-as-ocean ("the golden swell"). Americans will recognize the trope of the "amber waves of grain" from "America the Beautiful" transposed to Parisian fields.

18. "Si j'avais été dans un livre, je ne sais pas ce que j'aurais fait," reported in Joseph Reinach, *Histoire de l'affaire Dreyfus* 3:67, cited by Alain Pagès, *Émile Zola: Un intellectuel dans l'affaire Dreyfus* (Paris: Séguier, 1991), 31. The Pagès work is indispensable for a balanced view of this critical phase of Zola's career. On the Dreyfus affair more generally, see Jean-Louis Bredin's superb *L'Affaire* (Paris: Julliard, 1983). Translated by Jeffrey Mehlman, under the title *The Affair: The Case of Alfred Dreyfus* (New York: George Braziller, 1986). On the mobilization of intellectuals, see pp. 275–85, "Logicians of the Absolute."

19. Zola, "Lettre à M. Félix Faure" ("J'accuse"), in *L'Affaire Dreyfus—La Vérité en marche* (Paris: Garnier-Flammarion, 1969), 113–24. Further citations to "J'accuse" and to other writings by Zola concerning his participation in the Dreyfus affair will be to this edition and will be cited by page in the text.

20. The public writer is discussed at length in Priscilla Parkhurst Clark, *Literary France: The Making of a Culture* (Berkeley: University of California Press, 1987). See especially chapter 6 (on Voltaire and Hugo) and chapter 7 (on Zola and Sartre).

21. The basilica was built to fulfil a "vow" of national "expiation" for the "sins" that had brought the war and the Commune. See David Harvey, "Monument and Myth: The Building of the Basilica of the Sacred Heart," in *Consciousness and the Urban Experience: Studies in the History and Theory of Capitalist Urbanization* (Baltimore: Johns Hopkins, 1985), 221–49.

22. See Barthes' essay, *La Tour Eiffel* (Paris: Delpire, 1964). The essay, which features André Martin's tremendous photographs, was reissued in 1989

for the centennial by the Centre national de la photographie but is now out of print.

23. "Nous venons, écrivains, sculpteurs, architectes, peintres, amateurs passionnés de la beauté jusqu'ici intacte de Paris, protester de toutes nos forces, de toute notre indignation, au nom du goût français méconnu, au nom de l'art et de l'histoire français menacés, contre l'érection, en plein coeur de notre capitale, de l'inutile et monstrueuse Tour Eiffel. La Ville de Paris va-t-elle . . . se déshonorer et s'enlaidir irréparablement? Car la Tour Eiffel, dont la commerciale Amérique elle-même ne voudrait pas, c'est, n'en doutez pas, le déshonneur de Paris." "Protestation des artistes," *Le Temps*, 14 February 1887, cited on the frontispiece of Barthes, *La Tour Eiffel*. Among the signatories were the established painters Ernest Meissonier and William Bouguereau; the composer Charles Gounod; Charles Garnier (the architect of the Paris Opéra); the writers François Coppée, Leconte de Lisle, Sully Prudhomme, Dumas *fils* (members or future members of the Académie française), and Maupassant. The "intact beauty" of Paris is a startling affirmation in view of the bitter polemics over Haussmann's extensive manipulation of the city barely thirty years previously. But Haussmann's Paris fit within a recognizable tradition of city planning. Construction of the Tour Montparnasse in the 1970s raised many of the same protests.

24. "Faut-il renverser la Tour Eiffel?" in *Revue mondiale*, May-June 1929, cited by Henri Loyrette, in *1889—La Tour Eiffel et l'Exposition universelle* (Paris: Éditions de la Réunion des Musées nationaux, 1989), 218.

25. The emblematic text of this symbolic reconfiguration is surely *Le Tour de France par deux enfants,* originally published in 1877 with great numbers of printings; an edition with an epilogue was published in 1906. Two orphaned brothers from Lorraine, ages fourteen and seven, "choose France" in 1871 and travel across France in search of the uncle who will put their family papers in order and allow them to remain French legally. The adventures impress upon the boys not only the general civic virtues of economy, prudence, honesty, and hard work but also the supreme virtue of being French and the sublime duty of working to rebuild France—the subtitle of the book is *Devoir et Patrie [Duty and Fatherland]. Le Tour de France par deux enfants* teaches France. There is, of course, a visit to Paris, but it is only one site among many; and it is clear that the future of France lies in the land. The children are happy to leave the hustle and bustle of the city and finally settle on a farm located in the Beauce, the "breadbasket" of the country. Their diligence and intelligence bring the war-torn farm back to prosperity in a synecdochal projection of the country as a whole. The Revolution is safely locked up in the past. See Jacques and Mona Ozouf, "*Le Tour de France par deux enfants*—Le petit livre rouge de la République," in *Les Lieux de mémoire: La République,* ed. Pierre Nora (Paris: Gallimard, 1984), 1:291–321. Reflections of *Le Tour*'s conception of a sort of a French geography destined to greatness flicker even today. See, for example, the final work of Fernand Braudel, *L'Identité de la France I—Espace et histoire* (Paris: Arthaud, 1986).

26. "Il mito cadeva al benessere." Giovanni Macchia, *Il Mito de Parigi* (Turin: Einaudi, 1962), 344.

Index

Compositor: Impressions
Printer: Edwards Brothers, Inc.
Binder: Edwards Brothers, Inc.
Text: 10/13 Baskerville
Display: Baskerville